ORGANIZATIONS
FOR
CHILDREN AND YOUTH

ORGANIZATIONS
FOR
CHILDREN AND YOUTH

ROBERT F. HANSON
San Diego State University

and

REYNOLD E. CARLSON
Indiana University

PRENTICE-HALL, INC., *Englewood Cliffs, New Jersey*

© 1972 by Prentice-Hall, Inc.
Englewood Cliffs, N.J.

ISBN: 0–13–641563–6

Library of Congress Catalog Card Number: 74–38041
Printed in the United States of America

10   9   8   7   6   5   4   3   2

PRENTICE-HALL INTERNATIONAL, INC., *London*
PRENTICE-HALL OF AUSTRALIA PTY. LTD., *Sydney*
PRENTICE-HALL OF CANADA, LTD., *Toronto*
PRENTICE-HALL OF INDIA PRIVATE LIMITED, *New Delhi*
PRENTICE-HALL OF JAPAN, INC., *Tokyo*

CONTENTS

CHAPTER ELEVEN

VOCATIONALLY-ORIENTED ORGANIZATIONS   151

CHAPTER TWELVE

OTHER ORGANIZATIONS FOR YOUTH   167

CHAPTER THIRTEEN

COOPERATION, COORDINATION, AND PLANNING   189

CHAPTER FOURTEEN

WHAT OF THE FUTURE?   208

PREFACE

Youth groups are as old as the human race; but nationwide organizations with stated purposes, planned programs, definite structures, and voluntary memberships are a distinctive modern phenomenon. Never before has so much voluntary effort been devoted to providing wholesome and joyful leisure activities for the young of our country. Rare is the family that has not had some contact with an organized youth group.

In view of the pervasive influence of youth-serving agencies, it is surprising how little printed material is available besides that published by the organizations themselves. The many current books on children and youth deal with schooling, family life, maladjustments, and the like, giving no more than a passing glance at the youth organizations. In an effort to fill this gap in the literature, this book offers an objective survey of the field, with an introduction to the purposes, methods, and structures of the major voluntary organizations for children and youth in America.

This book is intended for several groups: first, students in social work and recreation who need the information it contains as part of their professional preparation; second, students from other disciplines interested in professional service; third, those already engaged in service who want an overview of youth services and a perspective of the agencies they serve; and fourth, the many volunteers, both young and old, who are or will be involved as parents, group leaders, consultants, board or committee chairmen or members, or civic workers supporting youth organizations.

When education is mentioned, schools come first to mind; but education is a continuing process in which youth agencies by their very nature have a significant role. Their influence reaches throughout the life span. It is the hope of the authors that this book will reveal how the voluntary organizations for children and youth have helped, generally favorably, in shaping the American way of life and how they remain relevant today as they adapt to new needs and new opportunities in a rapidly changing society.

Among the many persons who have contributed to the book, we are particularly grateful to the national headquarters staffs who so generously provided information about their organizations. Special recognition is due to Dr. Jack Stumpf, San Diego State School of Social Work; Dr. David Milne, San Diego State Department of Sociology; and Mrs. Thair Milne, San Diego State instructor in child development, for their suggestions relating to Chapters 2, 3, 4, and 5. Finally, thanks must be given to our wives, Ruth Carlson and June Hanson, for their continued encouragement and valuable assistance.

ROBERT F. HANSON
REYNOLD E. CARLSON

ORGANIZATIONS
FOR
CHILDREN AND YOUTH

THE PLACE
OF YOUTH AGENCIES
IN OUR SOCIETY

Chapter 1

American life has long been identified with voluntary, nongovernmental associations. When the French commentator Alexis de Tocqueville described his travels in the United States in 1840, he remarked, "Americans of all ages, all conditions and all dispositions constantly form associations."

Beginnings of the Agencies

Only a few years after de Tocqueville's visit, the first of the American youth organizations (the YMCA) was established to help young people cope with new conditions in the burgeoning industrial society. Its founders, and the founders of the other agencies which soon sprang up, believed that youth had common needs and problems and that answers to these could be found in associations, under competent adult leadership. By 1915, all of the major youth agencies in existence today were in operation (Figure 1-1).

Clubs for children and youth were certainly not new to Americans, or to others, in the mid-nineteenth century. Boys' and girls' clubs have probably existed for hundreds of years. They are found even in primitive societies, where they may be merely informal groups or very elaborate structures related to religious and educational functions.

The changing character of American life during the latter part of the nineteenth century, which has continued at an accelerated pace during the twentieth century, is largely responsible for the development of American organizations for youth. The second half of the nineteenth century saw a hitherto unprecedented increase in industrialization in the United States, with the resultant growth of our large cities and the decline of rural living. The period was marked by serious slum conditions, child labor, long working hours, poor health, and high rates of crime and delinquency. Several

1

Figure 1–1
Courtesy Girl Scouts of the United States of America.

organizations were established, in part at least, to counteract the drab and unpleasant conditions of crowded city life.

The writings of Jane Addams and other social reformers of that era pricked the public conscience as they told of the bleak situation facing city youth. Bluntly, they described and condemned the negative urban environment and its lack of wholesome recreation opportunities. Some of the pastimes drawing the most fire from Miss Addams were such commercial enterprises as dance halls, gin palaces, card rooms, and amusement parks. An abundance of profiteers capitalizing on youth's normal search for pleasure, the lack of wholesome outlets, and the monotonous labor of the factories combined to arouse the desire of many citizens to provide recreation and character education for the youth of the day.

The Young Men's Christian Association, the oldest of the youth-serving organizations still in existence today, was established in London by George Williams in 1844. It had materialized out of an effort to bring young working men of the city together into discussion groups for self-improvement and for the development and maintenance of Christian attitudes. The first YMCA in the United States was founded in 1851 in Boston, and other large cities across the land established associations during the next 25 years.

The Young Women's Christian Association also originated in England, in 1855. In 1866, the first group bearing the name YWCA was formed in Boston. The present national YWCA organization was established in 1906.

Boys' Clubs had been started in various cities at least as early as 1860, when a club was organized in Hartford, Connecticut. But it was not until 1906 that the individual clubs combined into a national organization.

All three of these organizations developed in large cities and were, in a sense, efforts to provide activities to counteract the problems accompanying industrialization and urbanization.

The rise of the settlement and community house movements may also be attributed to a reaction against conditions in the big cities. New York had its first settlement house by 1877; and Jane Addams' famous Hull House, in Chicago, opened its door in 1889. These settlement houses were directed at helping people of all ages in slum areas and offered a combination of social services, health facilities, and recreation. The settlements have continued to render their greatest service in large cities, whereas the YMCA, YWCA, and Boys' Clubs, although more prevalent in large cities, have expanded considerably into smaller cities and towns.

William Forbush, writing in 1902, listed over 70 organizations for boys in existence at the turn of the century.[1] Many of these were local in nature, sponsored by a church or settlement house. Of those groups listed, only the YMCA, Luther League, Christian Endeavor, and Baptist Union have survived until the present as national organizations.

In 1902, the Woodcraft Indians were organized under the leadership of Ernest Thompson Seton. This group was one of the forerunners of the Boy Scouts of America, which was organized by Lord Robert Baden-Powell in England in 1908. William D. Boyce brought the movement to America, and in 1910 the Boy Scouts of America was incorporated.

The Girl Scouts emerged as a part of the world Scout movement inspired by Lord Baden-Powell and his sister, Lady Agnes Baden-Powell, founders of the English Girl Guides. Their friend, Juliette Lowe, was instrumental in popularizing the idea in the United States. She organized "Girl Guide" troops in Savannah, Georgia, in 1912. The name in America was soon changed to "Girl Scouts," although the name "Girl Guides" is used in many other countries.

The Camp Fire Girls were founded in 1910 by Dr. and Mrs. Luther H. Gulick as an answer to the demand for an outdoor organization for girls. Camp Fire was incorporated in 1912.

The 4-H programs date their origin to about 1907, when C. D. Smith organized rural youth to improve farming techniques. In 1916, the Smith-Lever Act was passed by Congress, setting up machinery for the present program.

It is significant that all of the largest national youth-serving organiza-

1 William Byron Forbush, *The Boy Problem, A Study in Social Pedagogy* (Philadelphia: The Westminster Press, 1902), pp. 179–88.

tions were established by 1916. However, each of these organizations has altered in character with the passing years to meet the changing interests of young people.

As the various youth groups grew, local leaders began asking for assistance in starting programs in their communities. In response to this demand, national headquarters were set up by all the major youth-serving organizations. Printed materials were prepared and staffs engaged to assist communities in the establishment and development of programs. As a result, the growth of the agencies was accelerated.

Perhaps one of the basic reasons for the origin and growth of America's youth agencies is a national faith in the perfectability of man. Deeply imbedded in the American tradition is a firm belief in the power of the environment to mold people for good or evil (Figure 1–2). This belief may be traced back to our ancestors' willingness to pull up stakes in the Old World and to sail across the seas to relative wilderness in the conviction that in America they could somehow fashion a better world for themselves and for their children.

Figure 1–2
Conservation and beautification were primary interests of the youth-serving agencies long before the current public concern.
Courtesy Boy Scouts of America.

Acceptance of Youth Agencies Today

In our predominantly urban society, there is general agreement on the importance of such institutions as Scouting, "Y's," and Boys' Clubs as allies of the home, church, and school. Many of America's leading citizens give large credit to a youth organization for their start towards a successful life. So integral a part of modern American life are the youth organizations that they are usually taken for granted. In most homes, participation in their programs is considered a desirable, even essential, part of growing up.

The objectives of the various organizations are ones close to the heart of most parents: social, educational, vocational, health and character development; leadership training; inculcation of democratic ideals; development of a sense of responsibility; cleanliness of mind and body; fun and adventure; prevention of delinquency; and the like.

The degree to which these lofty objectives is attained is, of course, open to debate. Evaluations of the effectiveness of the organizations are, so far, largely limited to personal observations and testimony. For example, a county prosecuting attorney may be quoted as saying, "I'm convinced that boys and girls become better citizens through 4-H." A judge may remark on the small number of teen-agers he meets in juvenile court who have been Boy Scouts. Herbert Hoover credited the Boys' Clubs with being next in importance to the home and church in the prevention of delinquency. However, our research tools are not sufficiently refined at this point to measure precisely what benefits occur from participation in youth organizations. Undoubtedly, millions of youth have had rewarding, beneficial experiences that have added greatly to their lives, while others may have received little or nothing but disappointment from their involvement. The youth programs are only as good as their leadership, and most agency professionals would agree that there is never enough good leadership to go around.

Extent of Membership

In 1937, Chambers categorized some 330 youth-serving organizations in his survey for the American Youth Commission.[2] Eighty-one of these organizations were groups with membership composed primarily of children and youth. Twenty-one of the groups reported enrollments of 100,000 or more. A majority of these groups is in existence today.

Membership in the major traditional youth-serving agencies totaled well over 20 million in 1969. The Boy Scouts of America alone had approximately 6.25 million boys and adults enrolled in 152,312 troops, posts, and packs. Membership statistics on the youth agencies are somewhat difficult to evaluate, since some organizations, such as the Y's and settlement houses, serve a high percentage of adult members. The figure of 20 million is, however, a conservative one in that it does not include the 18.8 million membership claimed by the American Junior Red Cross, members of youth sports

2 Merritt Madison Chambers, *Youth-Serving Organizations* (Washington, D.C.: American Council on Education, 1937).

organizations such as the Little League, or any of the countless millions affiliated with young people's groups in churches and synagogues. It should also be remembered that these figures represent considerable duplication; a boy or girl may belong to two or three organizations at the same time. There is also a considerable difference in the extent of involvement; some youths are very active participants while others are members in name only.

Following are the membership statistics reported by several of the major youth agencies to the *World Almanac*.

American Youth Hostels	41,000
4-H Clubs	4,000,000
Boy Scouts of America	6,183,086
Camp Fire Girls	650,000
Girl Scouts	3,920,000
Girls' Clubs	100,000
Boys' Clubs	875,000
YMCA	5,200,000
YWCA	2,200,000[3]

Growth of the youth agencies has been little short of phenomenal since their beginnings. It took the Boy Scouts 26 years to reach one million members, but during the next 26 years they increased membership to over five million.[4] Most of the other prominent agencies have made similar strides.

The population in this country between the ages of 5 and 19 increased from 36 million in 1935 to 56.2 million in 1965, a gain of approximately 60 percent. In the same period, the Boy Scouts grew by over 400 percent; Camp Fire Girls by 158 percent; Boys' Clubs by 115 percent; Girl Scouts by 510 percent; 4-H Clubs by 123 percent; YMCA by 182 percent, and YWCA by 275 percent.

Membership trends continue to reflect the strength of the natural appeal youth groups have for young people. Following World War II, one boy in eight in the age range of those eligible belonged to the Boy Scouts. Today, one in six belongs. In the same period, Girl Scout and Camp Fire participation has increased from one girl in ten to one girl in seven.

There is no question that a majority of the youth growing up in America today belongs to or has had some relation with at least one of the youth agencies.

[3] *1971 Edition, The World Almanac and Book of Facts* (New York: Newspaper Enterprise Association, Inc., 1970), pp. 190–204.
[4] Boy Scouts of America, *1969 Report to Congress,* 91st Cong., 2nd Sess., House Document No. 291 (Washington, D.C.: Government Printing Office, 1970), pp. 34–35.

Categorizing the Agencies

The decision regarding a nomenclature for the organizations covered in this book has been a difficult one. Since each agency varies in some respect from all of the others, no one term has proven entirely satisfactory. "Character-building," "group work," "youth membership," "quasi-public," and "private" are all adjectives frequently used. The authors believe that "voluntary" is the most descriptive and most widely accepted term used to identify these agencies.

Reference will be made in subsequent chapters to church-sponsored youth groups, to organizations conducted under the auspices of the public schools, and to certain other types of groups. This book will not, however, cover programs for children and youth which are not nationally affiliated.

Any classification of youth-serving organizations is at best arbitrary. Although this book deals primarily with youth membership organizations, there are literally hundreds of adult organizations which designate service to youth as a primary or secondary purpose, and most of the youth-serving organizations include adults in their membership ranks. Some groups such as Protestant, Catholic, or Jewish youth groups can easily be categorized. However, many others do not fit into any clear-cut niche. An example is the YMCA. Although originally highly religious, the YMCA is now often quite secular; it offers a great variety of programs for all ages and both sexes; it may have an elaborate building or operate with no building at all.

Appendix A (on page 223) contains a list of the major youth-serving organizations of today, together with their addresses. The list is admittedly incomplete. The authors have used their personal judgment in selecting those organizations which they feel have the greatest influence and importance at the present time.

Most of the national organizations whose memberships are composed primarily of children and youth are discussed in some depth in Chapters 8 through 12.

Common Characteristics of the Voluntary Youth Agencies

There are several characteristics which the major voluntary youth-serving agencies have in common. In the first place, membership is usually voluntary on the part of the child. The program and leadership are designed to attract him of his own free will. The membership is open to all children regardless of race or religion, within the prescribed age and sex limitations.

The major organizations also tend to use similar methods of operation. They all function, in part at least, through small and continuous groups which have adult sponsorship but which retain a high degree of self-direction. The agencies attempt to base their programs on the interests and needs of youth, providing different groups for different age levels. Emphasis is placed on learning by doing. Although the goals are educational, in most cases the methods are recreational.

Membership fees are kept low, with finances coming chiefly from public contributions. Leadership is largely voluntary and involves millions of adults as advisors, leaders, board members, and committeemen. The organizations are directed by lay boards at both national and local levels.

Despite these similarities, each organization has a unique contribution to make, as we shall observe later.

Impact of the Agencies

Numbers of members alone do not justify the existence of the major organizations for youth. Their real value—impact on human lives—is extremely difficult to measure. The following example illustrates that the benefits of agency programs may not be seen for many years, if at all.

In South America, the YMCA's operate an international camp for youth from all over South America. The camp is called Piriapolis, and is located in Uruguay.

Some years ago a 13-year-old boy from Chile, named José Maza, attended Camp Piriapolis. His country had just been involved in a war with several neighboring countries; and at the camp, José met some boys from these other countries. They became close friends, and José had a wonderful time at camp.

On the closing night in camp, they held a Fire of Friendship—just as many camps in North America do today. Around the big campfire many of the boys had a chance to speak of their experiences at camp. When it came time for José to speak, his words were very simple. He said, "I have had a wonderful time at this camp. I have made many new friends. I have decided to dedicate my life to doing whatever I can to help my country be friends with her neighbors."

These simple words, said many year ago by a 13-year-old boy around a YMCA campfire in South America, might have been remembered by no one. They were remembered by José, however, because a few years ago, José Maza was elected President of the General Assembly of the United Nations!

Other world leaders have also had associations with the YMCA. Carlos Romulos was a very active YMCA layman for the Philippines. Charles Malik, from Lebanon, spent many years in the YMCA program of the Cairo, U.A.R., YMCA.

Is it perhaps more than just coincidence that three consecutive presidents of the General Assembly of the United Nations came out of strong YMCA backgrounds in their countries?

The YMCA and other youth agencies help provide one of the world's greatest needs—leadership.

Comparisons of Seven of the Major Organizations

For a clearer understanding of the youth organizations, it is helpful to compare seven of the major national organizations—the Boy Scouts, Camp Fire Girls, Girl Scouts, YMCA, YWCA, Boys' Clubs, and 4-H, as these demonstrate varied approaches and programs. All are voluntary in membership and generally accepted as a part of American life.

In terms of their common characteristics, the seven may be grouped as follows:

1. Boy Scouts, Camp Fire Girls, and Girl Scouts;
2. Boys' Clubs, YMCA, and YWCA;
3. 4-H.

PROGRAM

The three organizations in the first group have program structures that are developed on a national level. Continual revision of program, based on studies of interests and needs, takes place. Program progression is provided in terms of both age levels and accomplishments. Progression of individual members in terms of accomplishment takes place through the passing of tests or completion of projects. This program structure is often referred to as "stair-step" progression. It must be borne in mind that, even though there is a national program, it is not completely fixed as locally applied; the local leadership and the interests of members have a large part in determining how the program is implemented.

In the second group, national and regional program material may be available and there may be a general prescribed structure; but the program develops, in theory at least, out of group and community needs (Figure 1–3). The success of each unit is dependent to a large extent on the ability of its leaders and on the local setting, as well as the experiences of other groups within the organization. The fact that these organizations tend to be building-centered also affects their program.

The third group, the 4-H, have a somewhat different approach. State extension offices usually suggest program materials for their particular state. County units adjust these materials to meet their own needs.

Organizations of the first group emphasize small-group activities in the outdoors. Though their program covers a tremendous variety of fields, the

Figure 1–3
Sewing classes enable Y-Teens to try their hands at operating a sewing machine. *Courtesy National Board, YWCA.*

outdoor-related activities, including camping, have a major place. The second group tend to be more building-centered, with indoor recreation and education activities. The 4-H, originally working through agriculturally-oriented projects, is now wider in scope. Its programs vary from state to state but often maintain a rural flavor.

LEADERSHIP

The three groups differ considerably in use of leaders, both paid and volunteer. Without volunteers, the Boy Scouts, Girl Scouts, and Camp Fire Girls could not function. They maintain a relatively small paid staff, primarily administrative, that seldom works directly with boys and girls but is primarily responsible for the recruiting and training of volunteers, public relations, finances, and the handling of properties. Direct leadership is carried on by volunteers. As a result, a strong and continuing training program and a very active community relations program are necessary to assure adequate support from adults.

The YMCA, YWCA, and Boys' Clubs operate with paid staffs that not only handle administrative duties but also work directly with the members.

Figure 1–4
Camp is a happy experience for
members of many youth groups.
Courtesy Pioneer Girls.

Volunteers are used, but not as extensively as in the first group of organizations and often in a somewhat different way. There are some volunteers that have direct responsibility for groups such as Hi-Y Clubs, but many may assist only with particular program activities.

In 4-H, the Extension Service and local county agents' offices provide the administrative leadership, while most of the face-to-face leadership is given by volunteers.

It should be noted that the fixed and tested national programs, the national handbooks, and the stair-step progression system of the first three organizations help them to recruit and train volunteer leaders. The specific assistance that comes from these sources gives a sense of assurance and security to many adults in positions of leadership. On the other hand, it might be argued that the freer program of the organizations in the second group gives leaders more opportunity to exercise ingenuity and develop democratic leadership in their groups.

PROPERTIES

There are distinct differences between the three groups in property ownership. The Boy Scouts, Girl Scouts, and Camp Fire Girls seldom own or rent areas and facilities other than offices and camps. They use schools, churches, lodges, and homes for their meetings. The Y's and Boys' Clubs usually maintain buildings with club rooms, gymnasiums, activity rooms, and sometimes swimming pools. The 4-H club meetings are usually held in churches, schools, or homes, but the organization often has 4-H buildings located in county fairgrounds. All seven of the organizations own camps (Figure 1–4).

FINANCE

The organizations in the first two groups receive most of their funds from voluntary sources. The building-centered organizations usually require large budgets in orders to maintain their facilities. In the Y's, much of this cost is passed on to members in the form of moderately high fees. The Boys' Clubs, however, keep their fees very low so that their members coming from low-income families may be able to pay. Although the 4-H receives many contributions, it is financed largely through the federal, state, and local governments; and club fees are determined by individual clubs that use them for their own purposes.

Many other differences exist between the organizations, but the generalizations cited above suffice to illustrate the variations in modes of work.

CHARACTER EDUCATION AND PERSONALITY DEVELOPMENT

Adult responsibility for the development of children's morals and character has been accepted by each culture from the dawn of civilization. While moral instruction appears to be universal with man, the emphasis and techniques of conducting the training vary from society to society and from age to age, just as what men consider "moral" differs considerably.

Methods of Character Education

In this country, as well as throughout much of Europe, the major formal attempts to accomplish character education prior to the twentieth century were through religious *instruction in schools and churches.* Up until 1850, religious training in the schools was accepted without question and constituted one of the major areas of curriculum. With the growth of the public school system, religion was gradually excluded from study. This development was due in large measure to a long series of court cases wherein citizens' rights to freedom of thought and freedom from coercion were upheld. For 25 years or more after the teaching of religion per se was prohibited by most states, "morals and manners" or "conduct" continued to appear as subjects until educators began to realize that there is a low correlation between *knowing* what is right and *doing* what is right.

Although the schools today still include citizenship, ethical behavior, and high morals as major objectives, attempts at achieving these goals are primarily through experience—the participation in a "democratic classroom," and so on.

One universal tool in character education is the use of *stories.* Great faith has been placed in the examples of heroes down through the ages.

Most folk tales have some sort of moral which the teller hopes will influence the listener in a positive way. Outstanding examples of this type of character training are the parables of the Bible, American Indian legends, and Aesop's fables.

Another traditional technique used in developing character is *disciplinary or corrective action*. This method is the most spontaneous and probably by far the most universally practiced developmental technique. Before children are old enough to reason with, disciplinary action is, for many people, the only workable means of achieving acceptable behavior.

Most leaders feel that as a child becomes older, more positive methods of influencing behavior than punishment are preferable, since punitive measures are based on fear. Unless the child's attitudes are developed so that he can understand the reasons for socially acceptable behavior, he is apt to misbehave whenever he feels that the threat of punishment is no longer present. For example, if a child is kept out of the cookie jar by the threat of a spanking and the memory of previous spankings, he may leave the cookie jar alone. But should he get the chance to raid it on some occasion when he feels it is relatively safe to do so without fear of punishment, he is apt to eat the entire jarful of cookies at one sitting.

When socially approved behavior is based on fear alone, the good behavior is liable to be temporary and to disappear when the threat is removed. Many youths rebel against discipline if the reasons given for it are not convincing enough. Many parents of teen-agers find that when they attempt to forbid their son or daughter to date someone of whom they do not approve, their action tends to drive the young people closer together and to increase their determination to see each other. The end result may be an elopement or secret marriage.

Several years ago many teachers and parents subscribed to the point of view that all disciplinary measures were bad because they frustrated children and thwarted their self-expression and creativity. Modern leaders reject this theory, feeling that children need a set of limits and thoughtful adults to enforce them. The important consideration is, however, that children and youth gradually be given more and more responsibility for their actions, so that when they reach adulthood, they will be prepared to make intelligent decisions.

If our youth experience only situations in which they are told what to do, and act only under the threat of some type of punishment, we cannot expect them to assume intelligently the responsibilities of adulthood overnight when they gain their independence from school and home.

Another technique frequently employed to influence character development is *ritual and ceremony*. Many primitive cultures rely heavily on "magical" rites to indoctrinate their youth into the responsibilities of society. These are often associated with puberty and overnight transition from childhood to adulthood. Sometimes the ceremonies are accompanied by tests of endurance or hardship whereby the youth must prove his manhood.

Rites play an important part in many of our modern youth organizations: Scouting groups have pledges and oaths; fraternal groups such as De Molay and Job's Daughters use elaborate induction and installation ceremonies; and fraternities and sororities employ secret signs, passwords, handclasps, and initiations. Some fraternal groups place so much emphasis on the ritual that little else in the way of program is accomplished.

Founders of these groups believed that youth are highly impressionable and that beautiful ceremonies and idealistic vows would surely make a lasting impression on the new members. Undoubtedly this belief is true to an extent; and it is no doubt good to give members a knowledge of the high, virtuous ideals of an organization. But, today, less weight is placed on the value of these oaths and promises in actually influencing behavior than was formerly. It would be wonderful if a Boy Scout who had just memorized the Scout Law suddenly became trustworthy, loyal, helpful, friendly, courteous, and kind. However, there is no evidence of such a transformation.

Two of the most recent approaches to character development are *counseling* and *discussion*.

Counseling is much more prevalent than in the past. However, in most cases it is still used only for remedial cases—the child talks back to the teacher, so he is sent to the school counselor; a boy gets into trouble with the law, so he is assigned a probation officer to give him guidance. Some agencies such as the Y's, settlement houses, Boys' Clubs, and Big Brothers have utilized counseling to a fair extent. The greatest drawback to more extensive use is the expense involved in making possible the one-to-one interaction. Communities are often reluctant or unable to support such costly services.

Closely related to counseling is *lay advising* by the club leader. A strong argument for keeping group size relatively small is that thereby the leader or advisor can maintain a personal relationship with most, if not all, of the members. Often children and youth will discuss with a trusted adult leader a personal problem that they would not think of taking to their parents.

Discussion is the prime tool of group work and as such plays a vital role in the attainment of the objectives of most youth agencies. Many of the early school plans called for discussion of morals and character, often following a lecture. It is now felt that more can be accomplished when the discussion is related to an actual life situation, rather than handled in an unrelated lesson.

Many nations have tried, without much success, to give *moral instruction* in the schools. The chief weakness of these attempts to teach morals appears to be that they give the child little opportunity to exercise moral judgment.

Unfortunately, having a child repeat five hundred times, "Honesty is the best policy," does not make him honest. He must have an opportunity to make a choice between honest or dishonest behavior. The result of his choice—praise, reprimand, reward, punishment, satisfaction, etc.—will influence his reaction in a similar situation at a later date.

Doty believed that attitudes could be learned, and he presented five steps as the most efficient way of teaching an attitude: (1) exposure to a situation involving choice of behavior; (2) understanding; (3) repetition; (4) conviction; and (5) application.[1] He claimed that if we wish to alter a youngster's character in a desirable way, we were much more apt to succeed with a planned, deliberate, approach.

The power of systematic, planned programs for developing attitudes in youth can perhaps best be observed in the success of the Hitler Youth and Young Communist youth programs. Though we would certainly not subscribe to the methods and objectives of these programs, few would question their effectiveness. One of the real shortcomings of American programs for youth to date has been the lack of clearly defined objectives, together with concrete plans for reaching these objectives. Additional research in this area is sorely needed.

However, few would deny that the timeworn saying, "Example is better than precept," still holds true. Today we put it another way—"What you are speaks so loud, I can't hear a word you're saying." A youth leader should not expect the members of his group to be considerate and courteous if he is bossy and abrupt. The father who brags of cheating on his income tax and getting away with exceeding the speed limit should not be indignant or surprised when his son is caught stealing a comic book.

Youth agencies put great weight on the power of example, knowing that hero worship is at its peak during the years when young people are most likely to participate in youth organizations. Nearly all of us can look back to our childhood and recall a camp counselor, group leader, or teacher who we feel had a tremendous influence on our lives (Figure 2-1). John Dewey stated, "Everything the teacher does, as well as the manner in which he does it, incites the child to respond in some way or other, and each response tends to set the child's attitude in some way or other."[2]

Doty reported a significant relationship between the number of campers who returned to camp the following year and the quality of their counselor.[3] The personality of the counselor appeared to be more important than acceptance by one's group, the "cabin climate," or any other factor in predicting who would return.

[1] Richard S. Doty, *The Character Dimension of Camping* (New York: Association Press, 1960), pp. 55–56.
[2] John Dewey, *How We Think* (Boston: D.C. Heath and Company, 1933), p. 59.
[3] Doty, *The Character Dimension of Camping*, pp. 94–95.

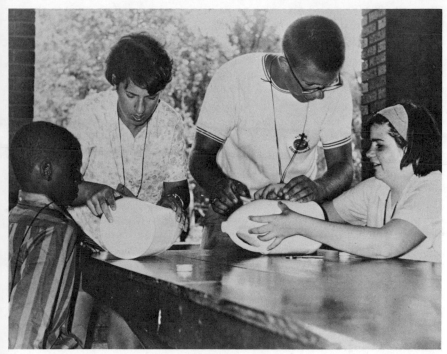

Figure 2–1
Volunteer teen-age counselors instruct young people at a children's day camp
of the East St. Louis, Illinois YWCA. *Courtesy National Board, YWCA.*

Early Programs for Character Development

The early part of this century brought forth a tremendous surge of interest
in character development, as was evidenced by the large number of organizations for youth which sprang up during that period. In addition to attempts
to develop character through the new agencies, a number of other approaches were tried—primarily through the public schools. Most of these
plans failed to survive the Depression, World War II, and the postwar
emphasis on science and basic education. However, their influence is still
felt in terms of class and school government, the "democratic classroom,"
and various plans whereby students "run" the city government for a day,
with student mayors, student police chiefs, and the like.

Some of the initial stimulus to character education through the schools
came in 1914 when an anonymous businessman, believing that democracy is
dependent on moral character, offered a $5,000 award for the best children's
morality code. Interest in the competition was so great that in 1919 he

offered a $20,000 award for the best public school plan of character educa-
tion. Twenty-six states entered the competition, which was eventually won
by the state of Iowa.[4]

The Iowa Plan was based on the principle that "the best way to prepare
for life in a democracy is by practicing it." The plan asserted that moral
education must be recognized as a definite end—not as a probable byproduct
—and therefore requires careful planning for desirable outcomes. Preparers
of the plan conducted a great deal of research in an attempt to discover (1)
what should be the subject matter each year that needed enriching in character education; (2) what projects and materials were consistent both with
character training and with the prevailing curricula, and (3) what materials
and aids were available which had proven useful. The researchers then
attempted to classify the tested and tried materials and to place them in a
form for convenient use. Some of the more important procedures suggested
included socialized recitations, projects, and attention to noble deeds.[5]

Collier's Magazine invited its readers in 1924 to produce a code of morals
for young people. The composite code, which dealt with areas such as
courage, wisdom, industry, truth, honesty, health, charity, humility, and
responsibility, was distributed to nearly every classroom in the country
through the efforts of Lions International.[6]

The School Republic was a plan originated by Mr. Wilson Gill of New
York City in 1897. The plan was adopted by many schools in this country
and abroad. The U.S. government used it for four years in Alaska, in
Cuba, and on Indian reservations. Under this plan, a whole school was
organized like a national government, electing a president and a vice-
president three times a year. Each schoolroom was organized like a city
government, with every child a member of the city council. The purpose of
the School Republic was to involve children in the responsibilities of
citizenry before the age of 21. The charter recognized children as legal,
responsible, practical citizens, not only of the future, but of the present.[7]

Another character-training program was originated by the Pathfinders
of America. First planned as a course in self-help for men and women in
penal institutions, the program was so successful that it was adapted for
school use. It differed from most other plans in that moral instruction was
a specialty to be presented, not by the classroom teacher, but by a specially
trained instructor from outside the school. This instructor would make the

4 Elizabeth R. Pendry and Hugh Hartshorne, *Organizations for Youth* (New York,
N.Y.: McGraw-Hill Book Co., 1935), p. 147.

5 *Ibid.,* pp. 147–154.

6 "Moral Code for School Children," *Collier's* LXXV, No. 3 (Jan. 17, 1925), p.
5. See also William G. Shepherd, "The Story of the Moral Code," *Collier's,* LXXV,
No. 3 (Jan. 17, 1925), pp. 7 and 43; Pendry and Hartshorne, *Organizations for
Youth,* pp. 155–160.

7 Pendry and Hartshorne, *Organizations for Youth,* pp. 161–166.

rounds of several schools, calling once a month at each classroom to lead a discussion on the subject elected for that month. At the end of the eighth grade, a diploma was awarded in "human engineering."[8]

The Knighthood of Youth was a program for children in elementary schools sponsored by the National Child Welfare Association. It was conceived in 1924 by Charles M. De Forest and had enrolled a million children by 1933. Children in the program called deeds of service "adventures," and their progress in various adventures was recorded as "stones" in a castle which they built on a wall chart. The class was organized as a club, with officers and committee chairmen who presented a variety of service projects. Booklets distributed by the national office offered suggestions along this line. Stories of famous men and women were used to inspire high ideals, and each child could progress to a higher rank (page, squire, knight, etc.) as he accomplished individual and group goals. The Association admitted the possibility that some of the children would do socially desirable acts solely for the reward but felt that the teacher's leadership could help negate this shortcoming.[9]

Need for Research in Character Education

Many agencies have made rather bold claims to be "character-building" organizations. If these claims are to be more than window dressing to acquire financial support, we must begin to measure, more accurately than we do at present, the effect of the youth agencies on the members they attempt to serve.

Research in character education is beset by many difficulties. It is not easy to get agreement on the patterns of character which are desirable in a particular society. It is even harder to identify with any assurance cause-and-effect relationships in a realm where there are so many variables. The studies by Hartshorne and May 40 years ago raised questions about the consistency with which any traits of character are transferred from one specific situation to another.[10] Nevertheless, there is a slowly emerging body of knowledge which represents a fairly widespread consensus among specialists in this field.

Parental Responsibility

In a series of long-term studies carried on under the guidance of Dr. Robert Havighurst of the University of Chicago, we have some of the best

8 *Ibid.*, 173–181.
9 *Ibid.*, 182–190.
10 Hugh Hartshorne and Mark A. May, *Studies in the Nature of Character* (New York: Macmillan, 1930).

findings to date.[11] These studies indicate that character is shaped predominantly by the intimate, emotionally powerful relationship between child and parent. Forces outside the family are not negligible or irrelevant in their indirect effect on character formation, but it seems that these forces operate mainly as they shape and guide parents' behavior, not that of the children.

Clearly, the basic qualities of personality are largely determined by the child's experience with his parents. Other persons and events can affect character development, exercising a curative or destructive influence, but seldom are these forces strong enough in the typical American community to make noteworthy changes. Therefore, youth agencies need to work in close partnership with the family. The findings indicate that an agency must maintain close contact with the home and give serious attention to programs of parent education and parent involvement.

Parents wonder what they can do to help their children to be good persons; to be honest, generous, independent, responsible, and respectful of others. Although there are differences of temperament that one seems to be born with, either a placid or an energetic child can turn out to be truthful or dishonest, industrious or negligent, as a result of what he experiences from life.

Not long ago, the answer to "What can we do to help?" would have been "Teach him good character." We now realize that character grows from within and appears to be fairly unrelated to a knowledge of what is right and wrong. Unfortunately, many parents perhaps do not realize that character formation begins in the crib. Confidence, trust, and love are vital to sound personality growth of the young child (Figure 2-2).

As the child matures, far too often he is either frustrated by the overly restrictive parent ("Stop that, you bad boy!"), or left without a set of limits by the overly-permissive parent. Neither of these extremes makes a positive contribution to the child's character.

At about age four or five, character begins to "set." This does not mean that whatever a child is by this time is unchangeable. It does mean that his character is pointed generally in the direction in which it will grow.

Responsibility of Youth Agencies

When parents have done a good job of instilling sound, basic values, the job of the youth agency is one of reinforcing these values and building on his early training. If the child has not had the benefit of a healthy home environment during the early formative years, then the job of the agency, school, or church becomes the much more difficult one of rebuilding values.

---

[11] Robert J. Havighurst and Hilda Taba, in collaboration with the Committee on Human Development, University of Chicago, *Adolescent Character and Personality* (New York: John Wiley & Sons, Inc., 1949).

Figure 2–2
Attitudes are "caught, not taught." *Courtesy Big Brothers of America.*

The older a child becomes, the more difficult this job is. Far too often, the child is rejected from the group in one manner or another, rather than having his character developed.

Outside the family, all research points to the peer group as the next most influential force in shaping the personality. Here is where moral values are tested and reinforced, or abandoned. Youth agencies concentrating on the small, closely-knit group relationships, therefore, are on solid ground in their efforts to instill positive values. Margaret Mead sees the process of character development as essentially divided into two periods.[12] The second period, which covers adolescence, is the one "in which the motivation of the members of one's age group is substituted for child-parent relationships and in which the child is swayed by age-group standards."

Many psychologists and group workers agree that the best, if not the only, way to develop mature, responsible individuals is to give the individual an incentive to behave ethically, together with the opportunity to make meaningful decisions. This belief is the basis of the theory behind the democratic, self-governing small groups which are advocated by all of the large national youth agencies and put into practice in varying degrees,

[12] Margaret Mead, in an address to the National Association of Deans of Women, as quoted in H.H. Remmers and D.H. Radler, *The American Teenager* (Indianapolis: The Bobbs-Merrill Company, Inc., 1957), p. 227.

depending upon the skill of the leader and the willingness of the group to act democratically and responsibly.

The wise leader will realize that "actions speak louder than words" and refrain from preaching and moralizing. On the other hand, he must realize that the activities themselves are not the goal. As has been said, "We must pay more attention to what the ball does to Johnny and less to what Johnny does to the ball."

It should be pointed out that even though an agency has character education or personality development as a major goal, it is doubtful whether any youngster has ever joined a youth group to have his character developed (Figure 2–3). This phase of the program is one which agency executives and club leaders hope will accompany the educational and recreational activities which attract and hold the boy or girl.

Figure 2–3
An AYH Camp Cookout.
*Courtesy American Youth
Hostels, Inc.*

NEEDS AND DESIRES
OF YOUTH

Chapter 3

The most pertinent justification for the voluntary youth organizations is that they help individuals to meet their basic needs, enabling them to lead healthy, happy lives.

Most psychologists now agree that neuroses are generally caused by the lack of gratification of basic needs such as security, belonging, love, respect, and prestige. Organized youth groups provide one of the most important mediums in our society for helping children and youth fulfill these essential needs. Further, they can play a vital part in shaping attitudes for lifelong growth.

Psychological Inquiries

Maslow believes that once people have achieved a satisfactory level of gratification of their basic needs, they can progress toward self-actualization, growth, and self-development.[1] He feels that absence of illness is not enough —that the fulfilled, meaningful life is one in which a person develops his talents, capacities, and creative tendencies. Growth in itself becomes a rewarding experience. People who are growth-motivated have a zest for living, become more independent and less anxious.

Youth agency programs of achievement can play a vital role in the self-actualization of young people by providing opportunities for individual growth, development of self-confidence, and widened experiences. The successful youth organization does more than meet basic needs; it helps the individual to reach his fullest potential as a human being.

1 Abraham Maslow, *Toward a Psychology of Being* (Princeton, N.J.: Van Nostrand Reinhold, 1968).

Many works in the field of adolescent and child psychology delve into the needs and desires of young people. One of the early attempts to explain behavior in terms of motivation toward basic needs was made by W.I. Thomas, a pioneer in the field of sociology. Thomas grouped human needs into four "wishes." They are:

1. the desire for new experience;
2. the desire for security;
3. the desire for response;
4. the desire for recognition.[2]

The desire for new experience is a human quality which is probably responsible for many of man's achievements, from the earliest explorations to the landing of man on the moon. It is also responsible for many a youth's going astray. Much of the adventure which was present in day-to-day life in ancient societies has been eliminated—the frontier is conquered, neighboring tribes no longer attack, and it is not necessary to kill buffalo to survive (Figure 3–1). But the desire for excitement and adventure remains. Children and youth will have their thrills one way or another. If they do not find them in exciting organized activities such as sports, canoeing, and exploring,

Figure 3–1

Scouts at Camp Shaganippi in Wisconsin enjoying a newly completed "monkey bridge." *Courtesy Boy Scouts of America.*

2 William I. Thomas, *The Unadjusted Girl* (Boston: Little, Brown, 1925), p. 4.

they may seek them through vandalism, breaking and entering, petty thievery, and gang fights.

Thomas considered the desire for security to be in opposition to the desire for new experience. He felt that the former was based on fear and therefore not healthy. Healthy or not, the security that comes from belonging—from being a member of an "in" group—is probably the source of much of the drawing power of youth groups, especially at the older levels. Many youth leaders realize this to be a factor and, when attempting to form new clubs, purposefully set out to interest and enroll key natural leaders in a school, so that the clubs will have high status and attract those who glory in the security of the company of the school "wheels."

The desire for response is closely related to love, affection, and Thomas' fourth wish, recognition. Youth agencies do much to help meet these basic needs through providing settings where a child or youth can be accepted, understood, and recognized for his achievements and growth. Good leaders almost unconsciously work toward meeting this need with a kind word, a pat on the back, and constant demonstration of interest and concern. The need for recognition is the basis for much of the youth agency's program, especially ranks, badges, and awards. Even the agencies which do not award ranks and badges are apt to use techniques such as selection of a "boy-of-the-month" or "outstanding camper." Recognition is gained also through being elected to office, wearing the group T-shirt, or being asked to lead the flag salute at a P.T.A. meeting (Figure 3–2).

Erikson stated, ". . . societies lighten the inescapable conflicts of childhood with a promise of some security, identity, and integrity. In thus reinforcing the values of the ego, societies create the only conditions under which human growth is possible."[3] One of the ways in which our society reinforces ego values is through its youth organizations.

Erikson developed the concept of "eight stages of man." He feels that a human child must demonstrate certain kinds of competencies in order to develop into a well-integrated personality. The eight vital qualities he stresses are: trust, autonomy, initiative, industry, identity, intimacy, generativity, and ego integrity.[4] Each individual, to become a mature adult, must develop all of the ego qualities mentioned. Although several of the qualities are best developed through a wholesome family experience, youth groups can and do play a vital supporting role, especially in the areas of industry, initiative, and identity (Figure 3–3).

One of the best explanations of the needs and desires of young people is found in Murray and Murray's *Guidelines for Group Leaders*. These authors believe:

[3] Erik H. Erikson, *Childhood and Society* (New York: W.W. Norton, 1950), p. 237.
[4] *Ibid.*, pp. 219–34.

Figure 3–2
Melanie Wight, FHA'er from
Muldrow, Oklahoma, displays a
Halloween centerpiece which
she and other FHA'ers prepared
for a local nursing home.
*Courtesy Future Homemakers
of America.*

Love is the most essential need of all humans and many of the other needs emerge from this. The fortunate person gets this from his home. Yet there are many who do not. When this happens, the person must have his need for love filled in some other way if he is to grow into an emotionally healthy person. This void may be filled by a teacher, group leader or someone else who shows an interest in him.[5]

Closely related to the need for love is the need for acceptance. Leaders of youth have a big responsibility in creating an atmosphere of acceptance. Many discipline problems relate to feelings of rejection. Many children do not know how to gain acceptance and need the help of a concerned adult. The leader must realize that the child who is very likeable and well-behaved is probably secure and accepted, while the child who presents problems for the group or who hangs back is the one to whom the leader especially needs to show affection and acceptance. The problem boy or girl must be shown that he or she is accepted, even when his behavior is not.

[5] Janet P. Murray and Clyde E. Murray, *Guidelines for Group Leaders* (New York: Whiteside, Inc. and Morrow, 1954), p. 144.

Figure 3–3
Marbles to music, science to swimming, the Boys' Clubs of America give a boy a chance to develop his interests. *Courtesy Boys' Clubs of America.*

Each of us has a need for some form of recognition. We need to feel that we have done something worthwhile. When children do not receive recognition for things they have done well, some are apt to seek attention in other ways—clowning, disrupting, vandalism. Others withdraw into themselves.

The youth agencies provide unlimited ways of satisfying this desire for attention—recognition banquets, volunteer leader awards, badges, ranks, offices, boy-of-the-month awards, newspaper publicity, and so on. The wise leader will be constantly on the lookout for opportunities to express approval for a job well done, knowing that in so doing he will be helping the individual to feel adequate and appreciated.

The fulfillment of a sense of belonging is another basic need we all have. The need is particularly acute during adolescence, although it is significant for all ages. Identification with an organization helps fill this desire, especially if the organization is a prestigious one. Undoubtedly, much of the appeal of Cub Scouts for boys is due to the uniform, which provides a visual image of "belonging."

The carrying of a membership card is not sufficient to satisfy this desire. Today almost everyone belongs to some organization, if only a book club or membership discount store. Real membership must involve an emotional experience. Persons who really belong have strong feelings toward the other members and for the group's purposes. Belonging to a group provides a youngster with a sense of identity and security necessary to his normal growth and development.

Agency officials realize that, even in the best organizations, "belonging" is not necessarily synonymous with membership. While membership is an official status usually involving the payment of dues and having one's name on a roster, "belonging" is essentially an emotional experience which may develop shortly after joining an organization, much later, or not at all. The challenge faced by youth agencies is to involve their members emotionally in the group to a point where they do indeed belong, and think in terms of "our" and "we" instead of "it" or "they."

Developing the Feeling of Belonging

There are several ways in which agency executives and group workers can help their members to develop a feeling of belonging. Some of these follow.

1. Giving the member a responsibility or role to play in the operation of the agency or group helps him feel a part of it. New members should not normally be given major responsibilities, but they should have a chance to grow into positions of responsible leadership.

2. Newcomers need to be made to feel welcome by the older members. New-member parties, membership manuals, and placement of newcomers on committees which are interesting and active are helpful techniques commonly used. There should be time at meetings to socialize informally, perhaps over refreshments. Leaders need to remind the "old-timers" periodically of their responsibilities in making the new members feel wanted and at home.

3. Orientation and induction are commonly used techniques for making the new member feel a part of the group and acquainting him with the goals and programs of the organization. Many of the youth agencies have developed elaborate induction ceremonies which stress the aims and ideals of the agencies.

4. Membership newsletters, open houses, exhibits, and other public relations techniques help acquaint new members with the history, purposes, and program of the organization.

5. Involvement in planning of the organization's program may well be the most important technique in developing a sense of belonging among the membership. A group with a large membership, only a few of whom are involved in planning and decision-making, will likely find a good deal of membership apathy and lack of identification with the agency. Organizations such as the YMCA and YWCA increase the percentage of members involved in planning and policy through the use of many committees, such as a camping committee, personnel committee, and a physical education or youth work committee. Care must be exercised to ensure that committees, when appointed, have definite assignments and enough activity so that members are not involved in a frustrating situation, which is soon viewed as a waste of time.

Problems of Prolonged Adolescence

Although many of the social and economic conditions which fostered the development of our organizations for youth in the early twentieth century are not the same today, today's youth is undoubtedly faced with as many as, if not more problems than youth of the past. This is particularly true of the adolescents in our society. Since 1900 there has been a general tendency to postpone adulthood. In less advanced cultures the 16-year-old youth is often economically capable of independence and is readily absorbed into the adult world. Most modern societies, however, seem to have a problem with their teen-agers. Children everywhere pass through the sudden crisis of puberty; but, whereas in many societies the onset of puberty and the strength of manhood qualify one for membership in the adult society, highly technologized, urbanized societies such as ours must postpone adulthood for several years. This creates what we call prolonged adolescence—an extended period during which youth must somehow balance between childhood and adulthood.

Many of the teen-ager's conflicts and tensions stem from the combination of an acceleration in the individual's physical and cultural growth with the continued refusal of the society to grant him the rights and opportunities of adulthood. When sexual drives are the strongest, sexual opportunities are fewest; obedience and submission are asked of youth at precisely the time when their strength, energy, and desire for autonomy are at a peak; responsible participation in major social institutions is denied or discouraged at the moment their interest in the world is awakened. A general decline of parental control and a world in a state of continuous crisis multiply teen-agers' tension and frustration. Erikson viewed the problem as follows.

> It is human to have a long childhood; it is civilized to have an even longer childhood. Long childhood makes a technical and mental virtuoso out of man, but it also leaves a lifelong residual of emotional immaturity in him.[6]

One of the basic reasons for the existence of the youth-serving organizations is to provide opportunities for growth toward maturity in a society which is more and more depriving its young people of the opportunity to mature in the manner that is normal in less developed cultures, through being assimilated into the work force at a young age.

Today most of our young people, males in particular, find themselves in one of two categories. Either the young people follow a long course of educational training that may require six to seven years beyond high-school graduation before they become self-supporting; or they drop out of school

[6] Erikson, *Childhood and Society,* p. 12.

somewhere before high-school graduation, in which case they may very well find themselves unemployable. Early in the century very few young people completed high school, but today the situation is reversed, and those who drop out generally have had a history of failure, frustration, and, very often, bad behavior. Some of them are fortunate enough to break into an adult role by hard work, good fortune, or marriage; but a high percentage face a prolonged period of disappointment.

Perhaps it is surprising that there is not more of an "adolescent problem" than there is. The great majority of teen-agers eventually make their way through to adult society and turn out to be constructive members of society. That most of them finally succeed is due in large part to the resources of the American community today—organized sports, youth centers, clubs, hobby groups, chaperoned dances, churches, and the comprehensive high school. However, the effectiveness of these organizational resources in coping with youth varies considerably.

Where adult leadership is poor and community resources are limited (as in urban slums and in certain new suburbs), where the population is highly mobile and rootless, or where failure in the academic process leaves some youth with a feeling of hopelessness, we can expect a high incidence of adolescent disorder.

Most of the young people who get into trouble, therefore, are those who are denied both the rights of adults and the compensation for this deprivation which the society has tried to set up. Since our culture is not likely to change its attitude toward teen-agers and to begin to give them adult status (if anything, the period of adolescence appears to be lengthening), it is important that we find means of giving our youth opportunities, responsibilities, and satisfactions in ways acceptable to the society.

Neglect of Teen-age Programs

The youth agencies face a great challenge in working with adolescents. Far too often, leaders have given up trying to work with them and have gradually included more and more programs and activities for elementary school children, since they are more eager, receptive, and easier to control.

Junior Legion baseball for teen-agers is successful, so we initiate the pony league, colt league, and Little League. These are also successful, so we think we should provide the same opportunities for the seven and eight-year-olds; and we organize pee wee leagues or minor leagues. Then we suddenly discover that the Legion program is gone—baseball is "old hat" to a teen-ager after he has participated in it for ten years.

As agencies have extended their services to include younger and older members via pre-school, old-age, and family programs, they have tended to push teen-agers out of the picture. A Y may build membership income and serve a large total of members through tiny-tot swims and family pot-luck suppers, but it is unlikely to increase its service to teen-agers concurrently. Adolescents may feel strongly possessive toward facilities that they think of as their own. They can be as dissatisfied with little children running in and out of their lounge as adults may be about noisy voices and rock music.

Specific Teen-age Needs

Specifically, what are the needs of today's teen-ager? If agencies are to work effectively with this age group, they must understand the unique needs and desires of modern youth. In addition to the basic needs which all human beings share, such as security, power, recognition, and affection, teens have many specific needs that are especially important to them.

The basic problem of the adolescent is that of *finding himself*, of changing his self-image from the familiar childhood one to conform to his new, more adult, environment. Finding answers to unverbalized questions such as "Who am I?" "Where do I belong?" "Where am I going?" is of vital concern to him. An outward show of cockiness and boisterousness often covers up a genuine confusion in the search for self.

Another need of youth is that of *conformity*. If the prevailing teen-age attitude toward an agency is that it is "square," few adolescents will ignore the label and participate anyway, even though the program might have considerable appeal. A Purdue University study of 18,000 teen-agers disclosed an almost neurotic fear of peer disapproval.[7]

One of the most ardent desires of the adolescent is to find *acceptance*. The young child in most cases finds this acceptance in his home and family. By mid-adolescence, however, the youth is no longer a child and needs acceptance by his peers (Figure 3–4). To be an outsider and rejected is one of the toughest crises for a teen-ager to face.

The growth of cliques, gangs, and high-school sororities and fraternities is an undesirable outcome of youth's search for acceptance. Generally, these groups thrive in areas where the schools and the community have done an inadequate job of providing more wholesome alternatives which would fulfill the need for acceptance and belonging.

Dropouts

One of the critical problems of many of the youth organizations that endeavor to serve varied age groups is the large dropout rate at older ages. The Boy Scouts, for example, find they have the largest membership and

[7] H.H. Remmers and D.H. Radler, *The American Teenager* (Indianapolis-New York: The Bobbs-Merrill Company, Inc., 1957).

Figure 3–4
Youth organizations offer programs which provide a young person with a chance
for adventure, new friendships, and the fellowship of others his age. *Courtesy
American Youth Hostels, Inc.*

greatest appeal during boys' Cub years and a continuing decrease in membership and appeal as boys get older. The need to adapt programs to meet
basic needs is evident. In a 1968 research report, *Is Scouting in Tune with
the Times?*,[8] an effort was made to determine the interests and values that
decline with age and those that either continue or expand. Being with boys
only, wearing a uniform, and having ceremonies tended to be of less interest
year by year as boys grew older. The desire to be with mixed groups of boys
and girls, to prepare for job opportunities, and to show what can be done
by oneself increased as boys matured. Team sports and outdoor activities
were two interests that remained high until older Explorer years.

Studies such as this are significant in that they provide guidelines for
varying age groups.

During 1950 and 1951, county extension agents in 11 western states
studied 205 boys and girls. These young people, chosen at random, had
been in 4-H club work for one year but had not re-enrolled. Case reports
written for each subject revealed many different local situations, but most
reports had one thing in common. The situation in which many first-year
members found themselves did not satisfy some of their basic developmental

[8] Daniel Yankelovich, Inc., *Is Scouting in Tune with the Times?* (New Brunswick, N.J.: Boy Scouts of America, 1968).

needs. The committee recommended that more attention be given to these three aspects of working with boys and girls:

1. their need for a sense of personal worth—desire for attention, desire for prestige, desire to excel;
2. their need for a continuing sense of personal security;
3. their desire for a feeling of accomplishment.[9]

Interests of Adolescents

Closely related to needs are an adolescent's interests. A study of adolescent boys conducted in 1954 by the Survey Research Center at the University of Michigan for the Boy Scouts pointed out the attraction of career exploration, team sports, swimming, hunting, working on cars, outdoor and

Figure 3–5
Most teen-age boys have a strong interest in automobiles. *Courtesy Big Brothers of America.*

[9] Laurel Sabrosky, *Western States Survey* (Washington, D.C.: Division of Extension Research, U.S. Department of Agricultural Extension, 1951).

social activities (Figure 3–5).[10] An interest study of youth in Schenectady, New York, showed that the leading interests of both boys and girls were television, movies, radio, dating, swimming, and church.

Interests change from year to year and from city to city. The alert adult advisor or agency staff member will need to keep in close touch with changing teen interests if his organization is to reach more than a minority of youth.

[10] Survey Research Center, Institute for Social Research, University of Michigan, A Study of Adolescent Boys (New Brunswick, N.J.: Boy Scouts of America, 1956).

COMMON GOALS
AND METHODS
OF ACHIEVING THEM

Chapter 4

The voluntary youth organizations operate on the assumption that the child's personality development and the acceptance of social responsibility can be furthered through participation in their programs. These programs are voluntarily selected activities, largely of a recreational nature, usually taking place in peer groups. Agencies also assume that the influence of the leader, functioning in an informal situation, is significant.

Although the programs of the youth-serving organizations are primarily recreational in method, they are educational in their objectives. Each organization has its own statement of objectives and its own unique methods of achieving them, but there are purposes common to all, variously expressed as development of "integrated personality," "character," "enriched living," and "social responsibility."

The Educational Policies Commission of the National Education Association listed as desirable objectives for a growing child the following: (1) self-realization; (2) human relationship; (3) economic efficiency; and (4) civic responsibility.[1] These goals may be achieved through the combined efforts of all agencies involved in the development of young people—home, school, church, and all groups concerned with the leisure-time activities of youth. Each agency may be striving in varying degrees for some or all of these goals.

Specific Objectives

Several specific objectives shared by the national youth agencies are described here.

[1] *The Purposes of Education in American Democracy* (Washington, D.C.: Educational Policies Commission, National Education Association of the United States, 1938), p. 47.

SOCIAL INTEGRATION

Agency officials hope that, through participation in their programs, young people will learn more effectively how to keep friends, adjust to others, work within groups, function democratically, and respect the rights of others. All of the agencies accept the democratic ideal as a major goal and try to instill the democratic method into the running of each group. All of the agencies agree on the need for giving youth opportunities to grow in responsibility. They recognize that achieving maturity is a long-term process and that progressive steps must be provided toward that end. The agencies are also interested in discovering leadership potential in young people, and in promoting such potential through wholesome activities.

DEVELOPING DEMOCRATIC LEADERSHIP

All of the agencies espouse the virtues of the democratic way of life (Figure 4–1). An important aim of the youth agencies is to teach the democratic process, through the experience of participation in a group conducted in a democratic manner.

Figure 4–1
Patriotism plays an important role in the Boy Scout program. *Courtesy Boy Scouts of America.*

PERSONALITY DEVELOPMENT

Most agencies realize that the process of personality development and character formation is an extremely complex affair. They have a strong feeling, however, that youth groups can be a potent force for the good in this process. Agency leaders realize the importance of working with the "whole child." At certain times in the past, physical education classes were conducted to develop the body; lectures were given to broaden the mind; the Bible was studied to improve the spirit. Today's professional youth worker understands that the child's life cannot be categorized and that good programs affect the member's total life (Figure 4–2). The agencies believe in the dignity of the individual—that the person is more important than the activity; that programs and groups are means to an end, not an end in themselves.

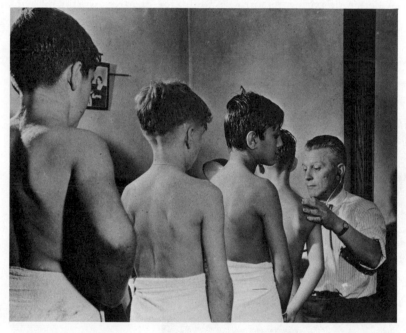

Figure 4–2

Regular physical examinations are offered Boys' Club members free of charge. Physical defects, abnormalities, malnutrition, or similar problems receive prompt corrective action. *Courtesy Boys' Clubs of America.*

CHARACTER DEVELOPMENT

While character development is closely related to the previous purposes, it has been stressed so much by the youth organizations that it probably deserves separate consideration. In our culture some of the traits associated with good character and hence promoted by youth organizations include: honesty, dependability, loyalty, thrift, sacrifice, sportsmanship, hard work, courage, loyalty, friendliness, courtesy, cleanliness, self-reliance, kindness, and reverence. Tolerance and the brotherhood of man are goals particularly relevant in today's interdependent world. Few will argue with any of these agency objectives; however, much more research is needed to determine the agencies' degree of effectiveness in reaching the objectives.

CONSTRUCTIVE USE OF LEISURE TIME

The youth organizations encourage high standards for the use of leisure time. As work hours are shortened and labor-saving devices become commonplace, Americans enjoy more leisure time each year. Experts feel that the future of America may well depend on our use of this abundant free time. One of the agencies' greatest potential contributions lies in the area of better preparing tomorrow's adults for creative, worthwhile, interesting lives (Figure 4-3).

Figure 4-3
Most youth agencies attempt to teach skills which, when mastered, will provide enjoyment the rest of one's life. *Courtesy Big Brothers of America.*

REALIZATION OF SPIRITUAL MEANINGS AND VALUES

Although the major youth-serving organizations are nondenominational, all are rooted in certain spiritual concepts. Each child is encouraged to be active in the faith of his choice, to show a reverence toward life, and to practice the Judeo-Christian concepts of brotherhood and tolerance. The Constitution of the Girl Scouts, for example, states that the motivating force in Girl Scouting is a spiritual one.

Achieving Objectives through Small Groups

The chief means of achieving these common objectives, as well as an agency's specific goals, is through the small group under adult leadership.

Youth agencies today place much faith in the potential of the group experience. Sociologists tell us that the way people learn and the attitudes they develop are influenced greatly by the groups to which they belong. The stronger the bonds of the group and the deeper the individual's involvement in the life of the group, the more influence the group exerts. Individual goalsetting is highly dependent upon group standards.

Group situations having the highest potential for influencing attitudes are small, intimate, or *primary* groups. The family, of course, is the outstanding example of the primary group. Most of the agencies attempt to organize into small, closely-knit units (Boy Scout patrols of eight boys; cabins in camp with a maximum of eight youngsters, etc.). Our value systems are largely conditioned by group membership, and it appears that groups are also very important in terms of security, psychological support, and self-understanding.

Not all groups, of course, exert a strong influence on their members. The strength of influence appears to be directly related to the degree of cohesiveness of the group, the amount of member involvement in the running of the group, and the climate that prevails at group meetings. Groups that are vital and make strong, positive contributions can be described as understanding, stimulating, flexible, cooperative, and democratic. Leadership is effective to the degree that it creates this atmosphere in the group.

In situations involving small groups, boys and girls can make new friends easily and are challenged by new ideas. They are introduced to new skills. They learn and experience the value of service to others (Figure 4–4). They get a chance to develop confidence in themselves. They learn to get along with others. Out of this experience comes leadership for the future because leadership skill is developed in a group situation.

In describing the importance of small groups, a representative of the Boys' Clubs wrote:

> We believe that the group experience can be one key to character building because groups influence the way we learn; groups influence our attitudes and our habits, beliefs and feelings; groups give us goals; groups set standards; group behavior is "catching"; groups give us support in time of trouble; groups sometimes provide us with limits within which we must learn to get along with others.

Figure 4–4
Working as volunteers in the Head Start program is a rewarding experience for members of the Tolleson High School FHA Chapter (Arizona). This FHA member works with a Head Start group on picture identification. Nancy uses a flannel board, placing different pictures on it while the children cover their eyes. *Courtesy Future Homemakers of America.*

It is through small group experience that youth have a chance to form close personal relationships with other boys and with an adult. Boys get something from the relationship with the group advisor that is so simple and commonplace, some of us forget how important it is—understanding. It is through groups that boys really have an opportunity to learn the practical problems, responsibilities and privileges of a democracy.

Out of these groups comes the leadership for the future, because leadership comes from within the group itself—with the adult in the role of an advisor.[2]

[2] Howard G. Gibbs, Director, Program Services, Boys' Clubs of America, Unpublished statement.

Since children and teen-agers are gregarious by nature, we can be almost certain that they will unite in groups of one kind or another. Community leaders throughout the country agree that it is most desirable to provide this social outlet through the national youth-serving agencies with proven programs and high ideals, rather than gamble on the outcome of informal neighborhood gangs without adult guidance.

Group work as a field of social work began in the youth-serving agencies. In fact, for some time there was a tendency to call the youth agencies "group work agencies." This title is not in vogue today because the agencies do much which cannot be classified as group work, and the term *group work* is now applied to many situations other than those found in voluntary agencies for youth.

Group work is commonly thought of as a process or a technique. It is one of three branches of social work, the other two being case work and community organization. Group work is dedicated to the task of assisting persons to attain a fuller and more satisfying life through group relationships. It is one method by which agencies attempt to fulfill their objectives.

Group work techniques may be applied to nearly any group of individuals in any setting—a club, committee, class, or team. The group worker is concerned with developing social responsibility and active citizenship for the improvement of society.

Trecker defined social group work as follows:

> Social group work is a method through which individuals in social agency settings are helped by a worker who guides their interaction in program activities so that they might relate themselves to others and experience growth opportunities in accordance with their needs and capabilities to the end of individual, group and community development.[3]

The group worker is not so much a "leader" as an "enabler" or "helper." The group will have its own leaders, official or unofficial.

Effectiveness of Group Work

Examination of two Y-Teen groups or other youth clubs may reveal that while the clubs are outwardly similar in appearance, one of the club advisors may use good group work techniques while the other advisor may not. The advisor not applying group work theory would probably be concerned primarily with such questions as "Was the meeting orderly?" "Who won the game?" or "Did the program go well?" While these questions may also interest the leader trained in group work theory, he would be

3 Harleigh B. Trecker, *Social Group Work, Principles and Practices* (New York: Association Press, 1955), p. 5.

more likely to ask such questions as "How meaningful an experience did the members have?" "How are the members reacting to one another?" and "Are the members growing in their concept and application of democracy?"

The group work method is neither the fastest nor the most efficient one for obtaining results. A group worker believes that more important than "getting a job done" is the task of providing group members with a satisfying experience involving personal growth. He recognizes that helping groups and individuals achieve independence and self-reliance is a slow task, but one that is essential if our youth are to develop into productive, responsible citizens.

Group work is founded on democratic principles, and therefore the individual is never subordinate to the activity. As many of the newly-emerging nations are discovering, democratic processes must be learned and practiced over a period of time before they can be effective. Youngsters who lack experience in democratic action cannot be expected suddenly to become contributing, concerned members of a democratic society when they reach their twenty-first birthdays. The truly effective citizens in our communities are those who have had progressively rewarding experiences in the democratic process from an early age and have been part of a successful organization or project.

One of the biggest problems associated with the continuing trend toward urbanization is the feeling of isolation and helplessness that often encompasses residents of a large metropolis. Groups of various kinds are vitally important not only as a means of feeling accepted and important, but also as a means of expression and community action.

It is very unfortunate that so many of our adults have no group affiliation. When asked why not, they will usually shrug their shoulders and reply, "I'm not a joiner." Those who are "not joiners" in most cases have had poor experience in groups of one kind or another or have had no experience at all in organized groups.

It is important that all individuals be given opportunities to belong and to gain acceptance as well as to create, share, express themselves, give service, and have fun—all functions of successful groups. The group worker's function is to make these opportunities available so that he may help young people along the road toward responsible and well-adjusted adulthood.

Factors in Successful Group Work

Certain factors are necessary if group work is to be possible. The first requirement is a worker or advisor from outside the group. This adult needs to possess at least some training and skills in human relationships. The second requirement is a group small enough to permit close relationships and similar enough in background (age, interests, education) to develop cohesiveness. Groups are formed by and for individuals with like concerns.

To function well, any group must also have a goal or goals. This goal may be in terms of member improvement (social, educational, recreational), or in terms of service to the community or world. One of the important tasks of the worker or advisor is to help the group formulate and express its goals.

The advisor is the intermediary between the group and the agency. He must help the group to understand agency goals and objectives. The way in which the advisor works is a distinguishing characteristic of social group action.

After extensive research with adolescent groups, the Sherifs concluded, "The crux of the matter for effective policy and action is not the busy work *as such,* not the programmed activities *as such,* or even the end products of training to exhibit for public display. The cardinal point is to insure throughout (whatever the activities) the youth's feeling of having a *function* in their initiation, development and execution. What we do not take part in initiating and developing and producing, what we engage in without our own choosing and aspiring, is not felt as ours. What we do not feel as ours lacks in the experience of inner-urgency and in sense of responsibility. The important thing to actualize at the very start is not immediate technical proficiency, but the feeling of participation, the feeling that we have functions in the larger scheme of things, the feeling that we have indispensable roles with others in things that all feel should be done."[4]

Mass Activities

Not all of the program of the youth-serving organizations takes place in small groups, however. "Mass" activities are used to a greater or lesser extent, depending upon the organization. Mass activities would include everything from a Boy Scout Jamboree drawing 40,000 boys to a dance for 50 teen-agers.

In all activities, however conducted, the important thing is not the activity itself but what happens to the individual who participates in it. A particular activity may be good or bad, depending on what it does to the individual.

[4] M. Sherif and Carolyn W. Sherif, *Reference Groups* (New York: Harper & Row, Publishers, 1964), pp. 314–15.

Differences between Agencies

Although there are many similarities in function and objectives between the various voluntary youth-serving agencies, there are also important differences between them which justify the number found in any good-sized community. Such differences include (1) specific focus of objectives; (2) choice of constituency with regard to age, sex, or background; (3) types of program made available by facilities and staff; (4) philosophy of program development, and (5) the role of the professional in the organization.

Duplication of services is probably not too great a concern because of the wide variety of approaches found. However, there often is competition for the time of the middle-class child, for adult leadership, and, of course, for finances. Competition within limits may be a good thing. The community with both Girl Scouts and Camp Fire Girls will probably have more girls participating than if it were served by only one or the other. Although the two organizations are similar in many ways, some girls will be attracted to one who would not join the other.

Any failures or shortcomings the youth agencies may have are not in terms of poor or unworthy goals but rather in terms of the abilities of staff and volunteers to find the means to reach these idealistic aims.

LEADERSHIP

The youth-serving agencies are concerned with leadership from two closely related standpoints. First, they seek to develop the leadership capabilities of the young people they serve. Through the democratic functioning of groups, the agencies hope to nurture both the ability to lead and the ability to follow. Second, they seek to promote a leadership-conscious staff of voluntary and paid workers. These adults must be familiar with the principles of group leadership and possess the personal qualities, training, and knowledge of techniques necessary to create a healthy environment for leadership growth.

Whether the goal of leadership development of youth is attained largely depends upon the agencies' success in obtaining a capable, well-trained staff. This chapter considers their concern with leadership development of both youth and staff.

Importance of Leadership

The destiny of America and perhaps of the world may well depend upon the kind of leaders this nation can produce. There is little doubt about our capacity to produce specialized leadership to maintain our place on the frontiers of engineering, science, medicine, and nearly all of the technical fields. There is some feeling, however, that whether we succeed or fail as a civilization will depend upon the amount of "generalized" leadership we can produce.

Specialists can solve many problems, but the really big issues of the day —war or peace, decay of our cities, eradication of poverty, etc.—depend upon great leaders who can see beyond the boundaries of any one academic field.

There has never been enough of this generalized leadership. The success of the Chinese Communists in breaking down the morale of American servicemen whom they had captured during the Korean War was due largely to the fact that they were able to isolate those men with leadership qualities from the others, who could then be turned against each other and become completely demoralized. The tragic part was that only about 5 percent of the captives demonstrated enough leadership to necessitate their isolation.

Leadership is a requisite in nearly all walks of life in America today—business, industry, education, government, and military service. How, then, does one become a leader? Why do some individuals have leadership capabilities while others do not?

Developing Leadership in the Group

Not many years ago there was much talk about "born" leaders or "natural" leaders. Modern leadership theory pretty well rejects this idea of predetermination. We now believe that leadership is learned and that most people possess the capacity to become leaders. Whether or not a child develops qualities of leadership depends on the experiences he undergoes. Leadership grows out of participation (Figure 5–1).

One of the biggest potential values of the voluntary youth agencies is that of serving as a laboratory where democratic leadership can be practiced and can flourish. The superintendent of recreation in a large city stated that his best recreation leaders on playgrounds were girls with a Girl Scout or Camp Fire background because of the years of leadership experience they brought with them to the job.

THE NATURE OF GROUP LEADERSHIP

Our concept of the nature of leadership has changed drastically in recent years, due to significant research in the area. We used to think in terms of "leaders and followers." We now know that there are different kinds of leadership and that any successful enterprise must have more than one leader. Many people still think of leaders and officers as synonymous terms. Objective studies of any group show that officers may exert little or no leadership, while others in the group may fulfill very valuable leadership functions. Evidence points to the conclusion that the more widely leadership functions are shared, the more successful any group will be.

A democratic society such as ours places responsibilities upon leaders of youth which are far different from those of leaders in totalitarian societies. In the latter, there is an effort to develop uniformity in thought and action in accordance with the ideals of the state. The individual is thought to exist for the service of the state. Efficiency and obedience to the leaders are regarded as primary virtues.

Figure 5–1
Leadership development...an
important goal of all youth
groups. *Courtesy Junior
Achievement, Inc.*

In contrast, in a democratic society there is respect for individual differences and recognition of the worth of the individual human being. The state is considered the servant of the individual. Leaders of youth should attempt to give each young person the opportunity to develop to the limit of his abilities and to accept his individual responsibility toward social improvement. The point of view that growth is dependent upon the interaction of human beings lies at the base of work with groups.

Many an adult leader of a Scout troop or Gra-Y club has taken on his position enthusiastic about the desirability of allowing the group to be self-directing and democratically run, only to find that by the second meeting there is so much havoc and confusion that he feels compelled to run the group in an authoritarian, strong-arm fashion. The ability to function democratically involves a process of gradually sharing more and more responsibilities. The amount of self-direction possible is closely related to the maturity of the members in the group. The wise adult leader will share responsibilities and authority to the extent that the members are prepared to handle it, hoping that they will gradually grow toward the capability of complete self-direction.

Although it may be easier to operate with an autocratic method, keeping everyone in line with "big stick" techniques, in the long run the democratically-run group will develop better *esprit de corps* and the members will be given an experience which will aid them throughout life. Evidence seems to indicate that if a youth group is to effect desirable changes in the attitudes and behavior of its members, the group must be self-directed, rather than run by a well-meaning adult. The adult role is to organize and establish an atmosphere in which youth-run groups can emerge (Figure 5–2). If the adult can refrain from taking over when the members make "wrong" decisions, unless such decisions are dangerous, the group may be able to mature into a responsible, democratically-oriented organization.

Figure 5–2
A company officer gets some help from an advisor. *Courtesy Junior Achievement, Inc.*

Kinds of Adult Leadership of Groups

A study by Lippitt and White considered the effects of three kinds of adult leadership (autocratic, democratic, and laissez-faire) on the behavior of four clubs of 11-year-old children.[1] They concluded that the pattern of interaction and the emotional development of the groups were directly influenced by the type of leadership. The differences in club behavior were established as being due to the effect of differences in leadership types, rather than to the characteristics of the clubs. In general, the democratic type of leadership proved more productive and beneficial to the group than either the authoritarian or the laissez-faire.

A national Girl Scout study found that eight out of ten intermediate

1 Ralph K. White and Ronald Lippitt, *Autocracy and Democracy* (New York: Harper & Row, 1960).

Scouts questioned felt that their opinions and preferences were taken into consideration by their leaders.[2] More than nine out of ten senior Scouts felt the same way. While younger children are often content to have an adult make all of the decisions and plans, older youth rightfully expect to have a voice in the affairs of their clubs.

Principles of Group Leadership

Assuming that there is general agreement on the desirability of democratic leadership, we offer several principles of leadership worthy of note. A good democratic leader:

1. leads by example;
2. helps a group to define its goals and work toward them;
3. knows when to stay in the background and work behind the scenes, rather than always "hogging" the limelight;
4. shares leadership with as many as possible, motivating members to accept as much responsibility as they can handle;
5. strives to develop teamwork and feelings of group cohesiveness;
6. does not ask a member of the group to do something he would not do himself—he pitches right in whenever there is a job to be done;
7. is concerned about the welfare and growth of *all* members of the group— not just those who are likeable and well-behaved;
8. is not easily discouraged; perseveres in spite of disappointment and temporary failure;
9. always plans with the group, not for them;
10. performs the function of enabler, coordinator, helper, and convener, rather than "director." He works to establish a climate of cooperation and friendliness.

TECHNIQUES OF GROUP LEADERSHIP

While there is no magic formula for making a group experience a success, our increased knowledge of group dynamics enables us to see some of the factors which appear to distinguish the successful leader from the mediocre leader.

Leadership studies indicate that the most successful leaders manage either consciously or unconsciously to:

1. Help the group to develop and understand group goals. The success of a group can best be measured in terms of the degree to which it has

[2] Survey Research Center, Institute for Social Research, University of Michigan, *Adolescent Girls* (New York: Girl Scouts of the United States of America, n.d.).

achieved its goals. This achievement can be reached only if a group understands what its goals are and sees the relation of program to the goals.

2. *Create a warm, friendly atmosphere.* Such relatively minor considera-
tions as chair arrangement, proper lighting, room temperature, and insula-
tion from interfering noise can make a big difference in the success of a
meeting. Getting people to know each other is essential—especially where
new members or visitors are concerned. A meeting may radiate feelings of
trust, good humor, and togetherness or feelings of suspicion, fear, and
apathy, according to the way the leader sets the stage. The good leader
must be sensitive to the needs of others present.

3. *Gain maximum participation in the affairs of the group.* This may
involve subtly preventing a few members from dominating the meeting as
well as actively drawing in those who tend to be withdrawn. Attendance and
drop-out rates are directly related to whether or not the individual member
feels he has an important role to play in the organization. Good leaders
maximize member involvement (Figure 5–3).

4. *Utilize a variety of program methods.* Depending on the nature and
size of the group, the program content, and many other factors, several
of the following techniques may prove useful: audio-visuals, role-playing,
panel discussions, buzz groups, demonstrations, "ice-breaker" games, lectures,
brainstorming, and field trips. The successful leader will incorporate a
variety of techniques and program formats to keep the meetings interesting
and exciting.

Agency Leadership Positions

The typical youth agency relies heavily on both paid and volunteer leadership. Without volunteers the tremendous size of the youth agency programs
would be impossible (Figure 5–4). On the other hand, the professional
plays an invaluable role in recruiting the volunteers, coordinating, admin-
istrating, training, and giving stability to the organizations. The paid and
volunteer leaders are equally important to the success of a modern youth
agency.

VOLUNTEERS

Three types of persons help fill millions of unpaid positions within the
agencies: (1) those who actually volunteer to work; (2) those who are
sought out by an organization because of their talents, and (3) those who
are "drafted" because there is nobody else to do the job. The latter two
groups cannot be considered as strictly volunteers. Unfortunately, there
is good reason to believe that the third category—those who get stuck—
comprises the largest group of the so-called volunteers. Many is the mother

Figure 5-3
A group of Girl Scouts singing. *Courtesy Girl Scouts of the United States of America.*

who discovers that if her boy is to be a Cub Scout, she must serve as den mother.

Volunteers are a tremendous resource for any agency and their value should not be ignored. Agencies utilizing large numbers of volunteers are able to offer infinitely more program opportunities than agencies using only paid staff. At the same time the presence of volunteers in the community assures a potent force of citizens knowledgeable about, and sold on, the value of the agency. They tend to interpret the agency to their associates and can be called on in time of need. Whenever a fund drive or membership campaign is organized, volunteer leaders and former volunteers generally form the nucleus of the work force.

Parents undoubtedly comprise the largest single source of volunteer leaders. Normally they are recruited because they are interested in a program through a son or daughter, and, frequently, because nobody else is available. For some types of jobs such as troop committees, agency boards, travel chairmen, and telephone callers, parents are the logical persons to carry the responsibility. Often they do not make the best adult leaders or advisors because of factors such as lack of experience, lack of patience, or the age difference between them and the children. Usually, problems arise when

Figure 5-4
Blue Birds, youngest members of the Camp Fire Girls, are assisted in their craft projects by their volunteer leader. *Courtesy Camp Fire Girls, Inc.*

the leader has his or her own children in the group—some show favoritism; some shortchange their own children in attempting to avoid favoritism; and even if neither of these happens, the leader's child is often put at a disadvantage in the group.

Since nearly all youth organizations in this country rely primarily on volunteers, planned procedures for recruitment, training, supervision, and recognition of volunteers are vital to the success of any agency.

A program for *recruitment* should logically begin with development of job descriptions. What will the duties and responsibilities of the volunteer be? What skills, education, and experience should he possess? Will he be reimbursed for travel expenses? What agency resources are available to him? These and other questions need to be answered before the volunteer is sought out.

Occasionally a good volunteer will walk into the office and announce his availability. In practice this seldom happens. Usually an organized effort must be made to recruit qualified persons. Much of this effort occurs as staff members continually keep their eyes and ears open for potential recruits, but often an organized campaign is needed. After a list of needed personnel is arrived at and job descriptions completed, key community leaders, board members, and friends of the organization are requested to suggest names.

If the community has a volunteer bureau, its staff might assist. The news media may help out. Records of past participants may yield names of people who either will help out themselves or can suggest names. Not all who are suggested or who volunteer should be accepted. Before an agency engages a volunteer, his background and references should be carefully checked. Agencies who have bypassed this step in their haste to get the person on the job, often regret their action later. The time and effort saved is not worthwhile when the possibility exists that the volunteer's real motivation could be that he is a homosexual or wants to gain access to the businessmen's locker combinations or the petty cash drawer. Only one incident is needed to mar the image of an agency in its community.

Usually volunteers will require at least some *training* before being put on the job. Even if they possess the technical background, they will need to be oriented to the agency and its purposes. The job description will help them to understand their assignment. An important aspect of training involves knowledge of the organization's resources (films, library, facilities, equipment, etc.) and how they can be obtained. They must know to whom to look for assistance and supervision, and they need to realize that they represent the agency to many people. Training may be formal, consisting of classes, staff meetings, conferences and retreats, or informal, consisting of reading, serving as an assistant on the job, or working closely with a paid staff worker. The important point is that training not be ignored or left to chance.

Special training and special opportunities for service as assistant or junior leaders may be offered to the older youth in the program. Though these young people should not be given full responsibility, they may be initiated into leadership activities so that they can give helpful service and prepare for greater responsibilities in the future.

Supervision should be given regularly and frequently through visits to the group with which the volunteer works and through private conferences. The volunteer's efforts should be evaluated with him. Care must be taken that the volunteer has a useful assignment and that his time and talents are being fully and profitably utilized.

Formal recognition of volunteer services is usually an annual event. It may take the form of giving awards or merely publicly thanking the volunteers. The recognition hopefully will serve as an inspiration and challenge to new recruits in the organization as well as a reward to those receiving the plaudits. Informal recognition may be constantly given through the expression of thanks, the giving of encouragement, and the interest shown in the problems and accomplishments of the volunteers.

Building-centered associations such as Y's and Jewish Community Centers often provide the volunteer with a family membership in exchange for his services. Youth volunteers are often encouraged by tangible evidences of recognition such as T-shirts, staff jackets, trips, dances, parties, and special privileges.

PART-TIME PAID STAFF

Those agencies with building-centered programs normally hire many part-time staff members for such jobs as lifeguards, instructors, locker-room attendants, or desk clerks. These are usually subprofessional positions held by college students, retired men, or housewives. Turnover rates are typically high and salaries traditionally low. Such organizations as Y's and Boys' Clubs have relied more and more on part-time workers in recent years as memberships have grown faster than budgets, and qualified full-time staffs have become harder to find. This policy has had the effect of increasing the ratio of members to professionals, forcing agencies to use the professional staff less and less for face-to-face leadership and more and more as administrators, supervisors, and trainers of part-time and volunteer staff.

PROFESSIONAL STAFF

All of the major agencies require a college degree for new professional staff members. The YMCA stipulates a fifth year of college prior to certification. Professional youth workers come from a variety of college majors. In general, the agencies are more interested in the personal qualities of the applicant than in the academic content of his education (Figure 5–5).

A student looking forward to a career in youth agency work is advised to include a strong liberal arts background in his preparation, with a major in social science, recreation administration, psychology, or education. The Boy Scouts also recommend work in business administration. The Master of Social Work degree is desired by several of the agencies for persons in executive positions. This is especially true of settlement houses, Jewish Community Centers, YMCA, and YWCA.

Job opportunities with the major agencies are plentiful. Median salaries have nearly doubled in the past ten years, with starting pay usually roughly equivalent to the salaries paid to public school teachers.

Desirable Traits of Youth Leaders

The youth agencies are only as good as their leaders. Many people have attempted to draw up lists of leadership traits. There is a good deal of disagreement and little evidence that any one list will ever be valid, since as soon as we accept one trait, we can think of a good leader who is an exception.

However, there are several basic qualifications which agency officials

Figure 5–5
Professional, skilled, full-time adult leadership is a "must" for all youth
agencies. Informal guidance shapes young lives and gives boys a start,
with basic values. *Courtesy Boys' Clubs of America.*

would do well to keep in mind in the never-ending search for leadership
talent.

1. A good youth leader is worthy of emulation. Young people need someone
   to look up to who is deserving of their respect and who can serve as an
   example of what they may become.
2. He likes and understands young people.
3. He has an understanding of and a sympathy for agency goals and objectives.
4. He has the specific skills required to do the job.

Since the major purposes of the youth organizations are related to
personality development, development of attitudes, and so forth, item
number four is probably the least important characteristic. Unfortunately,
it is often the main criterion used in the selection of leaders. Obviously, if
the group is a scuba-diving class or a karate group, it would be folly to
select a leader who was not well grounded in the activity. In technical

program areas such as these, it is important that the leader be both exemplary in character and skilled in the subject.

In most positions where volunteers are used, however, the skills are much less important than the motivation and personal qualities of the leaders. Yet far too often, the skills of the leader are the main consideration, with little thought given to what kind of influence the person will be on the group. It would be foolish to enlist an ex-professional baseball player as a Little League coach if he were to conduct the group on a "win at any cost" basis; unfortunately, this often happens when a group sees skills rather than values as the principal objective.

Common Problems Faced by Youth Leaders

All groups have problems, at least all groups composed of human beings. Certainly youth groups have their share of difficulties. The adult leader who is easily discouraged and half-heartedly motivated is not likely to remain with a youth group very long.

Experience has shown that, in general, those groups that have the strongest common purposes and goals have the fewest problems. Groups that lack purpose are apt to flounder. Any community has many groups and committees which drift along with little sense of purpose, sustained only by tradition and people's reluctance to end any group which has had some success in the past. Perhaps committees should be set up to abolish purposeless committees and clubs.

In a youth group situation the leader must help the members to set realistic goals and work toward them. Often a fund-raising drive, a challenge by another group, an appeal for aid in a disaster, or a proposal for a cross-country caravan will spark a group into unified action where previously conflict, bickering, and apathy were the rule. Real leadership often emerges when a group faces a difficult, demanding challenge.

A danger, of course, is that the group will become excited about a big project which proves to be too ambitious at the time, and which ends in failure or frustration.

Another big problem facing groups is that of factions or cliques within the organization. Teen-agers, especially, tend to be snobbish and clannish. An ounce of prevention is worth a pound of cure here. Successful leaders prevent cliques before they develop by carefully working new members in and by helping all members to get to know and appreciate each other through having fun together and working together in various combinations.

Conflicts often arise in groups. The way these are handled will determine whether the group is to be split or is to forge ahead. Voting is not the ideal way to settle differences of opinion. In a small group it tends to alienate those who are on the "losing" side. Often they will not give wholehearted support to the decision and may even get secret pleasure if the endeavor fails and they can say, "I told you so."

It is a much preferable leadership technique to work for a consensus of opinion. Often further discussion will resolve differences. If not, a compromise may be reached.

Several other problems which detract from the effectiveness of youth groups include:

1. failure to share responsibilities;
2. unwillingness to experiment or try new ideas;
3. poor communication at all levels;
4. getting bogged down by red tape or busy work;
5. indecision;
6. programming which lacks imagination.

Most of the major youth agencies place a good deal of emphasis on leadership training, both for adults and youth leaders. These efforts need to be increased, especially in the area of human relations, group dynamics, and leadership theory. The effectiveness of agencies in achieving their goals is dependent upon the quality of paid and volunteer leadership. It is of major importance to find, train, supervise, and give recognition to workers of high quality. The time is long past when good will alone was the requisite for leadership. An understanding of how to lead and how to develop leadership is essential.

PROGRAMS AND
PROGRAMMING

Chapter 6

Leaders or advisors of youth groups too often feel that their function is to "put on a good program." Although a good program is vital to the success and continuation of any group, the adult leader or advisor will have more success achieving the purposes and objectives of the organization if he assumes a role of helping the members develop their own program. Far too frequently, a program becomes an end unto itself rather than a tool to accomplish other goals and objectives.

How to Build a Program

The logical starting point in the process of program formation is with the organization's purposes and objectives. Careful consideration of these objectives will aid a group in deciding not only what to do but also how to go about doing it. Even with the more specific programs of Boy Scouts, Girl Scouts, and Camp Fire Girls, bringing the interest of the members into the planning process is possible. The choice of program activities is almost unlimited. The Durans' program encyclopedia includes 630 pages with over 3,200 suggestions.[1] The authors of the encyclopedia would probably be the first to admit that even this list could be expanded.

In planning programs with a group, we need to consider several other factors in addition to the group's objectives. It goes without saying that, unless a program has appeal to the members, it will be a failure no matter

[1] Dorothy B. Duran and Clement A. Duran, *New Encyclopedia of Successful Program Ideas* (New York: Association Press, 1968).

how lofty the purpose behind it. Too often, leaders superimpose a program of what they think the youth should be interested in, or what they need to know, without regard to interest. The inevitable result is poor attendance or disciplinary problems.

Interest-finder questionnaires are frequently used to get members' expression of interest, and these have the advantage of suggesting ideas that the group may never have thought of. The essential factor is that the members be included in the program-planning process.

It is important for the leader to introduce new ideas, rather than to limit programs to the members' expressed interest. Just asking a group what they want to do does not build a program. The leader must come with program possibilities, including the program suggestions of the agency under whose auspices the group functions. According to a national Girl Scout study, all activities in which girls had participated received considerably higher enjoyment ratings than the ratings of anticipation by girls who had not yet taken part in the activities.[2] In other words, a leader who asks the girls to decide whether or not to try a new activity can expect that the number of those who will eventually "have fun" will be greater by at least 20 percent than those who voted in favor of the experiment. The enthusiasm of the leader for the new activity must be sufficient to get the members to try it.

Many program areas require little skill; however, in some, such as sports, art, music and dance, the leader must be careful not to discourage members by activities which are either too advanced or too elementary (Figure 6–1). Junior high school members would be insulted by a game of "Red Rover," just as second graders are often frustrated by the complexities of football.

A program with appeal to typical middle-class youth may be a complete failure in a low-income neighborhood. It is important that the leader be aware of such factors as nationality background, education, and standards of living of the group members. It may be particularly difficult for the leader of a group of upper-class or upper-middle-class children to find activities which will interest and challenge them, since many of today's children have been to Europe, have flown in helicopters, have had judo lessons, and have played in junior symphonies by the time they are 12.

From the standpoint of practicability, there are many other factors which eliminate or make difficult certain program activities. These factors include cost, space, leadership, duplication of other programs, equipment, and time. The good leader will minimize these limitations by helping the group to work out solutions such as: earning money through a fund-raising project; adapting and modifying the rules to fit the activity to the space available;

2 Survey Research Center, Institute for Social Research, University of Michigan, *Adolescent Girls.*

Figure 6–1
Crafts such as woodworking are among the popular activities at The Salvation Army's network of youth clubs and community centers. *Courtesy of The Salvation Army.*

bringing in outside resource persons to provide specialized leadership; and making or borrowing necessary equipment.

Variety is important to keep interest alive (Figure 6–2). It is easy for a club to get into a rut and make each meeting a near duplication of the previous one in terms of agenda and activities. An occasional film, party, change of meeting place, or a get-together with another group will revive interest and raise spirits.

Participation rather than watching needs to be emphasized. Youngsters want to be active and involved, and they learn much better when they are actively participating. Group meetings can provide an outlet for creative expression in a number of ways.

Activities which stress teamwork and cooperation should be promoted, rather than those which are divisive and competitive. Competitive activities, when used, should be kept on a level of good fun, with awards minimized.

Leaders need to encourage activities in which the whole family can be involved in some way, and those which will have a carry-over value into later life. Sensitive leaders are aware of the interests and desires of the minority in their groups and avoid limiting programs to just what the majority wants.

Finally, constant evaluation of the program is needed. Much of this evaluation is done informally by the leader with an "ear to the ground," but on regular occasions it is helpful to sit down with the group for a critical program evaluation, as the lead-up to future program planning.

Figure 6-2
Crafts projects are employed in many youth programs, including Pioneer
Girls. *Courtesy Pioneer Girls.*

Basic Approaches to Program

Youth agency program is basically formed in two ways: the group work
approach and the national program approach. The Y clubs, Boys' Clubs,
Explorer Scout posts, Jewish Community Centers, and settlement houses
normally favor the first approach, whereby the direction of the program
evolves from the group (within the limits of agency policy and purpose).

Trecker summarizes the group work attitude toward program as follows:
"While program is important, the way in which the program is planned and
conducted is of greater importance." He then lists seven steps in the program development process: (1) the continuous discovery of needs and
interests; (2) the selection of a starting point in the program; (3) the
analysis of what is needed in way of work responsibilities to carry out the
program; (4) the allocation of duties to various members; (5) the coordination of individual efforts and the creation of group unity; (6) the program
itself, and (7) the evaluation.[3]

The chief advantage of this approach lies in the growth of the individual
as he becomes involved in the planning process. Under the guidance of a

[3] Harleigh B. Trecker, *Social Group Work* (New York: Association Press, 1955),
p. 161.

skilled group worker or advisor, members of the group can grow in responsibility, creativity, expression, and faith in the democratic process. The program is more apt to reflect the actual interests, and hopefully the needs, of the group members than a program which involves members less.

The primary drawbacks to this type of program development are that with poor or mediocre adult advisors the program may be unimaginative and lacking in purpose: for example, the junior high girls' club's only expressed interest may be in putting on dances. Many groups of children and teen-agers have not had adequate background for carrying out the responsibilities of a self-governing, democratically run group; and, unless the adult leadership is talented, the meetings may be one continual round of horseplay and chaos with nothing purposeful accomplished. In this case, instead of experiencing personal growth, the individuals may soon develop the attitude that the group is a farce, and may drop out with negative feelings toward the agency.

The advantages of strong national programs such as those followed by the Boy Scouts, Girl Scouts, Camp Fire Girls, and, to some extent, 4-H, lie in the use of national experts to work out activities and requirements which are educational, progressive, and purposeful (Figure 6–3). The average adult can, with a minimum of training, follow the national plan and do an adequate job of leading a group. Awards are used to a great extent in these national programs. The awards are a strong motivating factor and encourage members to participate in activities previously unknown to them. Sometimes the award, rather than the knowledge of or enjoyment of the activity, becomes the goal; but, on the other hand, a lifelong interest is often developed by a boy or girl in an area he would never have discovered if he had not been stimulated by the chance to earn a badge.

Weaknesses of national program planning, other than the false motivation mentioned above, include the following.

1. The program may not be related to the interests or the needs of a particular individual or group because of interests and needs varying from community to community and even within a community. The programs of the Scouting groups have had the most appeal and best success with middle-class children. Those from other social strata are more often than not deterred by the rigid requirements.

2. The member misses out on the experience of helping to develop the program. It is the agency's program or the adult leader's program, not "our" program.

A good leader or advisor in these organizations, of course, employs much of the best of the group work approach, along with the national program. The national program is then used as a foundation upon which the group

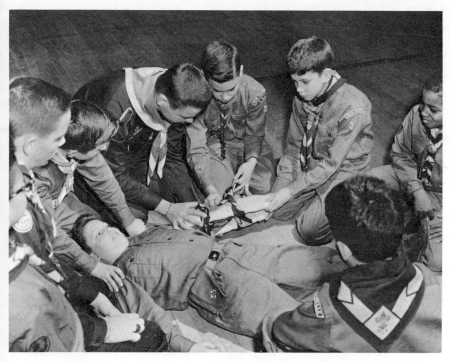

Figure 6–3
First aid is one of the many program skills emphasized in the Boy Scout
advancement program. *Courtesy Boy Scouts of America.*

program is expanded. Good Scout troops, for example, do much in the way
of program besides badge work and formal ceremony. The Scouts are
involved in the planning of the program as well as in the conduct of it.
Youngsters move up into increasingly responsible positions in the troop
as they become ready and they exert a good deal of leadership in the troop's
affairs.

Badge programs of the Scouting groups have been criticized as taking
some of the fun out of scouting. In an attempt to keep up with the times,
new badges such as World Brotherhood, My Government, and Community
Safety have been devised. Unfortunately, the requirements may present
unpleasant hurdles to get over on the way to a badge, and they may also
duplicate the content of the schools' curriculum. It is well to remember
that Lord Baden-Powell referred to the Boy Scout program as the scouting
game. Activities with fun and adventure can be expected to attract and hold
youngsters to a much greater extent than those which resemble classroom
work.

Some of the reasons that children and youth join groups are: to pursue interests and develop skills; to make or gain acceptance and status; to learn to relate to the opposite sex; to make friends; to become part of an influential body; to become free of parental control; to have fun; and, possibly most important, to belong because their friends belong and joining is "the thing to do." Wise group workers use this knowledge in forming new groups and in keeping existing ones vital. Opportunities need to be provided for developing new skills and interests; members need to be given a chance to make friendships and to gain some measure of status. The easiest way to start a new group is to interest a few key students who can easily influence their friends to join.

Most important of all, since membership is voluntary, the meetings must provide enjoyment and satisfaction. This does not mean that the entire program should be "fun and games." But in developing the program, some time should be devoted to sheer enjoyment.

Special Problems

Without question, one of the most pressing problems facing the large youth-serving agencies today is how to attract and hold the older youth in their programs. Median ages of members have shown a steady decline, with the agencies attracting a larger and larger percentage of elementary school children and a smaller and smaller percentage of junior high school and high school members. In most communities, programs for Y-Indian Guides, Cub Scouts, Bluebirds, and Brownies are booming, while the same agencies are reaching only a small fraction of adolescents through Hi-Ys, Explorer Scouts, Horizon Clubs, and Senior Girl Scouts. One reason often given for this failure to attract teen-agers is that the agencies, because of their size, tend to become institutionalized and resistant to the change which is necessary to keep up with the changing needs and interests of our youth. In fairness to the agencies, we must say that all have conducted studies of the needs and interests of the teen-ager and, as a result, have made many significant changes in their programs.

Explorer Scout officials point with pride to such examples of relating to youth's desires as the Coronado, California, Surfing Post which attracted a membership of over 100 in an area where scouting of any kind was formerly considered "square." Other Explorer posts are developed around interests as varied as Indian dancing and computer programming.[4] One Girl Scout Council discovered an immediate spurt of interest when their day camp for seniors was renamed "Archeological Dig."[5] Youth organiza-

[4] Hunsaker, Gordon D., "Explorers in the Surf", *Recreation Magazine,* Vol. LVIII, No. 6 (June, 1965) pp. 286–287, 308.
[5] Verbal report of Director of Camping of San Diego Council, Girl Scouts of U.S.A.

tions do have to be careful not to provide the older members with the "same old thing warmed over," if they hope to hold the interest of a boy or girl from ages eight through 18.

There has always been a generation gap, but there is some indication that it is wider today than it has been in the immediate past. Young people are exposed to a wider scope of influences than ever before and are usually far more sophisticated than young people of a past generation. They live in a new world in which financial insecurity seems to have disappeared for middle-income groups but to be more visible to the disadvantaged. The Korean and Vietnam wars, military service, and the ever-present threat of nuclear warfare provide a background that colors thinking in a different way than in the past. To meet the needs of this generation of young people demands understanding and new, ingenious approaches to program.

Older teen-age youth, particularly, need activities that relate them to the adult world, such as exploring careers, earning money, using cars, and participating in adult-type activities (Figure 6–4). Self-direction becomes increasingly important. They want the help of understanding adults, but they also want to make important decisions for themselves and to accept the responsibility for such decisions.

Programs that are adventurous and demanding now assume a large and

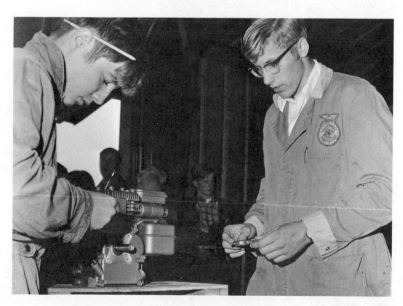

Figure 6–4
Care and maintenance of small gasoline engines is a skill being taught in many vocational agriculture classes. These FFA members sharpen their small engine skills by competing in an FFA trouble-shooting contest.
Courtesy Future Farmers of America.

important place. Climbing mountains, scuba diving, wilderness trips, and travel are examples. Team sports have a strong appeal, particularly for boys. Individual sports for both young men and women are important (Figure 6–5).

Youth are at an age of intense interest in personal and social problems. War and peace, sex relationships, religion, conservation, modern education, and the problems of race and poverty are the concern of many young people. Programs in music, art, and science must now be at a more significant level. Interests become more specialized as the youth mature.

As girls grow older their interests change from games and arts and crafts to the overwhelming choice of the older girls—the out-of-doors— reports the national Girl Scout study.[6] Nine out of 10 intermediate members

Figure 6–5
An adult leader in the Pioneer Girls assists a camper in learning correct archery form. *Courtesy Pioneer Girls.*

[6] Survey Research Center, Institute for Social Research, University of Michigan, *Adolescent Girls.*

and even more seniors listed camping, hikes, trips, and other outdoor activities as their favorite aspects of Scouting.

Program for teen-agers must be related to basic needs and drives. The same drives which lead to delinquent and anti-social behavior may be satisfied by socially acceptable recreational activities of a youth agency. As J. Edgar Hoover once put it, "Any boy would rather steal second base than steal an automobile."

Many activities planned by well-meaning adults do not meet the needs of today's teen. Programs with appeal are those with an element of glamor, thrill, status, and chance. Youth's entrancement with the automobile may be utilized to involve him in auto mechanics courses, adult-supervised car clubs, and auto safety campaigns, instead of illegal and dangerous dragging, thrill rides, and auto stealing. His natural interest in the other sex should be satisfied through wholesome coeducational programs which provide a sound preparation for marriage at a future date, rather than through unguided activities which may lead to serious problems.

For years surfing in Southern California had a reputation as a sport of the undisciplined. Many parents forbade their teens to participate because of all the anti-social behavior of the surfers—vandalism, narcotic use, lack of respect for property, and so on. Recently, the sport has been cleaned up to a considerable extent through the formation of clubs, clinics, and rules which regulate behavior, sponsor competition, and encourage high standards.[7]

Emphasis on the Family

Recreational programs have often been accused of separating families by pulling members off in a variety of different directions. Youth agencies are becoming increasingly aware of the importance of working through the family and in many cases offering programs for the entire family. Many YMCA's have changed their names to "Family YMCA's." The settlement houses and Jewish Community Centers have always attempted to work with the entire family. Cub scouting is called the world's largest home-centered organization; and, indeed, all of the major youth agencies realize the need for looking at their children and youth members in relation to their home environment. Activities such as family pot-lucks and picnics, father-son banquets, and mother-daughter teas are commonplace.

One study showed that a YMCA's effective contribution to family life does not depend upon how it is organized or whether it attempts to organize its program according to family groupings, but rather on how well it meets

[7] Michael C. Cronin, "Surf Safety Standards," *Parks and Recreation,* II, No. 7 (July, 1967) pp. 16–17, 34–36; J.R. White and D.R. White, "Surfers and Community Relations," *Parks and Recreation,* III, No. 8 (August, 1968) pp. 27–28, 58.

the following characteristics: (1) commitment to and recognition of the importance of familial influence in the development of character; (2) clear and precise objectives that are operationally specific and based on the best theoretical knowledge available, thus directing program toward identifiable family needs; (3) informed staff, laymen, and group leaders who are sensitive to the needs of families and knowledgeable in the field of family development and family-life education; (4) use of resources and the employment of creative imagination in effective program developments.[8] In other words, agencies can have a positive influence on family life in other ways than by providing programs for the entire family together.

The Importance of Service Projects

In those places where successful agency programs are functioning with older youth, it appears that a main attraction is service. Thousands of teen-agers are involved through their organizations in significant service to their communities. Millions more would probably respond if they were properly challenged.

Many of the projects taken on by older youth are truly adult-sized. Often the youth work with children less fortunate than themselves—both the culturally deprived and the physically and mentally handicapped. In many cases they work as hospital aides, rescue lost hikers, clean highways, plant trees, and do a hundred other productive tasks voluntarily.

Though the lives of American teens are crammed with activities, many of them cheerfully give up holidays, week-ends, and evenings to engage in jobs such as stuffing envelopes, making tray favors and nut cups for hospitals, tutoring classmates, and collecting food, clothing, and books for the needy.

The "Trick or Treat for UNICEF" (United Nations Children's Fund) program nets about $3,000,000 each fall through the efforts of youth who ring doorbells for the children of other lands, instead of candy for themselves.[9]

Seventeen thousand San Diego youth participated in a 33-mile "hike to fight hunger" in 1969. A total of $85,000 was raised in the one-day event. Each hiker signed up sponsors who agreed to pay from one cent to one dollar per mile. Half of the proceeds went to relief projects in India and half was used in the local food distribution program.[10]

Each year *Parents' Magazine* honors over 100 youth groups who have carried on outstanding service projects during the previous year. The following are examples of the projects reported.

A group of boys in Rockville, Connecticut, formed a daytime volunteer

8 The YMCA working with the family, A Report of the National Consultation (New York: National Board of Y.M.C.A.s, 1959) p. 28.
9 *The New York Times*, October 26, 1969, p. 74, Column 2.
10 Article in *San Diego Evening Tribume*, July 7, 1969, p. B–3.

ambulance contingent when the lack of volunteers for daytime calls threatened the community with the possible termination of its ambulance service. With the approval of the Board of Education, the boys evolved a plan whereby two boys, with an adult supervisor from the school faculty, would handle emergencies during the boys' school study periods. In preparation for the project, boys and supervisors took a ten-week advanced first-aid course. They were able to answer calls for several accidents and other emergencies. They even gave some night service.[11]

A migrant day camp was organized and conducted by Senior Girl Scouts of Geneva, New York, under the direction of their Senior Advisory Board. The interracial camp consisted of two one-week sessions for nearly 150 boys and girls from seven to twelve years of age. The outdoor program included hikes, games, arts and crafts, and—very important—a hot lunch. The project built up the self esteem of a neglected but needy group of children. Participating Scouts found satisfaction in planning a worthy project for those less fortunate than they.[12]

In Tulsa, Oklahoma, a 4-H group formed a volunteer fire department to fight grass fires during the daytime when the men of the community were at work.[13]

A Boy Scout troop of Leland and Lake Leelanau, Michigan, devoted 11,763 hours in one year to community service and conservation activities, including operating a youth center, constructing and distributing bird feeders and duck-nesting boxes, maintaining a public picnic area, aiding in a game and fish census, and repairing fishing equipment for donation to a nearby state hospital.[14]

The Ko Da Ta Hi Horizon Club Camp Fire Girls of Osburn, Idaho, filled Christmas ditty bags for servicemen in Vietnam, counseled at summer camp, assisted service organizations, and contributed to other community betterment projects.[15]

Members of the Key Club of Fullerton High School, Knoxville, Tennessee, collaborated in supporting a bowling league organized by the Easter Seal Society for physically handicapped children. The boys coached the youngsters, handled the wheelchairs of those who used them, and revitalized the entire program.[16]

[11] "Parents' Magazine's Sixteenth Annual Youth Group Awards," *Parents' Magazine* XLV, No. 10, October, 1970, p. 70.
[12] *Ibid.*, p. 71.
[13] "Parents' Magazine's 9th Annual Youth Group Achievement Awards," *"Parents' Magazine,* XXXVIII, No. 11, November, 1963.
[14] *Ibid.*, p. 125.
[15] "Parents' Magazine Award," *The Camp Fire Girl,* L, No. 2, November-December, 1970, p. 24.
[16] "Parents' Magazine's Fifteenth Annual Youth Group Awards," *Parents Magazine* XVIV, No. 10, October, 1969, p. 69.

The Baptist Youth Fellowship of Collingswood, New Jersey, decided "to help meet pressing needs in the lives of American Indians" by personally delivering gifts to a mission center in Anadarko, Oklahoma, and working in the center. Money for the project was raised by holding paper drives, washing cars, and collecting contributions.[17]

Since the awards program began in 1955, *Parents' Magazine* has recognized the accomplishments of hundreds of groups representing thousands of young people across the country. Youth wants to serve.

The importance of including *meaningful* service projects in the program of a youth group is pointed up by the fact that World War II provided the youth agencies with their biggest impetus. Youngsters were inspired by the need to work hard on the home front to support the war effort. Groups thrived as all lowered their shoulders to the task of collecting scrap metal and newspapers, writing letters to those in hospitals, growing food, and many other projects.

This fever to be of service is still present in our youth today. The task of the advisor is to help the group discover the battlegrounds of today— pollution, poverty, illness, citizen apathy, etc.—and then to guide them into meaningful experiences in combatting our problems.

Young people do not want to be categorized as performers of childish good deeds. They want to participate in activities that are worthy of adults.

[17] "Parents' Magazine's Fourteenth Annual Youth Awards," *Parents' Magazine,* XLIII, No. 11, p. 142–143.

ADMINISTRATION

Administration, the overall direction and management of an organization, is not an end in itself in the voluntary youth-serving organizations. Rather, it is the machinery for fulfilling their objectives. On the local level, administration functions through lay boards, trustees, and committees, as well as through certain professional workers (Figure 7–1). However, most of the

Figure 7–1
Activities such as this American Youth Hostel outing don't just happen. They require much planning and administrative detail weeks and often months in advance. *Courtesy American Youth Hostels, Inc.*

major voluntary youth-serving organizations are national in scope, and administration begins at the national level.

National Structures of the Organizations

The national structures of the organizations are governed by their certificates of incorporation, their bylaws, and the policies adopted by their governing bodies. The usual pattern includes a policy-making national board of directors or board of trustees made up of volunteers who serve without pay, and a paid professional staff to carry out its directives.

NATIONAL BOARDS AND COUNCILS

The membership on the national boards is generally selected from prominent, public-spirited individuals who have demonstrated interest in and given service to the organization. The board may be self-perpetuating; that is, its new members are nominated and selected by the board itself. In such cases, the board establishes the policies and operating procedures of the program. In other important instances, however, a large national council rather than a national board is considered the chief administrative body. In these cases, the council elects the board.

One agency that is led by a national council is the Boy Scouts. The Boy Scout National Council, which is elected from the membership on a regional basis and which consists of well over a thousand people, administers the program by means of an annual meeting to elect officers, executive board members, and members at large. The executive board of approximately 75 members meets three times annually to conduct the affairs of the organization. Similarly, the Camp Fire Girls' national board is elected by a national council. The national council is composed of members elected by official delegates to regional conferences and, in addition, regional chairmen and members of the national board. The national council sets board policies and recommends practices. The national board is the legally responsible body and must work within the policies of its national council. A small executive committee of the board functions for the board between meetings. The national council of the Boys' Clubs of America, made up of representatives of each autonomous member club, is the policy-making body of that organization; it elects officers and members of the board of directors.

STANDING COMMITTEES

The national organization may have numerous standing committees, depending on its size and nature. A typical large organization may have national committees concerned with finance, public relations, camping, field services, program, personnel and training, properties, supplies, international relations, educational and institutional relationships, and other areas. Some of these committees may have several subcommittees. For example, subcommittees of the Boy Scout Relationships Committee at the end of 1969 included committees on community relationships, religious relationships, organization relationships, and school relationships.

NATIONAL STAFF

The executive or director of the national organization is employed by and responsible to the national board. The national professional staff assists the executive in carrying out the directives of the board. National staff positions may include specialists in all aspects of the program as well as specialists in the training of volunteer and professional workers, organization, public relations, publications, personnel, fund-raising, research, business administration, merchandising, and other areas.

NATIONAL SERVICES

With its council and board, executive committee, staff, and director, the national organization performs on a national level many of the functions that a local organization performs on the local level, rendering a variety of services as far as its funds and leadership permit. These services are described briefly in the following. The various national organizations differ in the emphasis they place upon each of these offerings.

Giving field service to local communities. Personal advice and counsel to communities which are organizing new programs and expanding programs in operation are major functions. Services related to programs, facilities, leadership, interpretation, and finance are made available to local groups. The patterns for successful local operations have been developed through years of experience.

Setting Standards. Another major function of the national organization is the setting of standards for the conduct of local constituent groups. The standards may concentrate on areas such as professional and volunteer leadership qualifications, program content, facility construction, methods of financing, and organizational structure.

These standards provide the basis for evaluation of a local unit. The evaluation may take the form of self-study or it may involve a visitation by regional staff or other consultants.

The results of the evaluation then form the basis of a program of self-improvement. In a few cases the local organization may be found to be so deficient that it is placed on probation or expelled from the national organization.

Carrying on Work in Public Relations and Interpretation. Through conferences, workshops, personal contacts, special events such as nationally-proclaimed "weeks," special publications, and material prepared for the mass media, the national organization assumes leadership in interpreting the agency to its own members, educational groups, governmental agencies, and the general public. This public relations work is essential in maintaining moral and financial support and in securing leadership necessary for the ongoing program.

Upgrading Professional Services.   The national office is responsible in large measure for the quality of the professional leadership of the organization, and therefore it is concerned with the recruitment, training, and placement of local professional workers. Among its responsibilities are drawing up specifications for training; making job analyses; establishing guides for salaries, working hours, vacations, pensions, insurance, health and safety, and other conditions of work; and providing incentives for professional growth through promotions and variety of job experiences. The professional worker in service is assisted by special publications, conferences, training programs, and personal consultations so that he may keep his morale and his performance of duty at high levels.

Special training opportunities offered at the national level may vary from brief institutes, seminars, and training courses to four-year undergraduate curricula offered through numerous cooperating colleges and universities. One-year graduate training may also be offered. In some instances, scholarships are made available for this training. National training may be offered to volunteers as well as professionals.

Certain colleges and universities, including New York University, Springfield College, and George Williams College, are especially concerned with training young people who wish to seek careers in the youth agencies. The two latter institutions were originally established for YMCA training but have expanded their programs to wider curricula serving other youth agencies.

Preparing Publications and Audio-Visual Materials.   Many kinds of publications are issued by the national offices. Magazines may be published for leaders, professional staff members, and child members. Program materials and leadership training materials may range from handbooks to pamphlets and newsletters. Materials to interpret the organization to the general public or particular groups may be issued. Miscellaneous forms and various types of brochures may be prepared.

Audio-visual materials are frequently an important aid offered by the national offices. They may include movies, slides, filmstrips, recordings, photographs, and posters.

Offering supplies and equipment.   Uniforms, insignia, books, camping equipment, and supplies of all kinds needed in the program are usually offered for sale by the national organizations, which may designate certain merchandise as "official." Distributors throughout the country may be licensed, and certain materials may be purchased through the national or local offices.

Making Specialists' Services Available. Many national organizations maintain technical staffs to assist local groups. The staffs may include specialists in the conduct of program activities, financial consultants, community organizers, architects, engineers, journalists, camp planners, and others.

Conducting Research and Developing Program. The major national organizations maintain a continual study of their program, structure, achievements, membership trends, and changing interests of the organization as well as of social needs which they might serve. Such self-examination is essential to keep the organization abreast of changing times and has meant success and survival to the organizations that have adapted themselves to meet new needs. In organizations with prescribed national programs, such as the Boy Scouts, Girl Scouts, and Camp Fire Girls, a heavy responsibility rests with the national office to present programs that are of value to the individual and to society. The programs must be analyzed, tested, and revised periodically. Changes and refinements in program substance, age groupings, advancement requirements, and procedures result from these studies.

The research may be quite extensive. An example is a survey of the relevance of Scouting to the needs and interests of American boys made in 1968 by Daniel Yankelovich, Inc. for the Boy Scouts.[1] More than 3,600 Scouts and non-Scouts, parents, and volunteer Scouters throughout the contiguous states were interviewed and a mass of data was recorded and analyzed. Results were studied by national committees and changes in policies and program were considered in the light of the research. Research may be conducted not only by private concerns but also by colleges and universities, which may make their results available to professional or lay leaders of the organizations.

Operating Nationally-Owned Areas and Facilities. National properties such as certain camps and training centers are operated at the national level.

Maintaining Contact with Other National Organizations. Chapter 13 discusses ways in which national organizations cooperate. By participating with other voluntary and governmental agencies in conferences and workshops, the national office exchanges ideas, keeps pace with current needs and developments, and establishes new guidelines for action.

Encouraging International Relations. Organizations with international

---

[1] Daniel Yankelovich, Inc., *Is Scouting in Tune with the Times?* (New Brunswick, N.J.: Boy Scouts of America, 1968).

affiliations may maintain these contacts in large measure through branch offices of the international organization in the national office, with special staff designation for this function. International projects may include strengthening the program in other countries through money, materials, and personnel; exchange of young people; scholarships; tours; and correspondence. World organizations with constitutions, bylaws, international offices, and regular conferences function in some of the organizations.

Organizing National Events.   The responsibility for organizing national conventions, council meetings, workshops, contests, and other special national events falls on the shoulders of the national office or committees set up through it (Figure 7–2). Specific themes such as the Boy Scout "Scouting rounds a guy out," or special programs such as the Camp Fire Girls' "Adventure '68," may be used to attract nationwide attention to the organization.

Maintaining Governmental Relationships.   Inasmuch as youth organizations are voluntary, their relationships with the government are voluntary and vary considerably from organization to organization. All of the major agencies enjoy a tax-exempt status. The Boy Scouts, Boys' Clubs, and Girl

Figure 7–2

FHA national officers work on plans for the 1971 national meeting of Future Homemakers of America. (l to r) Debbi Godwin, Debi Hegi, Jean Pederson, and Jane Nemke. *Courtesy Future Homemakers of America.*

Scouts are chartered by Congress and report annually to Congress. Numerous government agencies cooperate with the youth organizations in forwarding their work. A few organizations, notably 4-H, have an even closer tie with government. The U.S. Department of Agriculture finances the national administrative office of 4-H, which also works with the Cooperative Extension Service of the state land-grant colleges and universities and with the county extension agencies.

Unifying the Organization. One of the vital functions of the national office is to serve as the unifying center of the organization and as its official voice before other groups and the general public. It clarifies the purposes and objectives of the organization and plans ways of achieving them. Through its many services it gives impetus, direction, character, and purpose to the total organization.

FINANCING THE NATIONAL SERVICES

The organizations' national services are financed in many ways. Individual national membership dues or registration fees are a major source of income in some. Payment by local units of fixed sums or percentages of their local budgets is a means of support in others. The sale of literature, supplies, and equipment is an important source of revenue. Additional money may be received from royalties; income from investments and properties; charges for special services; and gifts from foundations, industries, and individuals to support both regular budgets and special programs.

Regional and State Offices

The administrative work of the national organization is broken down geographically in many cases to a regional level in order to carry the functions of the national organization to the members and to provide bases of operation for members of the national staff assigned to regions. In 1968 the Boys' Clubs maintained eight regional offices, the Boy Scouts 12, the Girl Scouts six, and the Camp Fire Girls seven. The numbers of regional offices may change from time to time. For example, there were 12 Girl Scout regions in 1967.

Conferences and planning sessions may be held on a regional basis even in organizations that are not large enough to maintain paid regional staffs or for other reasons do not do so. In Junior Achievement there are five regional boards, each directly represented on the national executive committee. The state is somewhat analogous to the region in 4-H Clubs in that it is the smaller-than-national division that works with local units.

Administration on a Local Area Level

The constituent unit of a national organization may comprise a number of counties, a metropolitan area, a neighborhood, or even a single facility, such as a Boys' Club. A large area may be subdivided for administrative purposes into districts. The administrative functions have some similarity to those on a national level but are scaled to the smaller area of service.

Each of the major organizations has its own distinct outline or manual of practices for constituent units, which differentiates it from other organizations. In order to become part of a national organization, a local group usually receives a charter or franchise for operation within a geographical area. As they accept the charter from the parent organization, they must agree to conform with its national policies. The charter, granted frequently for one year, is renewable but may be withdrawn if the local body fails to meet the national requirements. The local unit is incorporated under the laws of the state in which it is located. Its responsibilities are to maintain a program of high quality, to provide personnel, to obtain facilities for the program, to secure financing, to set up necessary committees, to carry on a public relations program, and to work with the community (Figure 7–3).

Figure 7–3
One Junior Achievement company member receives an award for selling the most products. *Courtesy Junior Achievement.*

LOCAL COUNCILS

Local councils, where they exist, are constituent units of the national organization. Their jurisdiction covers a definite geographical area. Some councils consist of all members of the organization, although voting rights may be restricted to adult members serving in defined capacities, such as leaders, board members, committee members, or sponsors. Other councils consist of representatives. The local Boy Scout council consists of one person from each institution sponsoring a troop and members-at-large. An annual meeting at which at least some of the board members are elected is a common feature of a local council. The wishes of the general membership may be made known to the board through the local council meetings.

LOCAL BOARDS

A local lay board of directors, if there is no local council, is usually self-perpetuating. The board is the legally responsible unit of the organization, and the business of the organization is carried on in its name. The board determines the local policies of the organization; initiates and carries out plans to serve the membership; employs the professional executive director; secures land and facilities; evaluates the group's operation; participates in regional and national meetings of the parent organization; cooperates with other community groups, perhaps through a council of social agencies; and maintains rapport with the community. The board is responsible for adopting a budget and securing funds for operating the program. If the organization is a participant in a united fund or other community fund-raising group, the board is expected to submit reports, explain and defend its budget in order to secure its allocation from the fund, and provide workers to solicit funds. Many of its duties are delegated to the executive director employed by the board.

The board may maintain several standing committees, such as an executive committee and committees for finance, personnel, program, property management, camp, public relations, and awards. Generally committee chairmen are members of the board while other committee members may or may not be.

LOCAL EXECUTIVE AND STAFF

The local executive is employed by the board commonly as a result of recommendations by the national organization. He is usually professionally trained and meets standards of the national organization in terms of training, age, and experience. He should have business and administrative ability, understand the ways of working with youth, and be thoroughly grounded in the philosophy of the organization by which he is employed. He needs to be both an organizer and a promoter. He is the administrative officer of the board responsible for carrying out the decisions of the board in its name. He usually employs the staff, and the top staff are responsible directly to him. The morale of the staff largely reflects his own attitude. It is up to him to see that the staff members clearly understand and accept their responsibilities. Through regular staff meetings he encourages democratic and creative participation in the conduct of the work. In an ex-officio capacity he attends board meetings and advises the board on the needs and progress of the program.

Other local or area staff members may include assistant directors, field directors, district directors, or directors of specialized areas, such as training. If the program is building-centered, as in a Boys' Club or YMCA, and if paid workers are used in direct leadership, the professional full-time staff may also include directors of particular aspects of the program, such as physical education, swimming, social activities, or arts and crafts. In a Girls Club, sewing and homemaking directors might be added. Part-time employees and volunteers add to the leadership staff.

It should be pointed out that in agencies in which direct leadership is carried on only by volunteers, the executive and staff give much of their attention to organizing, planning, recruiting and training leaders, raising money, and interpreting the organization. In other agencies, the executive may give his time to administrative duties, but the rest of the staff may give the majority of their time to direct leadership; and in small organizations, the executive may divide his time between administration and direct leadership.

LOCAL ADMINISTRATIVE RESPONSIBILITIES

The board may designate the following responsibilities to the local executive:

1. *Liaison with the national organization:* The administrative officer serves as a liaison between the national organization and the local unit. This duty involves translating national policy into local action. The national organization must be kept informed regarding needs, programs, and services used to implement local programs. Making reports, arranging for visits of national staff, participating in workshops, and attending national and regional meetings are part of maintaining relationships with the national organization.

2. *Business management:* Responsibility for business management falls on the executive. Without financing and accurate records, the agency cannot function. Where agencies must raise their own money, this function becomes a major responsibility of the executive. Financing involves not only working with a money-raising staff but also interpreting the worth of the agency program to prospective givers. If a group such as the united fund acts as the money-raising agent, executives of member agencies are

responsible for financial accountability to the united fund as well as their own board.

Business management includes not only money-raising but also the preparation of budgets, budget control, accounting, payment of bills, and handling of contracts of various kinds. It requires the keeping of records on membership, program, staff, materials, facilities, insurance, inventories, agreements, and contracts. The making of financial reports is also essential.

3. *Maintaining of standards:* The executive sees to it that the standards set up by the national organization provide the basis for local operations. There are standards for staff employment, facilities, finance, and operation of program. The national organization also prepares standards for health and safety in program operations and insurance standards for the protection of the staff and members.

4. *Planning:* If an organization is to keep abreast of the times, continual planning is required for program, finance, staff, and facilities. Though the administrator is responsible for seeing that planning is done, he does not necessarily do it himself. Actual planning may require the services of the staff, board, committees, and, in many cases, technical specialists. The administrator must see that the agency works closely with community planning agencies so that the needs of the community can be met effectively.

5. *Directing and managing:* The resources of leadership can be most effectively harnessed to serve the major objectives of the organization only when routines are well organized to save time. The executive must see to it that management of facilities, including repairs, maintenance, and protection, are efficient. Operations ranging from bookkeeping to maintenance should be routinized.

Scheduling to make the maximum use of facilities and leadership is necessary. A calendar of activities should be kept.

6. *Interpretation and public relations:* The executive must take a leading role in interpreting the organization to the public. Preparing releases for the press, radio, and television and giving talks and reports to civic groups and others interested are vital for community understanding of an agency. The agency may also interpret its work through cooperating with other welfare and recreation groups on committees, through community councils, and in special projects.

7. *Personnel relationships:* The selection and guidance of personnel, both professional and volunteer, is one of the greatest responsibilities of administration. The executive is the most influential person in the maintenance of morale. He should provide opportunities for the staff to participate in decision-making so that each person may exercise initiative and make the best use of his abilities.

The preparation of job descriptions and analyses of personal qualifications are steps preparatory to the selection of staff. Every worker, when selected, needs to be oriented to his assignment. This orientation may include explanations of the purposes and structure of the agency, descriptions of the particular duties, and information as to resources available. Supervising and evaluating must continue after the worker is placed. Praise or other recognition bestowed when earned is necessary to the maintenance of high morale.

The recruitment, training, supervision, and evaluation of volunteers may follow somewhat the patterns used for professional workers. Sources of potential volunteers include the sponsoring institutions, PTA's, volunteer bureaus, clubs, parents, college students, young adults who have themselves gone through the program, and older youth in the program who may be able to assist with younger members. Requests for help may be made through talks to civic-minded groups, personal contacts, radio, television, and newspapers. Volunteers may be used as resource consultants, club leaders, camp counselors, committee members, board members, or special project leaders. Extensive training may be necessary. Particular skills and knowledge needed by the leaders may be taught by professionals or other volunteers. Several local organizations may present a combined training course, perhaps under the auspices of a local council of social agencies.

Probably the most important administrative task of the executive is to recruit an excellent staff of paid and volunteer workers and then provide them with the backing and freedom they need to do the job for which they are capable (Figure 7–4).

8. *Evaluation of the agency:* Evaluation, which is a continuing process, may be conducted through staff, boards, committees, community agencies, national organization members, and sometimes technical specialists. Only those organizations that are able to look at themselves and their operations in the light of their objectives will be able to meet those objectives under the rapidly changing conditions of today.

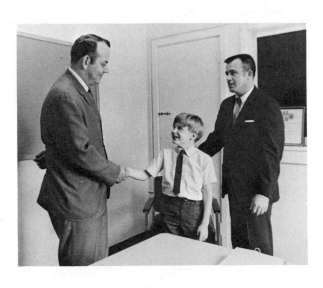

Figure 7–4
A staff member of Big Brothers of America introduces a volunteer to his new "little brother." *Courtesy Big Brothers of America.*

9. *Focusing on purposes:* The purposes of the organization must be kept in the foreground, and all members of the staff must be kept aware of the central focus of the organization. The administrator who is able to direct the efforts of his staff unfailingly toward the achievement of the purposes is performing one of his most important functions.

Summary

The purpose of administration is to provide an effective means of achieving the goals and objectives of the organization. National and regional administrative services are established to serve local administrative units. Their services encompass assisting in establishing new programs, setting standards, advising in problems of finance and personnel, providing publications and supplies, conducting research, planning program improvements, providing public relation services, and acting as unifying voices for their organizations.

The local administrative organizations have as their primary concerns the provision of the best programs and leadership available for pursuing the objectives of their agencies. The success of administration is assessed in terms of how well the objectives of the organization are achieved.

OUTDOOR-ORIENTED
AGENCIES

Chapter 8

It is impossible to sort youth organizations into neat categories. However, because it seems desirable for purposes of study to group together agencies having important features in common, the agencies discussed in this book are categorized as follows: outdoor-oriented agencies; religious-oriented agencies; organizations serving the disadvantaged; vocationally-oriented organizations; and, last, organizations that do not fit well into any of the preceding categories. The difficulty of categorizing can be illustrated by noticing that many religious-based groups offer very strong outdoor programs; that many agencies specializing in serving low-income areas also offer programs for boys and girls from more affluent areas; and that outdoor-oriented agencies seldom restrict their activities to the outdoors. Other examples of overlapping purposes and programs are numerous.

In terms of total membership and influence, the organizations described in this chapter probably rank first. Boy Scout troops and, to a lesser extent, Girl Scouts and Camp Fire Girls are found in nearly every community in the nation. Throughout the country today nearly one boy in four between the ages of eight and 16 is enrolled in a Boy Scout unit. Nearly as many girls are affiliated with either the Girl Scouts or Camp Fire Girls.

Boy Scouts of America

The Boy Scouts of America ranks as America's largest youth organization, with over 1,590,000 adult volunteers and a total membership of over six million.[1]

---

[1] Boy Scouts of America, *1969 Report to Congress,* 91st Cong., 2nd sess., House Document No. 271 (Washington, D. C.: Government Printing Office, 1970), p. 33.

ORIGIN OF SCOUTING

Scouting began in England in 1908, when Lord Robert Baden-Powell developed a handbook, *Scouting for Boys*. He had long felt the need for a training program to make young men more self-sufficient. Although he did not start out to found an organization, his following grew so fast that soon patrols were springing up throughout England.[2]

In 1910, an American publisher named William D. Boyce was helped to find his way through London fog by a young lad. When he tried to tip the boy, his money was refused.

Inquiring why, he learned about scouting. Boyce was so impressed that he sought out more information about scouting, and upon his return to the United States he founded the Boy Scouts of America. Several other similar groups had sprung up throughout the country by this time—the Woodcraft Indians, Sons of Daniel Boone, Boy Scouts of the United States, National Scouts of America, and others. The national secretary of the Committee on Boys' Work of the YMCA, Edgar Robinson, saw the need for one strong scout organization and was instrumental in getting most of these groups to combine into the Boy Scouts of America as a strong centralized association.

Ernest Thompson Seton, founder of the Woodcraft movement, Dan Beard, an artist who founded Sons of Daniel Boone, and James E. West, a Washington lawyer who was named the first Chief Scout Executive, guided the new organization through its formative years. Seton left Scouting after five years because he felt it was becoming too organized and too vocational. Beard served as National Commissioner and wrote illustrated articles for the Boy Scout magazine, *Boys' Life,* until his death in 1941 at 90 years of age.

West was the active leader from 1911 until 1943, when the membership had grown to 1.5 million.

HOW SCOUTING IS ADMINISTERED

New Brunswick, New Jersey, is the site of Scouting's beautiful national headquarters. A staff of hundreds, working in areas such as publications, supplies, training, and program aids, is supported largely by dues of $1.00 per year per boy ($2.00 per adult) and profits from sales.

---

[2] Boy Scouts of America, *Report to Congress* (Washington, D. C.: Government Printing Office, annual).
Publications of Boy Scouts of America, New Brunswick, N. J.:
Scoutmaster's Handbook, 1963
Cubmaster's Packbook, 1967
Den Mother's Denbook, 1967
Webelos Den Leader's Book, 1967
Boy Scout Handbook, 7th ed., 1966
Explorer Leaders' Reference Book, 1969
Scouting Magazine, monthly.

The National Council, elected annually, administers the program and elects Executive Board members. The Executive Board meets three times a year.

Administration and services are decentralized through 12 regional offices and about 500 local councils. Most of the local councils are supported by United Funds. Several important functions are carried on by the councils— leadership training, recruitment of volunteers and sponsors, development of council-wide camping programs, sponsorship of Scout circuses, selling of supplies, etc. Each council is further divided into districts, with one or more district Scout executives to coordinate activities within a smaller geographical area.

Scouting today is broken into three programs—Cub Scouting, Boy Scouting, and Exploring.

CUB SCOUTING

Almost immediately after the formation of the Boy Scouts, younger brothers began to show up at meetings, wishing they could belong. It soon became apparent that there was a need for an organization for younger boys. Lord Baden-Powell devised the program of Cub Scouting for boys in England about 1916. However, much study and debate preceded its official beginnings in the United States in 1930.

Since that time, the membership of the Cub Scouts has grown tremendously. In fact, in 1956, it passed the regular Scout enrollment and by 1970 was approaching 2.5 million boys.

Cub Scouting today is a home-and-family-centered program for boys eight through ten years of age. It features a weekly den meeting directed by a Den Mother or Den Leader and a monthly gathering of several dens together at a "pack meeting" under the leadership of a Cubmaster—usually one of the fathers.

The program encourages parents to work with their boy on a series of achievements. Some of the activities included are safety, helping around the home, construction projects, and hobbies. The parents observe the achievement and sign the Cub's book. This participation encourages the parents to be interested in what their son is doing.

The weekly den meetings are usually held in a home. The Den Mother provides crafts, games, stories, and refreshments for the boys. She tries to help them learn to be better citizens, to be more civic-minded, and to become well-rounded individuals.

Much of the organization's appeal to a young boy has been in its distinctive uniform. This is proudly worn to school on days of meetings and during Scout Week.

There are three stages of advancement in Cub Scouting—Wolf, Bear, and Webelos. Following a reorganization of the Cub program in 1967, Webelos

Cubs became organized in separate dens within the pack. These ten-year-olds work under the direction of a man in preparation for advancement to Boy Scouting. Webelos activity is more specialized than Wolf or Bear activity; in addition to passing their Boy Scout Tenderfoot requirements, Webelos Cubs work on badges in areas such as aquanaut, athlete, forester, scientist, naturalist, engineer, and artist.

The new Webelos program, which stands for "We'll be loyal Scouts," was the result of a five-year study and replaced the former Lion rank. It is hoped that the new Webelos dens will overcome one of the problems of the past—that of ten-year-olds becoming bored with Cubs and dropping out prior to moving into Boy Scouting.

In recent years, Scouting has recognized the need to involve more men in Cub Scouting and to provide a program that is challenging, exciting and outdoor-related.

BOY SCOUTS

Boy Scouting, an outdoor program of scoutcraft and leadership skills, is for boys 11 through 17 years old. Most Scouts join and belong to "troops." The ideal troop consists of 30 to 35 boys, divided into four "patrols." In a well-run troop, the boys themselves occupy most of the key leadership positions such as patrol leader, senior patrol leader, and junior assistant scoutmaster.

Each troop has a sponsoring institution such a church, a service club, a PTA, or a civic group. Approximately half of all troops are sponsored by churches. The sponsoring institution is responsible for developing an active troop committee that oversees the program, provides a meeting place, secures a man over 21 years old to serve as Scoutmaster, and assists in areas such as equipment and transportation.

Scouting utilizes a highly structured, national program of achievements and awards. Each boy works at his own pace in progressing through the ranks of Tenderfoot, Second Class, First Class, Star Scout, Life Scout, and Eagle Scout. The requirements through First Class are standard for all boys and include tests in subjects such as knot-tying, knowledge and care of the flag, map and compass, hiking, fire building, and first aid.

After the rank of First Class, achievement is centered on "merit badges." A few of these are specified as requirements for attaining the rank of Eagle, but most are voluntary according to the boy's interest. There are at this writing 117 different badges ranging alphabetically from Agriculture and Atomic Energy to World Brotherhood and Zoology. Swimming, first-aid, and cooking badges have each been awarded to more than two million boys since 1911, when Scouting began in this country. Nearly every year one or more new subjects are announced, and often obsolete badges are discontinued.

The Eagle Scout award calls for the achievement of 21 merit badges and other requirements. To date, about 630,000 boys out of 25 million past and present Boy Scouts have achieved the Eagle Scout award.

As any old-time Scouter will tell you, "Outing is the heart of Scouting." In general, the most successful troops have been those who regularly—once a month or more—are involved in camping, hiking, and other outdoor programs (Figure 8–1).

Service is another important aspect of Scouting. The Scout motto of "Do a good turn daily" is promoted today as enthusiastically as it was 60 years ago (Figure 8–2).

BOYPOWER '76 is an eight-year program, begun in 1969, which will climax with the country's two-hundredth anniversary. The program sets national goals and standards in the areas of membership, trained leaders, troop quality, and finance. If the goals of the Boy Scouts of America are reached, one boy in three of Scout age will be enrolled in a troop, pack, or Explorer unit for a total of 6.5 million boys. Sixty-five percent of the leaders will complete training courses. Troops will be expected to meet minimum standards, including ten days and nights of camping per year; re-registering at least 55 percent of their members each year; and advancing 50 percent of those registered at least one rank.

Figure 8–1
Enjoyment of life in the out-of-doors is the secret behind the success of the Boy Scout program. *Courtesy of Boy Scouts of America.*

Figure 8–2

The Boy Scout motto, "Do a good turn daily," translates into hundreds
of different community service projects.
Courtesy Boy Scouts of America.

Like most other youth agencies, Scouting is concerned about reaching
more minority groups and poor boys. Greater professional resources are
being allotted to poverty areas, with some financial assistance to selected
councils.

The Philmont Scout Ranch in New Mexico and the Schiff Scout Reserva-
tion in New Jersey, owned by the national Boy Scouts, are outstanding
centers for camping and training. Both are valued at several millions of
dollars and serve thousands of Scouts and leaders each year.

National and international jamborees provide the highlight of many a
boy's days in Scouting. Held periodically, they currently attract over 50,000
boys for a sharing of ideas and fun.

EXPLORING

Exploring is for young men and women of high-school age, who plan
and run their post programs under elected leadership guided by an adult
advisor. At present there are two kinds of posts—general interest and special
interest. A general interest post program is broad and develops according
to the interests of the members. A special interest post focuses on a specialty.

Special programs for older boys originated with the Sea Scouts, which were started in 1912. This program boomed after World War I because of the large surplus of ships. In 1935, the Explorer Scout program was begun. In its early stages it was primarily an extension of Boy Scouting with ranks, badges, and a heavy emphasis on camping and citizenship.

In 1941, the Air Explorer program was begun, giving boys another option. After World War II, Scout leaders became distressed with the relatively small number of boys being attracted to and held by the Explorer programs and contracted with the University of Michigan to study the problem. The study indicated that traditional Scout programs were not of interest to the majority of high-school-age boys and suggested that the program be modified to meet better the changing needs and interests of adolescents.[3]

In 1956, a pilot project was attempted in Orange County, California. The experiment involved developing "special-interest" Explorer posts along career and vocational lines. Posts were organized in such areas as medicine, forestry, law, business, electronics, law enforcement, science, hotel management, and automotives. Sponsors were sought from among the specialized organizations and professional groups in the area—a bank sponsoring a post specializing in finance; the sheriff's department sponsoring the law enforcement post; and so on.

In 1959, the special-interest idea was officially adopted, and today most of the posts have accepted this format. Although most posts are vocationally-oriented, some special-interest posts specialize in avocational interests such as Indian dance, surfing, or mountain rescue.

Two factors contribute particularly to the success of these special-interest Explorer posts. First, top-ranking men in their fields actually take boys behind the scenes and let them experience the careers instead of just talking about them. The second factor is the method used by the post to recruit boys. Instead of recruiting from a small neighborhood area, the special-interest post recruits from the area of one or more high schools, thus reaching many boys with similar interests.

Each post should have at least 16 members—preferably 25 to 30—to justify use of top-flight consultants. Less emphasis is put on the uniform today than previously. Another trend is the inclusion of girls in some specialty posts where they have a definite interest. All-girl posts began to emerge in 1971, when girls were formally admitted as Explorer Scouts. Until this time, girls held "associate" memberships only. Coeducational activities are an important part of most posts' programs. Members are encouraged to refer to the program as "Exploring," rather than "Explorer Scouts," to help create the new contemporary image.

Posts are encouraged to have two regular meetings, an officers' meeting, and a special event each month. Much helpful guidance on running the

[3] Survey Research Center, Institute for Social Research, University of Michigan, *A Study of Adolescent Boys* (New Brunswick, N. J.: Boy Scouts of America, 1956).

post and program ideas are included in the organization's national publication, *Exploring the Scene*. Scouting is making a determined effort to provide a relevant, contemporary program with appeal to the nation's youth of the Seventies.

Girl Scouts of the United States of America

After the Boy Scouts were established in England by Sir Robert Baden-Powell, a program along the same lines was demanded by the girls of England. As a result, in 1909 Miss Agnes Baden-Powell, sister of the Boy Scout founder, started an organization called the *Girl Guides*. The movement flourished and soon began to spread to other countries.[4]

During a visit to England, Mrs. Juliette Gordon Low realized that there was a need for such a program in the United States. In 1912 she established a Girl Guide program in Savannah, Georgia. Acceptance of the organization was instantaneous, and in 1915 a headquarters was established in Washington, D.C. The name of the American organization was changed to *Girl Scouts*. Since then, its growth has been rapid. It is today the largest voluntary youth organization for girls in the country; by the end of 1969 3,920,533 girls and leaders were enrolled—one girl out of every seven between the ages of seven and17.[5]

Since its initial spread beyond England, Girl Guiding-Girl Scouting has emphasized international affiliations. In 1928, the World Association of Girl Guides and Girl Scouts, in which the autonomous organizations from numerous countries meet to foster international understanding through the organization, was formed. Today a Girl Scout has counterparts in 68 countries. What happens to the Girl Scouts or Girl Guides in England, France, Japan, or Brazil makes a difference to her. She has a commitment to learn about them, to understand them, and to share responsibility with them in a world grown small. International gatherings are common, and a visit to the Girl Guide chalet in Switzerland or the cabaña in Mexico is the highlight of many a girl's life.

[4] Girl Scouts of the United States of America, *Annual Report,* (Washington, D. C.: U. S. Government Printing Office, annual); *Trefoil Around the World, Girl Guiding and Girl Scouting in Many Lands,* 5th ed., Revised. (London: World Association of Girl Guides and Girl Scouts, 1968).
  Publications of Girl Scouts of the United States of America, New York N.Y.:
  Elizabeth Sheehy, *Girl Scout Leader Notebook,* 1963
  Brownie Girl Scout Handbook, 1963
  Cadette Girl Scout Handbook, 1963
  Junior Girl Scout Handbook, 1963
  Senior Girl Scout Handbook, 1963
  Girl Scout Leader, 8 times yearly.
[5] Girl Scouts of the United States of America, *Annual Report, Girl Scouts, 1969,* 91st Cong., 2nd sess., House Document No. 91–302 (Washington, D. C.: U. S. Government Printing Office, 1970), p. 49.

Girl Scouting, through its informal educational program, influences girls by reinforcing and supplementing the teachings of the home, the school, and the church or synagogue. Its purpose, as stated in the preamble to the Girl Scout constitution, is that of "inspiring girls with the highest ideals of character, conduct, patriotism, and service that they may become happy and resourceful citizens."

There is one Girl Scout program with four age levels, each in harmony with the needs and interests of the girls of the particular age level. The basic unit of Girl Scouting is the troop, which includes from 16 to 20 girls in the Brownies and from 24 to 32 girls in the older Scouts. The troops, with the exception of Brownies, are subdivided into patrols of five to eight members. Each patrol elects a patrol leader to represent it at the Court of Honor, which is the planning body of the troop and consists of the adult troop leaders, patrol leaders, troop treasurer, and troop scribe.

Troop activities for all ages reflect the six elements that give the program its distinctive character: the ethical code embodied in the Girl Scout Promise and Laws; training in citizenship; troop management; service to others; international friendship; and emphasis on health and safety at all times. On this foundation is built a wide range of activities in the arts, the home, and the out-of-doors.

Inspiring the members is the frequently-repeated Girl Scout Promise: "On my honor, I will try: to do my duty to God and my country, to help other people at all times, to obey the Girl Scout Laws." The laws, similar in many ways to the Boy Scout Law, are:

1. A Girl Scout's honor is to be trusted.
2. A Girl Scout is loyal.
3. A Girl Scout's duty is to be useful and to help others.
4. A Girl Scout is a friend to all and a sister to every other Girl Scout.
5. A Girl Scout is courteous.
6. A Girl Scout is a friend to animals.
7. A Girl Scout obeys orders.
8. A Girl Scout is cheerful.
9. A Girl Scout is thrifty.
10. A Girl Scout is clean in thought, word, and deed.

The symbol of the trefoil, standing for the three parts of the Promise, is worn as a pin and used in other ways.

Each age group has its own handbook and its own distinctive uniform. The Brownies wear light brown cotton dresses with brown felt beanies and orange ties. The Junior Girl Scouts appear in light green cotton dresses with yellow ties, whereas the Cadettes wear dark green skirts with white blouses.

The Senior Girl Scout uniform is a tailored two-piece outfit of dark green. The four levels of Girl Scouting may be briefly described as follows.

BROWNIE GIRL SCOUTS

The Brownies, named by Lord Baden-Powell for the elves who like to help as well as play, are seven or eight years old or are in the second and third grades. The Brownies have a Promise of their own, differing from that of their older sisters: "I promise to do my best to love God and my country, to help other people every day, especially those at home." The program, informal and less structured than that of the older Scouts, is based on the three B's:

Be a discoverer.
Be a ready helper.
Be a friend maker.

Figure 8–3
Visits to places of interest are enjoyed by Brownies. *Courtesy Girl Scouts of the United States of America.*

Meeting weekly with their leaders and assistant leaders, the Brownies play, sing, explore their neighborhoods, learn simple crafts and skills, and begin to learn how to take care of themselves outdoors (Figure 8–3). The program is more home-centered than that of older Scouts.

JUNIOR GIRL SCOUTS

As the girls grow, their program expands to meet their widening horizons. At the Junior Girl Scout level, girls from nine through 11 years of age, or in the fourth through sixth grades, begin the more formal Girl Scout program. They may choose to work on any of over 40 proficiency badges. Badges earned are presented at a "Court of Awards" and may thereafter be displayed on a sash worn across the front of the girls' uniforms. After earning a certain number of badges and meeting other requirements, the Junior Girl Scout may receive the honors of Sign of the Arrow or Sign of the Star.

The largest proportion of members are either Brownies or Junior Girl Scouts.

CADETTE GIRL SCOUTS

At this level, girls aged 12, 13, and 14 years, or in the seventh, eighth, and ninth grades, find in Girl Scouting those experiences that will help them in growing up. Their choice of proficiency badges on which to work increases; and the girls are confronted with "Challenges," which are real-life situations that test the girls' abilities to use the knowledge and understanding they have gained in the four areas of social dependability, emergency preparedness, active citizenship, and the Girl Scout Promise. The Cadette may become a First Class Scout, the highest award of her age group, which usually takes three years as a Cadette to complete.

SENIOR GIRL SCOUTS

Freedom of choice through a "wheel of opportunities" opens up to girls from 15 through 17 years of age, or in the tenth through twelfth grades, who join the Senior Girl Scouts. Opportunities for explorations of possible careers and for community service are offered through nine types of troop activities: arts, community action, homemaker, international friendship, mariner, mounted, trail blazer, wing, and panorama (which offers variety rather than specialization). There are 15 areas in which the girls may take training and give service, including library aide, child care aide, aide to handicapped persons, hospital aide, and teacher aide. Girl Scout national and international events are designed for this age group.

Supplementing these four age groups is *Campus Girl Scouts*, organized in 1968 to encourage girls to continue affiliation with Scouts. By combining these opportunities with social events and chances to work in partnership with interested adult advisors, Senior Girl Scouting helps prepare teen-age girls as citizens.

GIRL SCOUT CAMPING

Through the four stages of Girl Scouting, camping programs progress from brief outings under close supervision to wilderness living in which all the resources and skills learned over the years are put to use. Day camping for younger girls is followed by established camping, in which girls reside for an extended period in camp, and by troop camping, in which troops go camping for varying lengths of time with their own leaders. Senior Girl Scouts with camping experience may attend nationwide encampments, such as the Roundups and the two-week All-States Rendezvous of 1969.

During 1968 the Girl Scouts took an historic step by establishing a new national center on 13,000 acres in Wyoming. The property, known as the Girl Scout National Center West, offers great opportunities for troop camping, geological expeditions, and large encampments, as well as for experiencing the reality of mountains, plains, and Western history. For city girls throughout the nation, it offers a chance to sample the wonders of wildlife and the true untouched outdoors.

LOCAL STRUCTURE

The Girl Scout Councils are the local units of Girl Scouting. They are made up of adults engaged in Girl Scouting. The council determines the general policies of the local organization and elects the officers. During recent years the councils have tended to encompass larger geographic areas than previously in order that all girls might have the opportunity of joining. It is through the local council that Scouting is brought to girls.

The Board is the local administrative unit of the council. The local executive is responsible to the board. Various committees made up of lay leaders function in such areas as program, camping, leadership training, finances, and public relations.

One of the great strengths of the Girl Scouts is their ability to secure the volunteer services of men and women to carry on their program. As in most organizations, there is a shortage of good leaders to assume direct responsibility; and recruiting, training, and assisting leaders are major concerns. A continuing program of training is conducted, and every possible help and recognition are given to the troop leaders, all of whom are volunteers.

NATIONAL STRUCTURE

The national administration of the Girl Scouts reaches down to the grass roots through its National Council, which is made up of representatives elected by local councils as well as some general members. The council plans the program emphasis of the national organization and elects the Girl Scout National Board of Directors. The board of directors maintains the national headquarters and supervises the six regional offices. An executive committee carries on the business of the organization between meetings of the board.

PRESENT-DAY CONCERNS

To keep pace with the changing scene, Girl Scouting is trying hard to stay relevant. Major changes in regional boundaries and establishment of national branch offices for six new regions were accomplished in 1968; the new structure offers additional and more decentralized services to the 399 local councils. These changes and an organizational realignment, based on recommendations of a management study, were authorized by the national board of directors.

Meaningful steps were taken to bring councils face to face with social problems and to deal with them within the framework of Girl Scouting. As citizens concerned about justice and unrest, the Girl Scout National Board of Directors, in spring 1968, voted to support the major goal and objectives of the Report of the National Advisory Commission on Civil Disorders.[6] Councils were urged to study the findings and to implement in every way possible through the Girl Scout program the creation of a "true union—a single society and a single American identity." Many pledged enthusiastic support and established ad hoc committees and task force groups to study ways to accept this challenge.

A task group, appointed at the same board meeting to study the critical problems of racism and poverty, identified several major areas of concern: the seeming increase of polarity between races, cultural deprivation, the need for greater sensitivity toward others, and understanding of others. The report was referred to national committees to relate findings to areas which seemed relevant.

"Girl Scouting in the Year 2,000" was the thrust of a colloquium in the summer of 1968. Future social, cultural, educational, and economic environmental conditions were discussed in light of their implications for Girl Scouting. Examination is continuing on major points to provide information for developing broad goals in the areas of program, human relations, and organizational structure.

The organization has moved recently in the direction of employing greater numbers of specialists to staff the council, regional, and national offices in such areas as finance, public relations, personnel, facility development, and program.

6 Girl Scouts of the United States of America, *1968 Annual Report,* 91st Cong., 1st sess., House Document Nos. 91–95 (Washington, D. C.: U. S. Government Printing Office, 1969), p. ix.

Girl Scouting today is very different from the stereotyped ideas still strongly implanted in the mind of the general public—those of camping, crafts, and cookies; and yet the seeds of today's program design have always been in the Girl Scout movement. In the tumultuous modern scene neither the girls themselves, nor their adult leaders, or even the members of co-operating organizations, many of which sponsor Girl Scout troops, seem content with an ingrown philosophy and carefree educational and recreational activities. The concept of service to others and, in particular, of service to disadvantaged children and families living in urban, rural, and suburban areas, has taken hold. The challenges of indigenous leadership and of holding the older girls in the organization have captured the imagination of the organization.

Girls still work for various badges. They learn to know, love, and live in the outdoors. They learn, particularly the Brownies and Juniors, to use their hands and acquire knowledge and appreciation of the arts taught them by adults who are dedicated to helping young people.

However, emphasis has shifted. The concept of closer relationships between girls from more affluent families and those from so-called disadvantaged areas has set the Girl Scout movement on fire with determination to reach and encourage girls disheartened by their seeming lack of personal opportunity to grow, learn, belong, and be somebody.[7]

As a major national organization serving girls, the Girl Scouts have endeavored to stay in tune with the times, without abandoning their traditional outdoor role. Today they continue the best of the program of the past but seek to serve in the broader capacity of human relationships and civic responsibility.

Camp Fire Girls, Inc.

The Camp Fire Girls were founded in 1910 as the first national nonsectarian, interracial organization for girls in the United States. This was about the time the Boy Scouts were having their beginnings, and there were many inquiries about the possibilities of forming a girls' organization. Dr. Luther H. Gulick, a pioneer in health education, an innovator in the YMCA, and one of the founders of the Boy Scouts, became interested in work with girls.[8]

---

[7] Girl Scouts of the United States of America, *Girl Scouting Today* (New York: Public Affairs Division of the Girl Scouts of U.S.A., 1969) p. 1.

[8] Helen Buckler, Mary F. Fiedler, and Martha F. Allen, eds., *Wo-He-Lo, the Story of Camp Fire Girls, 1910–1960* (New York, N. Y.: Holt, Rinehart and Winston, 1961).
Publications of Camp Fire Girls, Inc., New York, N.Y.:
Annual Report
Book of the Camp Fire Girls, rev. ed., 1966.
Handbook for Guardians of Camp Fire Girls, rev. ed. 1966.

Two separate groups were organized which became the core of Camp Fire. With the help of Dr. Gulick, William Chauncey Langdon in 1910 planned a pageant in Thedford, Vermont. He organized girls under the name of "Camp Fire Girls," setting up the ranks (Wood-Gatherer, Fire-Maker, and Torch-Bearer), various activities, and a uniform. Also in 1910, Dr. Gulick and his wife started a camp for girls near South Casco, Maine, emphasizing handicrafts and social experiences. The Camp was named Wo-He-Lo (Work, Health, Love), and the decision was made to permeate the program with Indian lore and ceremonials. In their attempts to start a national organization for girls, the Gulicks wanted to be sure that they were not making a copy of the Boy Scouts. From the first they emphasized the womanliness of girls and their work. Gulick felt that awarding badges was fundamentally wrong for girls. Incorporation papers were signed on May 15, 1912. Any girl could join who wanted to: seek beauty, give service, pursue knowledge, be trustworthy, hold on to health, glorify work, and be happy. These goals became the Law of the Camp Fire Girls.

In 1912 the first manual was published, and in 1913 came the announcement of the establishment of Blue Birds, an auxiliary of Camp Fire Girls for seven, eight, and nine-year-old girls. It was not until 1941 that Horizon Clubs were organized for girls in ninth through twelfth grades. Horizon Clubs stressed the development of a well-rounded personality, wholesome relationships with others, social activities with boys and girls, vocational exploration, and community service.

TODAY'S PROGRAM

A national study in the late 1950's resulted in the organizational pattern that we find in the Camp Fire Girls today.[9] The study determined that Blue Birds needed only a two-year program; that nine-year-olds were ready for Camp Fire; and that Junior High needed their own program and insignia. The program was modified at this time to take into consideration the needs and interests of today's girls. It was decided that the program had to undergo modification from time to time, but that the philosophy and method would not change.

A Camp Fire Girl may choose from programs in the areas of home, outdoors, creative arts, business, citizenship, science, and sports and games. The idea behind these activities came from Dr. Gulick, who believed that

---

Handbook for Junior Hi Camp Fire Guardians, 1965
Advisor's Guide to Horizon Club, 1963
The Blue Bird Book for Leaders, 1962
The Camp Fire Girl, monthly except July and August.
9 *Leadership-Program Studies,* conducted by Audience Research, Gallup Enterprises, New Jersey, for Camp Fire Girls, 1957 and 1958.

character is built to a great degree through self-fulfilling activities that the individual chooses for himself. The Gulicks were great believers in the decision-making ability of youth, a point of view that has influenced the Camp Fire program a great deal.

An important aspect of the Camp Fire Girls is its use of the Indian theme. The Gulicks found that their most successful summer programs were built around this theme. In carrying out the Indian theme, the program places great emphasis on symbolism and is highlighted with ceremonies. Symbolism starts when a Blue Bird flies up to Camp Fire Girls and chooses her own Indian name symbolic of what she is or wants to be. As the young Camp Fire Girl earns beads and acquires honors, she begins to design her ceremonial jacket or gown. Ceremonials are planned by the girls with many purposes in mind. They may be held for presenting awards, hearing an honored guest, welcoming a new member, saying goodbye to an old member, honoring a special person, and many other reasons. The ceremonials are usually held out-of-doors after dark. The use of candles and the tunes of old Indian songs give them a very mystic air.

OBJECTIVES

The objectives of the Camp Fire Girls are:

1. the application of the girl's religious, spiritual, and ethical teachings to her daily living;
2. a love of home and family that grows as she grows;
3. pride in women's traditional qualities—tenderness, affection, and skill in human relations;
4. deep love of her country, the practice of democracy, readiness to serve;
5. the capacity for fun, friendship and happy group relations;
6. the formation of healthful habits;
7. the ability to take care of herself, to do her work skillfully, and to take pleasure in it;
8. interests and hobbies she can enjoy with others and alone;
9. love of the out-of-doors and skill in outdoor living;
10. a happy heart that will help her find beauty, romance, and adventure in the common things of daily life.

Like many other youth organizations, Camp Fire became concerned during the 1960s about its difficulty in reaching girls in low income and minority sections of the large cities. In 1964, a demonstration project was funded by the Children's Bureau. The program, known as the Metropolitan Critical Areas Project, proved beneficial not only in reaching new members but also in developing techniques for more effective work in inner-city areas.

The Camp Fire Girl program is divided into four age-brackets: *Blue Birds, Camp Fire Girls, Junior Hi Camp Fire Girls,* and *Horizon Club.* The youngest members of the Camp Fire Girls are the *Blue Birds,* girls who are seven and eight years old, or in second and third grades. Groups must have at least six members and no more than 20. They enjoy creative play and learn about their community—the grocer, the baker, the newspaper, and so on. They play games, sing, do simple craft work, and undertake small service projects. The groups meet once a week in homes, schools, churches, synagogues, or community centers. The Blue Bird wish is "to have fun, to learn to make beautiful things, to remember to finish what I begin, to want to keep my temper most of the time, to go to interesting places, to know about trees and flowers and birds, to make friends."

Camp Fire Girl groups are composed of girls who are nine, ten, and 11 years old or in the fourth, fifth, and sixth grades. Size of the groups ranges between six and 20. There are 1001 honors or activities in which they may choose to engage. Girls earn colored honor beads which they use in their own original decorative patterns on their ceremonial gowns. Individual skills are developed through work in seven areas: home, outdoors, creative arts, science, business, sports and games, and citizenship. They attain rank, not by competition, but by moving from one achievement to another. The three ranks, in order, are: Trail-Seeker, Wood-Gatherer, and Fire-Maker. Each has its own symbolism and ceremonial. Emphasis is put on outdoor living, sports, crafts, and other active programs.

Girls 12 and 13 years old, or in the seventh and eighth grades, form the *Junior Hi Camp Fire Girls.* They experience group activities in numerous areas, leading to the Group Torch-Bearer rank; and later they achieve the Individual Torch-Bearer rank in any one of 25 specialized fields of interest. Parliamentary procedures and intergroup cabinet activities are introduced to give girls a more adult experience, with increasing responsibility and leadership. Promotional materials stress opportunities for experiences such as style shows, progressive dinner parties, sox hops, train trips, service projects, and teaching games to young children (Figure 8–4).

Horizon Club members, 14 and over, or in the ninth through twelfth grades, enjoy experiences which stress personality development, coeducational parties and dances, community service, and career possibilities. They find useful ways to serve the community, such as volunteering in children's clinics and hospitals and assisting in museums, welfare agencies, and community chest activities. The Wo-He-Lo Medallion is awarded *Horizon Club* members who finish a specialized two-year project. *Horizon Club* attempts to prepare girls for entering the adult world. The program is theirs to develop, plan, and carry out.

Figure 8–4
Junior Hi members of Camp Fire Girls are doing needlework on a service project. *Courtesy Camp Fire Girls, Inc.*

Camp Fire, like many other youth agencies, is making a genuine attempt to hold the older girl through special national programs. During 1967, girls from throughout the land traveled together on a Caribbean cruise. In 1968, 223 Horizon Girls were selected to participate in "Adventure '68." After an orientation at Estes Park, Colorado, they broke into seven groups, which fanned out throughout the West to learn firsthand some of the conservation issues facing the nation.

NATIONAL ORGANIZATION

The National Council of Camp Fire Girls is the policy-making body of the organization. It is composed of 150 members elected by the regional conference from boards of directors of local councils, plus a national board of directors. Thus, local experience and opinion are brought to bear on the making of national policies and recommended practices by which all units of the organization are governed. The national Board of Directors, composed of no more than 50 members, is elected by the national council. Working through its committees, it sets goals, and, with the national staff, carries out policies and programs as directed by the national council. The national board of directors meets at least twice a year and is on call for special meetings.

American Youth Hostels, Inc.

PURPOSE OF AYH

American Youth Hostels is a nonprofit, nonsectarian, nonpolitical corporation organized exclusively for charitable and educational purposes and open to all, regardless of age, race, creed, or religion. The purpose of AYH is to help all, especially young people, gain a greater understanding of the world and its people, through outdoor activities, educational and recreational travel, and related programs; to develop fit, self-reliant, well-informed citizens; to provide youth hostels—simple overnight accommodations in scenic, historic, and cultural areas—with supervising house-parents and local sponsorship. AYH is a service organization supported by voluntary contributions, memberships and program fees, and is a member of the International Youth Hostel Federation.[10]

YOUTH HOSTELING

The youth hostel idea was conceived by Richard Schirrmann, a young German school teacher, in 1909. Realizing the need to get his students out of the smoke-filled city into the countryside, he took them on excursions. The trips were so well enjoyed by the students that they wished to have extended adventures, and it became necessary to find overnight accommodations. With the help of friends, Mr. Schirrmann established hostels—low-cost overnight facilities. Soon the movement spread to other nations. Isabel and Monroe Smith, two American teachers, were exposed to hosteling while on a trip to Europe; and in 1934 they established the first youth hostel in Northfield, Massachusetts, thus founding AYH. There are now 47 member associations in the International Federation and 4,200 hostels throughout the world. The road to adventure reaches to every continent on earth, and is available to anyone who appreciates inexpensive "under-your-own-steam" types of travel—bicycling, hiking, canoeing, horseback riding, skiing —and who appreciates the fun of making friends and the thrill of new trails.

By the end of 1970, AYH membership had reached more than 52,000. World membership neared 2 million.[11]

QUALIFICATIONS FOR TRIP MEMBERS

Any AYH member aged 15 years or above by July 1 of a given year is eligible for all trips in the United States and Canada. Those aged 16 by

10 Publications of American Youth Hostels, New York, N. Y.:
Annual Report
What Is Hosteling?, brochure, n.d.
The AYH Hostel Guide & Handbook, annual.
Facts about AYH, mimeographed, Dec., 1970.
11 *Facts about AYH,* p. 2.

July 1 are eligible for the special high-school European trips. Applicants for all other trips must be over 17 years old. Ages usually range from 15 to 35 years.

The most important qualifications are a sense of adventure, a liking for the outdoors, the ability to get along well with others, and a willingness to share in making the trip a success.

By international agreement, each hosteler carries a Youth Pass, issued by his own national youth hostel association.

AYH GROUPS

AYH has specialized in a unique small-group educational travel program under trained leadership since 1934. There are many advantages to limiting groups to seven to nine persons plus a leader. On-the-spot decisions can be made with a flexibility unknown in larger groups; small groups can go places and see things that a large group often misses. Groups are organized, as far as possible, according to age and interests. Members represent various parts of the United States. Families are a growing part of AYH, and some hostels have family accommodations.

Each person becomes skilled in cooperative living, bearing a share of the responsibility while maintaining individual freedom. For example, a group member is expected to help in the cooking and other chores except when hotels and restaurants are used. Cooperation and sharing of this sort is a long-established hosteling tradition, Although a group often does things together, there is opportunity for members to sightsee on their own.

AYH LEADERS

Youth hostel leaders are chosen from a variety of countries and backgrounds. They share a common interest in furthering international friendship and in providing a meaningful summer for their groups and themselves. All leaders are adults who have successfully passed the AYH National Leadership Course. Typically, they are teachers, graduate students, and group workers. Many have hosteled as trip members. They are selected for their skill in working with groups as well as with individual personalities, their practical hosteling experience, and their ability to handle group funds. Leaders are not travel guides; their main responsibility is the well-being and safety of the group members. It is up to each member of the group to cooperate in discovering what there is to do and see every day.

OVERNIGHT ACCOMMODATIONS

Groups generally stay overnight in youth hostels. A hostel (from the Old English meaning "resting place") is an inexpensive accommodation. In the United States and Canada it can be a school, camp, church, student house, mountain lodge, community center, farm home, or specially built facility. Overseas, hostels can be found in old castles, villas, modern buildings, and even in retired sailing ships! There are separate dorms and washrooms for fellows and girls, a kitchen where hostelers may cook their own meals, and, usually, a recreation room. Bunks, blankets, cooking utensils, and cleaning equipment are provided; but everything is self-service. Most hostels abroad serve meals. House-parents supervise hostels; in the United States they are often the owners of the hostel, so they take a personal interest in the hostel's appearance and in the observance of hostel customs.

AYH members use other accommodations in addition to hostels. Y's, inexpensive hotels, pensions, student houses, and camping grounds may also be stopping places (8–5). Some groups have opportunities to enjoy home hospitality.

Figure 8–5
Kayaking, an AYH "under your own steam" activity. *Courtesy American Youth Hostels.*

MEANS OF TRANSPORTATION

AYH offers three types of hosteling trips: bicycles, station wagons, and public transportation. On bicycle trips, an average of 35 miles is covered daily on cycling days at a leisurely pace (Figure 8–6). At times the group

Figure 8–6
American Youth Hostel members
on a Cape Cod cycling tour.
*Courtesy American Youth
Hostels.*

may cycle ten to 15 miles and at other times 40 to 45. Groups do not cycle every day.

AYH tries to route groups on country roads to avoid heavy traffic. Long distances and rough terrain are covered by train, steamer, bus. Station-wagon camping groups drive about 200 miles on traveling days. Wayfarer groups use public transportation—train, bus, steamer, and plane. A moderate amount of hiking is included on wayfarer trips.

EQUIPMENT

Hostelers need simple and easy-to-care-for equipment. A lightweight bicycle with gears is essential for bicycle trips. Saddlebags that rest on the back of the bicycle hold all equipment and clothing. All non-bicycle groups use rucksacks. An AYH membership card and sheet sleeping sack are required items. Sleeping bags are necessary for some trips. Bicycling, long popular in Europe, is growing rapidly in this country. If adequate bicycle trails can be developed, this activity should continue to grow and become one of the most beneficial youth activities available.

NEW VISTAS IN HOSTELING

The AYH recognizes the differences in the European and American scenes as they relate to hosteling. The "on-your-own-steam" modes of travel are sometimes better adapted to the compact countries of Europe than to the vast open areas of the United States. The AYH has sought new ways of serving through its distinctive character.

The AYH now encourages other youth agencies to use youth hostels in their programs. Schools are finding that hostels are usable for outdoor education purposes.

AYH councils are developing broad programs, with lectures, training courses, recreation activities, and outings. Local hostel clubs are affiliated with a council if they are established within the jurisdiction of a council.

Woodcraft Rangers

The Woodcraft Rangers are an outdoor-oriented organization for both boys and girls. The Woodcraft movement was founded by Ernest Thompson Seton in 1902. This renowned naturalist also was co-founder of the Boy Scout movement in the United States and became the group's first Chief Scout. In the early years of the twentieth century, many established camps, both private and agency, used the Woodcraft program. Much of the Boy Scout program was based on the Woodcraft idea started by Seton, who later broke with the Boy Scouts because he felt they were becoming too organized and placed too much emphasis on the military idea.

The Woodcraft League failed to expand, probably because of Seton's ideas about local autonomy and lack of national direction. The only strong Woodcraft League program existing today is that of the Woodcraft Rangers in Los Angeles County. This organization serves approximately 6,000 boys and girls, from age seven through the teens, who are organized into 300 tribes.[12]

The primary objective of Woodcraft Rangers is to promote good citizenship through a program of fun, friendship, and adventure. Its secondary purpose is to preserve the Indian lore and crafts which are a part of our heritage. The Indian theme has great fascination and appeal for youngsters of all ages.

The organization believes that citizenship training is best obtained through a program of wholesome recreation based on the principles of cleanliness, reverence, integrity, and service. Tribal meetings are held weekly, and here youngsters plan the activities, learn to conduct meetings, and govern themselves under the leadership of adult guides. The organization owns and

12 Woodcraft Rangers Fact Sheet, p. 1.

operates four Woodcraft Rangers Camps and stresses the outdoor life in all of its programs. The program avoids uniforms but does place great emphasis on achievements as the youngsters earn *coups* (Indian Word for honors).

Other Outdoor-Oriented Groups

Many religious organizations conduct youth programs somewhat resembling those of the Boy Scouts and Girl Scouts. These include Pioneer Girls, Christian Service Brigade, Boys' Brigade, the Salvation Army's Girl Guards and Sunbeams, J.M.V. Pathfinders (Seventh-Day Adventist), and the Mormon's Mutual Improvement Association. These groups are described in Chapter 9.

Several other organizations in which outdoor camping, hikes, and excursions are prominent, such as the YMCA, YWCA, Boys' Club, and 4-H, are included in later chapters. Additional agencies and private groups which collectively make a great impact but which are too numerous to describe individually, offer camping, tours, hiking, horseback riding, canoeing, sailing, mountain climbing, skiing, and other outdoor-related activities. An unusual example is Outward Bound, which operates survival schools that present tremendous challenges to older youth.

RELIGIOUS-ORIENTED
ORGANIZATIONS

Chapter 9

The agencies covered in this chapter are religious-oriented to a greater or lesser extent. Some of them restrict their memberships to young people who adhere to their particular faiths. Others open their memberships to anyone, retaining their religious connections in terms of their social ideals rather than their creeds. In some instances, organizations which began with programs that were primarily religious have expanded their scope in other areas to such an extent that their religious origins survive chiefly as guiding principles rather than as program elements.

Even though organizations described in other chapters in this book are not labeled as "religious-based," they are not necessarily nonreligious in character. Many churches sponsor youth organizations, such as Scouts. Most of the youth organizations encourage participation by their members in the life of religious institutions of their choice.

Young Men's Christian Association of the United States of America

In 1840, a group of 11 young London clerks began meeting in the room of George Williams for prayer and mutual help. Their desire to make this type of opportunity available to other young men away from home led to the formation of the Young Men's Christian Association on June 6, 1844. Membership was limited to members of evangelical churches, but nonmembers were invited to activities.[1]

---

[1] *YMCA Yearbook* (New York: Association Press, annual); Charles Howard Hopkins, *History of the YMCA in North America* (New York: Association Press, 1951); *Programs for Urban Action* (New York, N. Y.: National Board of Young Men's Christian Association, 1969); *The YMCA in the Next Decade* (New York, N.Y.: Research and Development Services, National Council of Young Men's Christian Associations, 1970). Brochure.

The association grew rapidly because of the very poor conditions under which youth of that day lived. Associations soon sprang up in many other English cities; and in 1851, Boston formed the United States' first YMCA. Had the various churches been working effectively with young people at that time, it is doubtful that the "Y" would have enjoyed such growth, since its primary motivation and program were religious in nature.

With the erection of buildings and the hiring of paid staff, programs began to expand, until today Y's serve all ages—men, women, boys, and girls —in an infinitely wide variety of programs. In 1969 there were nearly 2,000 branches of the YMCA in the country. Among the Y's 5,458,848 members were 1,570,493 women and girls.[2]

INNOVATIONS OF THE YMCA

From the beginning, the association has been most adaptive and willing to pioneer.

A few of the "firsts" for which the YMCA deserves credit include: invention of the sports of basketball and volleyball, physical fitness programs for men, night schools, camping (the oldest camp in the country, YMCA Camp Dudley in New York State, was opened in 1885), youth and government programs, learn-to-swim campaigns, and toastmasters' clubs. The Y inaugurated prisoner-of-war aid during the Civil War, performed 90 percent of the welfare work with the U.S. forces in World War I, and operated 646 USO units in World War II. The Y helped launch the Boy Scouts; and a Y Secretary, Luther Gulick, founded the Camp Fire Girls. Work among college students was begun in 1858, and today college Y's are found on most major college and university campuses.

The organization is still pioneering, as may be indicated by mentioning just a few of the new programs initiated by different associations during one recent year: courses on "how to avoid being a college dropout," fitness counseling, cigarettes and health clinics, measured-mile program to encourage walking, welcome to foreign visitors, international camper exchange, parent-teen communications program, camping for older adults, model United Nations, tutorial programs for college students to help elementary school low-achievers, and YMCA-on-Wheels, a motorized program office.

WORLD SERVICE

YMCA World Service donations provide over $2,500,000 each year to assist Y's in 40 foreign countries. The program is a self-help operation very similar to the Peace Corps and predating it by more than 70 years. Of the

2 Earle Buckley and Richard L. Batchelder, eds., *YMCA Yearbook and Official Roster* (New York, N.Y.: Association Press, 1970). p. 155.

83 countries with YMCA's today, 46 were begun with the help of the World Service program.[3]

In the Middle East today, the YMCA is the only place where Jews and Arabs associate together freely and work together.

PROGRAMS AND FACILITIES

Programs and facilities vary greatly from one Y to another. This variety is due to the fact that each association is an autonomous organization governed by a board of directors selected from its own membership.

Down through the years, the YMCA has placed less and less emphasis on evangelical Christianity and more and more on character education, group work, physical fitness, and a host of other aspects of its work. Persons of all faiths are accepted into membership.

The YMCA has been a powerful force in the ecumenical movement. A YMCA secretary, John R. Mott, was one of the most influential persons in this respect.

The typical YMCA today is de-emphasizing dormitory services, cafeterias, and other building features for which it has long been noted. Major emphasis is now being placed on Y-Indian Guides, adult and youth physical fitness programs, camping, and aquatics.

Some Y's with elaborate facilities and recreational programs have been charged with being no more than "middle-class country clubs." The process of institutionalization probably has provided some basis for this criticism. When any organization develops a large budget and becomes dependent on the community at large for support, there is a natural tendency to emphasize activities with good income potential and to avoid taking stands on controversial social and religious issues which could alienate certain influential segments of the population.

There does, however, appear to be a trend in the Y toward more involvement in social issues. An emergency fund was set up at the 1966 triennial convention of Y secretaries for members of their ranks who had been fired for taking stands on issues of social consequence.

YMCA CLUBS

Although YMCA's have long been associated with large buildings, programs are in no sense wholly dependent on them. Hundreds of Y's have little more than offices or small meeting rooms. In these "non-equipment" branches, the club program has been the heart of the work. The Y today operates what is known as a "four-front" club program designed to give a boy or girl a continuous experience from the lower elementary through the

3 *Questions and Answers About the Work of the International Committee of YMCAs of the United States* (New York, N.Y.: The International Committee of YMCAs, 1971). Brochure.

intermediate grades, junior high school, and high school. A description of the various parts of this club program follows.

Y-Indian Guides

The fastest growing and most successful club program of the YMCA today is the father and son Y-Indian Guides. This is a program in which six-to-eight-year-old boys participate together with their fathers as "big and little braves" in small units known as "tribes." Its purpose is to multiply the number of things that fathers and sons do together. The Y believes that the comradeship of father and son strengthens the family and enriches the community.

Here is a program for the well-meaning but busy father who always intends to spend more time with his son but has a hard time getting around to it. As the name indicates, the Y-Indian Guide program is built on the lore of the American Indian, which has great appeal to the imagination of the primary-aged boy. Tribes, usually composed of six to ten boys and their fathers, meet every other week for a program of games, crafts, stories, and other activities. Special events such as swim parties, fishing or camping trips, hikes, and outings to points of historical interest are often held.

The Indian flavor is promoted through the use of Indian headbands, Indian games and stories, and the making of totem poles, tom-toms, and other Indian articles for use in the short ceremonies of a tribe. One significant rule that is enforced is that neither a father nor a son may attend a meeting without the other.

Meetings are rotated from home to home of the members and do not last more than an hour except on special occasions.

When two or more tribes exist in a community, a governing council known as a "long house" is created. This organization provides the medium for exchange of ideas, joint programs, and expansion of the Y-Indian Guide program.

There is an official manual, but each tribe exercises a great deal of freedom. No national tests or requirements to pass are used.

The slogan "pals forever" has been criticized by some, including many YMCA leaders, on the grounds that a father should not be a "pal" to his boy, but rather a father. However, the ideal of a close and permanent relationship between father and son is certainly a worthy one.

The organization's stated aims, which boys are encouraged to learn, are:

1. to be clean in body and pure in heart.
2. to be "pals forever" with my dad/son.
3. to love the sacred circle of my family.
4. to be attentive when others speak.
5. to love my neighbor as myself.

6. to seek to preserve the beauty of the Great Spirit's work in forest, field and stream.[4]

Some mothers have been so enthusiastic regarding the Y-Indian Guides that they have agitated for a program of their own; and now many communities also have Y-Indian Maidens, a similar program for mothers and daughters.

Although the Y-Indian Guides tribes normally disband after two or three years, some tribes continue to get together unofficially now and then until the boys finish high school.

At the time of this writing, there were over 450,000 fathers and sons enrolled in the Y-Indian Guides, representing a growth of 190 percent in ten years.[5]

GRA-Y

The second "front" of the YMCA club program is known as the Gra-Y, which had its beginnings in Morris Cove, Connecticut, in 1924. Many YMCA's do not push Gra-Y because they feel that fourth, fifth, and sixth grade boys have enough to do; Little League, Cub Scouts, music lessons, and a multitude of other activities are available to this age group. As a result, the Gra-Y clubs vary from community to community.

The clubs usually have these characteristics:

1. They consist of at least eight boys of about nine, ten, and 11 years of age, who may be in the same school or may be brought together at the YMCA building.
2. They usually have a sponsoring committee of which two or more are parents.
3. They build their programs around the needs, interests, and capabilities of younger boys through helping boys carry out the Gra-Y purpose.
4. They have an adult leader.
5. They meet about once or twice a week.
6. Each club has its own boy leaders.
7. They are affiliated with the local YMCA.

Most Gra-Y clubs promote better father-and-son relationships by encouraging them to do things together, such as going on hikes and trips. There are no ranks or special requirements, and the leaders attempt to involve the boys in planning the kind of program that will meet their interests as well as

[4] *The Father and Son Y-Indian Guides* (New York, N.Y.: Association Press, 1962), p. 5.
[5] *YMCA Yearbook and Official Roster, 1970,* (New York, N.Y.: Association Press, 1971), p. 171.

needs. A well-balanced program provides opportunities for decision-making, problem-solving, service projects, religious and educational experiences, physical activities, and social activities.

Some YMCAs organize similar programs for girls known as Tri-Gra-Y.

Junior Hi-Y

Junior Hi-Y and Junior Tri-Hi-Y are programs for boys and girls of junior high school age. These, as well as Tri-Hi-Y for high-school girls, are fairly well modeled after Hi-Y.

Hi-Y

The first high-school YMCA of which there is any record was organized in Ionia, Michigan, in 1870. Although the high-school YMCA movement spread rapidly to other communities, the name *Hi-Y* was not used until after the turn of the century. The National Hi-Y Fellowship was created in 1933 to bring together in one national organization thousands of Hi-Y and Tri-Hi-Y clubs. Its establishment has resulted in the development and general acceptance of common standards for club leadership and operation and a framework of mutual cooperation. Across the United States, in large cities, small towns, and rural areas, there are more than 11,000 Senior-Hi-Y and Tri-Hi-Y clubs with a total membership of over 220,000.[6]

The Hi-Y purpose, which has remained unchanged since its development in 1913 is: "To create, maintain, and extend throughout the home, school and community high standards of Christian character." The name "Hi-Y" stands for "High School YMCA." Members join Hi-Y Clubs because of expectations for good times, friendships, activities such as trips, parties, and sports, and opportunities to learn many of the skills of social relations and leadership. Although in the past some clubs have been selective in their membership, today the accepted practice is to open the club's membership to any interested youth. The program of Hi-Y clubs varies according to the interests of the members, but often includes speakers and discussions on matters of interest.

One of the outstanding programs of Hi-Y is its Youth-in-Government program. This program is now found in most states. Club members elect representatives to model legislatures and have the opportunity to study and write bills which the representatives attempt to put through when the sessions convene at the state capitol. The model legislatures themselves are run on a basis very similar to that of the actual legislatures. The program has won the acclaim of officials in both major political parties throughout the country. While overall membership in the YMCA has been booming, programs for older youth, such as Hi-Y, have found themselves hard-pressed

6 *Ibid,* p. 171.

to hold their own. This is a typical problem shared by nearly all of the youth agencies. It would appear that, as more and more younger members are enrolled in an organization, it becomes more and more difficult to hold the older youth.

VOLUNTEERS IN THE YMCA

Although the total YMCA membership climbed by 45 percent from 1959 to 1969, the number of YMCA professional workers grew much more slowly.[7] This has resulted in an increasing number of members per worker, and it is necessary to rely heavily on part-time and volunteer help.

In a recent year, over half a million different persons rendered volunteer service through the YMCA. One out of nine members served as a member of a board, officer of a group, club advisor, coach, instructor, or in some other capacity.

YMCA FINANCES AND MEMBERSHIPS

YMCA's in 1969 received $41 million from community chests and united funds. This was 15.7 percent of their total income. Membership dues brought in 21.7 percent of the total income; program fees, 23.3 percent; contributions, 5.6 percent; residences, 14.3 percent; club services, 9.9 percent; endowments, 2.1 percent; and miscellaneous, 7.4 percent. Total income was $261 million.[8]

The national organization is supported by a contribution from each local YMCA, the amount of which equals a certain percentage of the local budget.

Membership policies of most associations require adults to pay fees equivalent to the actual cost of providing the membership services. Young adult fees are typically set at half to three-quarters of the actual cost; and youth memberships are from 10 to 50 percent of the actual cost, with the rest being subsidized by United Fund contributions or sustaining memberships.

Although 5,650,610 different persons were members of the YMCA during 1968, 43 percent of the total different members did not renew membership.[9] This statistic suggests that membership is rather unstable and that perhaps many persons look upon joining the YMCA as buying a service rather than as belonging to an organization. To alter this attitude is one of the great challenges facing YMCA directors today.

[7] *Ibid*, p. 52.

[8] *Ibid.*, p. 164.

[9] *YMCA Yearbook and Official Roster, 1969* (National Council of the Young Men's Christian Association of Canada and the United States of America, 1969), pp. 56–57.

Young Women's Christian Association of the United States of America

The YWCA is a women's organization. It came into being in the middle of the nineteenth century when women faced opportunities and responsibilities for which neither they nor society were prepared.

NATURE OF THE YWCA

The YWCA is a membership organization. Many uninformed persons think of the "Y" as a building—or a place to get an inexpensive room, hot shower, or swimming lessons. However, it is an association, which may or may not own a building. Its members determine policy and share in the leadership.[10]

The YWCA is an international organization. Mutual understanding and concern has always been a major emphasis of the association, which now is found in 78 countries.

The YWCA is an organization with a Christian purpose. That purpose is basic to all of its programs. Because the YWCA has always felt the vital relationship between the material and spiritual aspects of human life, it has performed many social service functions in the communities in which it has been located. The present statement of purpose adopted at the 1967 Convention reads as follows:

> The Young Women's Christian Association of the United States of America, a movement rooted in the Christian faith as known in Jesus and nourished by the resources of that faith, seeks to respond to the barrier-breaking love of God in this day. The Association draws together into responsible membership women and girls of diverse experiences and faiths, that their lives may be open to new understanding and deeper relationships and that together they may join in the struggle for peace and justice, freedom and dignity for all people.[11]

Women and girls of 12 years and over are eligible for membership; men and boys of 12 years and over who participate in programs are called YWCA associates. Each branch has its own board of directors elected by the members.

[10] Mary S. Sims, *The YWCA, An Unfolding Purpose* (New York, N.Y.: Woman's Press, 1950); Mary S. Sims, *The Purpose Widens* (New York: Bureau of Communications, National Board, Young Women's Christian Association, 1969); Sara-Alyce P. Wright, *Y-Teen Club Adviser's Handbook* (New York, N.Y.: Young Women's Christian Association, revised 1964); *The YWCA Magazine,* monthly except July, August, and September.

[11] *Report, Twenty-Fourth National Convention, Young Women's Christian Association of the United States of America* (New York, N.Y.: Young Women's Christian Association of the U.S.A., 1967), p. 53.

HISTORICAL BACKGROUNDS

In the middle of the nineteenth century, the association idea grew simultaneously in England, Germany, and Switzerland. In each of these countries the vitality of the movement came from the evangelical churches.

The YWCA had its beginnings in England in 1855 when the North London Home and a group known as the Prayer Union opened simultaneously. In 1859, the name Young Women's Christian Association was adopted. The time was ripe for such an organization. The Mid-Victorian age brought many changes in the lives of women, particularly in work opportunities outside their own homes. The developments of the Industrial Revolution were rapidly making the old statement, "A woman's place is in the home," obsolete.

While there is no clear line of connection between association beginnings in England and the United States, in 1858 a group of New York women gathered to form the Union Prayer Circle, which later evolved into the Ladies' Christian Association of the City of New York. The Boston YWCA, organized in 1866, was the first in this country to use the full name— Young Women's Christian Association. Similar groups were organized in many eastern cities in the years following without any direct promotion. By 1875, 28 associations reported the following work: 13 boarding homes, 10 Bible classes, 21 prayer meetings, 15 employment services. Other early activities included libraries and classes in sewing, history, writing, and bookkeeping.

The specific goal of these early associations was that of providing the influence and protection of a Christian home for women and girls who had left their own homes to come to the city.

The present national organization was not started until 1906, at which time there were 608 local YWCA's with a membership of 186,330. By this time, many of the associations were not content to limit themselves to work with young women away from home and began to extend into the community. YWCA's organized homes for the aged; distributed flowers, food, and clothing to prisons, hospitals, and soldiers' homes; set up day nurseries; and supported efforts to increase wages for women and girls. Their leadership was "fired with missionary zeal for all who suffered or were unfortunate."

NATIONAL RELATIONSHIPS TO LOCAL ASSOCIATIONS

Each association is an autonomous organization, responsible for its own fund-raising, policy development, and programming. The national organization is a voluntary grouping of local associations. Until 1949 the only requirement that a local YWCA was obliged to meet was the so-called basis of membership—restricting voting power and office-holding to those members who individually accepted the Christian purpose spelled out in the National Constitution. In 1949, the requirement of contributing to the expenses of the national organization was added; and, in 1967, a strict requirement of nondiscrimination was added. Any action by an association which prevents achieving full integration, or expresses intent to become or remain segregated, is grounds for disaffiliation.

National conventions are held every three years. At these meetings, women representing each of the local associations gather to develop areas of emphasis for the next three years. The 1967–1970 program priorities, for example, were in the areas of: (1) Christian movement—new dimensions, (2) education, (3) work and leisure, (4) racial integration, (5) social isolation, (6) sex values, (7) health, (8) world responsibility, and (9) political responsibility.[12]

The 1970–1973 program, by way of contrast, concentrated on one imperative—the elimination of racism. Adopted unanimously at the Twenty-fifth National Convention, the program read, in part:

> We determine, as members of the YWCA in Associations—local and national—to thrust our collective power toward the elimination of racism wherever it exists and by any means necessary. This is our imperative for 1970–1973.
>
> Within the context of our primary concern to achieve a just society we will need to work to:
> Eliminate poverty
> End war—build peace
> Reshape the quality of the environment
> Revolutionize society's expectations of women and their own self-perception
> Involve youth intentionally in leadership and decision making.[13]

YWCA PROGRAM AND POLICY

Although the YWCA has programs for all ages, and for men and boys occasionally, highest priority is given to the needs of girls and young women in their teens and early twenties. Subsidies received from gifts and united fund drives are usually spent primarily on that age group while other programs are intended to be self-supporting.

Down through the years the YWCA has spoken out on controversial issues more than any other youth agency. It has been willing to be criticized and to take unpopular stands when necessary. Racial integration, support of the

---

[12] *National YWCA Emphases, 1967–70* (New York, N.Y.: Board of Communications, National Board, Young Women's Christian Association, n.d.), pp. 3–5.

[13] *Report, Twenty-Fifth National Convention, Young Women's Christian Association of the United States of America* (New York, N.Y.: National Board of the Young Women's Christian Association of the U.S.A., 1971), p. 164.

United Nations and other international institutions, the ecumenical movement, and labor legislation are just a few of the causes for which the YWCA has worked and fought.

There has never been any one activity or group of activities found uniformly in all associations. Each association strives to meet its Christian purpose in the ways most appropriate to its own community.

The YWCA, unlike most social agencies, is not organized to provide some particular service. It exists to carry out what it considers to be its Christian purpose principally with women and girls, in whatever ways are best suited to the time and place. Change is a dominant characteristic; and the YWCA has tried to take on new programs, accept new opportunities, and abandon old, less-needed work.

Y-TEENS

The first youth work of the YWCA began with the inception of the Little Girls' Christian Association in 1881 in Oakland. The association was established chiefly for the purpose of protection and to promote interest in literary and art studies. From this time on, the program with girls grew rapidly, and in 1918 the national organization decided that the movement needed unity. The name Girl Reserves was selected. A code, uniforms, insignia, and emblems came into being.

Unofficially before 1934, and officially after the Convention that year, the minimum age of 12 years was accepted for the YWCA work with youth. It has been generally felt that with the number of agencies reaching younger girls, the YW could make its greatest contribution as girls enter puberty and move through adolescence to young womanhood.

By 1946, the younger members organized in the Girl Reserves clubs were looked upon more and more widely as an integral part of the whole association. In this year, the name was changed from Girl Reserves to Y-Teens. The name Y-Teens seemed to more accurately describe the goal of youth participation and identification with the total YWCA *now,* in contrast to the idea of Reserves for the future.

The Y-Teens (girls from 12 to 17) now constitutes one of the major concerns of the YWCA. The program is not rigidly structured, but rather allows each club to determine its own program within the limits of the general purposes of the organization (Figure 9–1). Material and aids are provided, but the aim is to utilize the mutual interests and needs of the girls.

Y-Teens number over 400,000 today.[14] Service projects and world fellowship programs open new vistas for teen-age girls in the areas of citizenship and responsibility.

The Y-Teens goals are a summation of YWCA purpose—to grow as a

[14] *The Story of the YWCA,* (New York N.Y.: National Board, YWCA, 1969), Mimeographed, p. 3.

Figure 9–1
More than 400,000 girls take part in Y-Teen clubs and activities. They plan their own programs, elect their officers, and work in partnership with adults on YWCA and community projects. Here, a group discusses ideas for the World Fellowship program. *Courtesy National Board, YWCA.*

person; to grow in friendship with people of all races, religions, and nationalities; and to grow in knowledge and love of God. Clubs are often deliberately set up as interracial groups to help implement these purposes.

Each club is run in a democratic manner with elected officers and an adult volunteer advisor. One of the main purposes of Y-Teens is to develop leadership; therefore leadership conferences and workshops play an important role in the program. Programs are usually devised in each of six areas: human relations, creative arts, citizenship and service, vocations, spiritual growth, and health and recreation.

National Jewish Welfare Board

Under the guidance of the National Jewish Welfare Board, an extensive program for Jewish people is carried on through the Jewish Community Centers, the Young Men's Hebrew Association, and the Young Women's Hebrew Association.[15]

The Jewish Community Center, open to all Jews, is a powerful force

[15] *Jewish Community Centers* (New York, N.Y.: National Jewish Welfare Board, n.d.). Mimeographed.

for unity among the Jews. The Center attempts to mold character, develop creativity and self-respect among Jewish people, provide opportunities for learning the deeper meaning of democracy and Judaism, and train leaders for citizenship responsibilities and community service.

Forerunners of the Young Men's Hebrew Association were in existence as early as 1854. The growth was accelerated by the formation of the New York City Young Men's Hebrew Association in 1874 and the Philadelphia YMHA in 1875. These two associations are the oldest Jewish youth groups with continuous histories.

Although women were admitted to either full or partial membership in a number of YMHA's as early as 1868, the Young Women's Hebrew Association as such did not develop until 1888, when the New York YMHA organized an auxiliary. The oldest existing separate association for girls and women is the YWHA of New York City, established in 1902.

The Jewish Community Center movement came into being during the second decade of the twentieth century and has become the dominant type of organization in the field of Jewish group work. It represents the embodiment of the concept of a center of Jewish life that has been actively stimulated by the Jewish Welfare Board, the parent organization since 1921.

The Jewish Welfare Board was particularly active in stimulating mergers and combinations of existing YMHA's and YWHA's and other local agencies and their development into Jewish Community Centers, with equal privileges for all age groups of both sexes.

THE CENTER ITSELF

A fully equipped Jewish Community Center provides social rooms, game rooms, classrooms, clubrooms, a gymnasium, a swimming pool, and an auditorium. The center offers its members a well-rounded program of recreational and educational activities, including physical education and swimming classes, socials, games, dances, entertainments, lectures, concerts, and forums. Jewish interests are specifically encouraged and, whenever feasible, Jewish elements are introduced into the general program.

All centers provide for the special interests of boys and girls of elementary and high-school age. The boys and girls participate in recreational activities and are also organized into councils and other self-governing bodies for the purpose of conducting interclub activities of a competitive and cooperative character. A summer program is customarily conducted. Play schools and day camps have been established in some centers, and others conduct resident camps under their own auspices or in association with neighboring organizations.

For the adult there are social clubs, arts, crafts, sewing, discussions, holiday programs, luncheons, trips, and motor camping.

Centers often participate in civic movements, stimulate discussion of public questions, and observe civic holidays. In more recent years the program has emphasized adult education through formal and informal instruction.

FAMILY EMPHASIS

The basic membership in a center is the family unit. Although many other organizations admit the importance of family programs, the Jewish Community Centers have probably done a better job than any other agency in carrying on a wide array of activities appealing to families as well as to individuals in the family.

CLUBS

Club programs are given strong emphasis in the Centers. Most of them offer club programs for all age groups, from nursery school to senior citizens. Larger Centers may hire group workers who specialize in work with particular age groups, such as small children or teen-agers.

LEADERSHIP

Educational qualifications for professional workers in the Centers are probably higher than those in any other youth organization. Most professionals are expected to hold Master's degrees in social group work, but other degrees are acceptable in some positions.

FINANCING THE PROGRAM

Financing for the Centers in obtained from United Jewish Federation appeals, community chests, united funds, membership dues, fees for services and activities, rentals and sales of products, special fund-raising, and contributions. The major portion comes from united funds, membership dues, and fees for services.

MEMBERSHIP POLICIES

Although the Centers focus their efforts on serving Jews, with the objective of deepening Jewish identification, most of them follow the Jewish Welfare Board's guiding policy of being open to non-Jews. Surveys show that non-Jewish membership has increased from 5 percent in 1957 to about 10 percent today. A few centers have as high as 25 percent non-Jewish members. While reaffirming its nonrestrictive policy, the Jewish Welfare Board is concerned that the Jewish character of the organization be maintained.

EXTENT OF TODAY'S PROGRAM

The Jewish Community Centers and the YM-YWHA's affiliated with the Jewish Welfare Board are expanding in an unparalleled fashion. Today, there are more than 200 Centers and Y's which operate 450 major units, branches, country and day camps in over 200 cities. They serve about 745,000 members ranging in age from three to 83. An estimated service to additional people doubles the figure.[16]

Aggregate local expenditures of the Centers and Y's total more than $40 million annually. Facilities owned are valued at $150 million. A staff of about 1,420 professional social workers and several hundred specialists in the arts, child education, health and physical education, and adult Jewish education serve the Centers and Y's.[17]

FUNCTIONS OF THE JEWISH WELFARE BOARD

The Jewish Welfare Board helps the Centers carry out their local programs and fulfill their Jewish and community responsibilities. The Board provides the Centers with program and educational resources, technical and advisory services, and regional and national consultation. Regional consultants and eight regional groups of Centers and Y's are maintained. A national executive staff and specialists are based at national headquarters.

The Board issues program materials dealing with all aspects of Center work; it organizes and conducts regional and national conferences, institutes, seminars, and many kinds of inter-center activities. It gives skilled guidance in developing, improving, and evaluating Center programs in camping, health and physical education, the performing and graphic arts, Jewish cultural projects, holiday observances, and public affairs. It offers technical advice in community planning, building construction, equipment planning, administration, fund-raising, and public relations.

Another responsibility of the Board lies in the recruitment, orientation, and placement of professional Center workers. It also administers a scholarship program for the graduate training of Center workers and recruits college students for professional careers. Its research center develops data to keep the Centers abreast of changing trends and needs.

REACH INTO OTHER COUNTRIES

The Jewish Community Center idea has spread into other countries. There are YMHA's and Jewish Community Centers in Bombay, India; Tokyo, Japan; Buenos Aires, Argentina; São Paulo, Brazil; La Paz, Bolivia; Santiago, Chile; Lima, Peru; the Dominican Republic; Mexico City; Australia and Canada, and throughout Europe and Israel.

[16] *Ibid.*
[17] *Ibid.*

The B'nai B'rith Youth Organization

The B'nai B'rith Youth Organization, founded in 1924, is the world's largest Jewish youth movement. Approximately 45,000 Jewish youth in 1,100 North American communities and many on five other continents belong to BBYO. Professional social workers and educators supervise BBYO district and regional offices.[18]

BBYO, a federation of three youth groups, attracts a cross-section of the young Jewish community, including future leaders of the adult community. The BBYO components are: Aleph Zadik Aleph for teen-age boys; B'nai B'rith Girls for teen-age girls; B'nai B'rith Young Adults for 18-to-26-year-olds.

BBYO's programs and activities are designed to meet the needs and interests of its diversified membership (Figure 9–3). Specifically, BBYO strives to help its members "feel at home" as Jews through knowledge of their religious and cultural heritage; to provide a meaningful experience in democratic self-government; to meet and work with many friends under responsible adult guidance; and to develop and practice a sense of community responsibility.

Service projects play an important role in the BBYO program. The organization contributes about $50,000 to charitable causes each year. Social, athletic, and cultural activities are also emphasized. Creative writing, art, and public speaking contests have Jewish themes, so that contestants not only develop a skill, but also have a deeper exposure to Judaisim.

Other Jewish Youth Groups

Each of the three main branches of Judaism in this country has its own youth movement which is affiliated with local synagogues. In general, the groups operate very similarly to Christian denominational groups, with a loose structure and local self-determination. Camping, social, and educational activities tend to prevail.[19] The three organizations are:

> 1. *National Federation of Temple Youth (Reform)*. The NFTY seeks to train Reform Jewish youth in the values of the synagogue and their application to daily life through service to the community and congregation. The organization also sponsors study programs, cultural activities, summer camps, leadership seminars, overseas tours, work programs, an international student exchange, and community service projects.
>
> 2. *United Synagogue Youth (Conservative)*. This group states as its purpose

[18] *Facts and Faces of B'nai B'rith Youth Organization* (Washington, D.C.: B'nai B'rith Youth Organization, n.d.) Mimeographed.
[19] American Jewish Committee, *American Jewish Yearbook,* (New York, N.Y.: American Book-Stratford Press, Inc., 1967).

the development of a program for strengthening identification with Judaism, based on the personality development, needs, and interests of the adolescent.

3. *National Council of Young Israel (Orthodox)*. This group maintains a program of spiritual, cultural, and communal activity directed toward the advancement and perpetuation of traditional Judaism. It seeks to instill in its youth an understanding of and an appreciation for the ethical and spiritual values of Judaism.

The Salvation Army Youth Programs

The Salvation Army is an international religious and charitable movement, a branch of the Christian faith, organized and operated on a military pattern. Conditions of membership are: religious conversion, the acceptance of Salvation Army doctrines, abstinence from liquor, and a pledge to support actively the Army's principles and work. There are two categories of membership: commissioned officers, trained in Salvation Army schools for officers, who devote their lives fully to the religious and social welfare activities and administration of the organization; and soldiers who, as members of the congregation, belong to a local neighborhood church fellowship known as the Corps.[20]

ORIGIN AND SPREAD

The Salvation Army commenced as a ministry to the unchurched. William Booth, who left the Methodist ministry in 1865 to become an independent evangelist, began to preach in the slums of London's East End. It was not his plan to found a church; but when he attempted to send converts to the churches, they did not feel at home because of their poor appearance. Booth established Christian Mission Centers for these converts.

Today the Salvation Army operates in more than 70 countries and territories, maintaining over 20,000 religious and charitable centers. Its work is supported by contributions of members, collections, fees, donations, and gifts.

WAYS OF WORK

Salvation Army Centers often work through other youth agencies, sponsoring Boy Scout troops, Little League baseball teams, and Pop Warner football teams. Drop-in centers known as Red Shield Youth Centers are often maintained, featuring crafts rooms, gymnasiums, auditoriums, and game rooms.

[20] *Girl Guard Handbook* (New York, N.Y.: The Salvation Army, 1961); *Sunbeam Handbook* (New York, N.Y.: The Salvation Army, 1960); *The Salvation Army...Definition, History, Services, Organization* (New York, N.Y.: The Salvation Army, n.d.) Mimeographed, 8 pages.

Daycare centers, camps, and boys' clubs are other means by which the Salvation Army provides for children and youth in inner-city areas.

SUNBEAMS AND GIRL GUARDS

The organization has several groups for girls, the Sunbeams and two divisions of Girl Guards. Sunbeams are the youngest members, six to ten years old; Girl Guards are the middle group, ten to 13 years, and Senior Guards are the oldest group, girls 14 to 18 years of age. Sunbeams and Girl Guards have their own leaders, tests, interests, and meeting place (Figure 9–2). The ranks and proficiency badge program resemble those of the Girl Scouts; however, considerably more religion is included in the program. There are requirements such as: "Recite five verses of Scripture," "Attend Sunday School regularly," and so on. Sunbeams work on proficiency badges such as cooking, flower study, helper, friend to animal, and nurse's aide. Girl Guards may win honors in such activities as canoeing, chemistry, crocheting, fingerpainting, landscape gardening, and needlework. Second-class and first-class tests contain many of the same elements as Scouting: citizenship, first-aid, campcrafts, and nature study. All uniforms are troop property.

Figure 9–2
Sunbeams have lots of fun as they learn to "Do Right" in The Salvation Army's program for girls six through ten. Older girls may participate in the Girl Guards and Senior Guards. *Courtesy The Salvation Army.*

The stated purpose of the Girl Guards is to help each girl become a happy, resourceful person, who is a responsible member of her group; to help her grow up into a useful citizen; and to build a love for God.

Protestant Denominational Youth Programs

The character of youth work in the major Protestant denominations has changed radically in recent years. As late as 1960, emphasis was on the building of strong national church-related youth movements. The Methodist Youth Fellowship alone claimed 1,518,486 members in 1961.[21] Luther League, Christian Endeavor, the Congregational Pilgrim Fellowships, Baptist youth organizations and many others quoted membership statistics in the hundreds of thousands or millions.

However, in the 1960s there was a strong movement away from church youth programs on a highly organized club basis. In 1966 the Girls Friendly Society of the Episcopal church was disbanded. In 1968 the Methodist Youth Fellowship ceased to exist, and the Luther League of the Lutheran Church in America was terminated. Basic reasons given were a lack of interest on the part of young people, a rejection of old ways of doing things, a feeling that local situations were too diverse to be accommodated by a national program, and the desire to bring the youth into the mainstream of the life of the church.

CHANGES IN YOUTH PROGRAMS

The demise of the large, national church youth organizational structure does not, however, signify the end of church youth programs. On the contrary, many churches are finding a renewed interest on the part of their young people.

Paradoxically, while many churches have nearly given up on youth activities for lack of interest, other local churches are enjoying the greatest youth attendance in history. It would seem that those groups that are flourishing are those which have been able to break away from the old patterns and develop programs more in tune with changing interests and values.

Some of the changes that are apparent are:

1. An interest in new forms of worship, such as creative litany writing in contemporary language, rock music services, and folk masses.

2. A desire to engage in intensive "rap sessions" or discussions. Encounter games, sensitivity training techniques, and situation games are being widely used. Interest in social games, dancing, and organized competitive athletics has waned. Popular movies are often the springboard for in-depth discussions.

3. An increased interest in music in its many forms.

4. An effort to remain detached from the formal organization of the church, which is often considered irrelevant. Many youth groups gather in homes and other places instead of the church.

5. A desire to avoid the trappings of organized groups, such as minutes, officers, and record-keeping.

6. An emphasis on being involved. Work projects, social-concern action,

---

[21] Information included in a letter from Charles W. Courtoy, Director, United Methodist Church Ministries with Senior High Youth, dated 12/22/69.

and political involvement are more and more being considered "where it's at."

7. An increased emphasis on ecumenical, interchurch programs, many co-sponsored by two or more denominations. In many areas, Catholics and Protestants now work together.

ADULT LEADERSHIP

In the main, it appears that those groups which are successful today are those which have the guidance of personally concerned adults who are willing not only to give generously of their own time but also to allow youth the freedom they need to develop a program consistent with their own life-style.

Of paramount importance is the type of leadership provided by the adult advisor. This should be active at first, then be gradually relinquished as the youth are able to carry the load themselves. The adult must be supportive in that he is there when needed to help the youth work out their problems without doing it for them, and to serve as a constant source of new and creative ideas. It is important that the relationship between the youth and adult be one in which the youth have a genuine opportunity to accept or reject the adult suggestions.

The primary role of the national church offices is now not one of organizing and coordinating, but rather one of serving as a resource for materials which may be used in a number of ways by local youth groups. Several churches print monthly magazines which are primarily problem-and-issue oriented.

Churches are beginning to discover that the youth of today are not the youth of 1950 or 1960. In order for youth programs to survive they must be meaningful and relevant to today's young people living in a rapidly changing world.

Youth Program of the Church of Jesus Christ of Latter-day Saints

The youth program of the Mormon Church had its beginnings as early as 1843. However, it was not until November 28, 1869, that President Brigham Young formally organized the young women of the Church. Some five years later, June 10, 1875, the young men were similarly organized into an association by President Young.[22]

MUTUAL IMPROVEMENT ASSOCIATION

Throughout the Church of Jesus Christ of Latter-day Saints this weekday teaching and activity program is popularly known as the "MIA," or

[22] *Mutual Improvement Association Executive Manual* (Salt Lake City, Utah: General Boards of the M.I.A. of the Church of Jesus Christ of Latter Day Saints, 1966).

"Mutual" (Mutual Improvement Association), and is customarily held on a Tuesday or Wednesday night. For approximately an hour and a half, the participants in Mutual enjoy a program including assembly numbers, religious class instruction, and cultural arts activities. There is a regular schedule of sporting and athletic events and competition. Those who direct the events for Mormon youth are selected from among the lay membership of the Church. The entire operation proceeds under the close supervision and direction of the Bishopric, the three men who are the spiritual heads of the church unit—the "ward."

Careful attention is given to assure each member of the Mutual a full opportunity to have an experience in depth in the various cultural activity programs. Regardless of capability, the individual is assisted in such a way as to afford him social development and aesthetic appreciation in music, drama and speech, and the dance.

The motto of the MIA is found in the thirty-sixth verse of the ninety-third section of the Doctrine and Covenants and expresses one of the great guiding principles of the organization—"The glory of God is intelligence."

MIA is divided into an organization of the young men (YMMIA) and an organization of the young women (YWMIA)—two organizations working cooperatively together. MIA purposes are:

    a. to develop testimonies of the Gospel;
    b. to develop talents;
    c. to provide social activities;
    d. to provide recreational activities;
    e. to develop faithful Latter-day Saints.[23]

All interested young men and women 12 years of age and older—both members and nonmembers of the Church—may attend MIA.

PROGRAM FOR TEEN-AGERS

The MIA course of study and activity for boys 12 and 13 years old is the Boy Scout program. It is the desire of the authorities of the Church that a Boy Scout troop be organized in every ward, giving every boy the opportunity to participate in scouting.

The program for 12 and 13-year-old girls is known as the *Beehive*. This program has remained basically unchanged since its inauguration in 1914. The idea is founded on the symbolism of the bees gathering honey as they are motivated by the spirit of the hive. Beehive objectives are:

    1. to build testimonies;
    2. to enrich girlhood;

[23] *Ibid.,* p. 13.

3. to strengthen home ties;

4. to build toward noble womanhood;

5. to develop social skills.

Mia Maid is the name given to the 14 and 15-year-old girls in the MIA program. The Mia Maid program is also planned to guide the girls into projects and activities of a social, cultural, recreational, and spiritual nature.

The Boy Scout Explorer program has been adopted by the YMMIA for the young men in the four-year age-range, from the ninth through the twelfth grade in school (14, 15, 16, and 17 years).

The *Laurel* program is designed for the 16 and 17-year-old girls in the MIA program. Eighteen-year-old girls, who have not graduated from high school, may also be enrolled in this age group.

OLDER YOUTH

Programs are also provided for unmarried young men and women out of high school and for young married couples.

The MIA Cultural Arts program of dance, drama, speech, and music teaches all to dance, to enjoy dramatic experiences, to speak properly, and to give talks in public, as well as to participate in various musical events.

The athletic program of the YMMIA provides for physical and social development through enjoyable group activities for the young men of the Church. The success of the Latter-day Saints athletic program has attracted international attention and acclaim through its All-Church basketball and softball tournaments, which are reported to be the largest tournaments in the world in terms of the numbers of teams participating and young men playing.

Young Life

Young Life is a relatively new interdenominational Christian organization for youth. It began when a Texas church assigned its student assistant, Jim Rayburn, to the unique project of conducting a program for teen-agers who would not attend church. Rayburn, a seminary student, was so successful that the experiment grew into a national organization with headquarters in Dallas by 1941. Today the work of Young Life is carried on by a staff of more than 250 men and women, assisted by several hundred volunteer leaders, largely college and seminary students and young businessmen.[24]

[24] *An Adventure in Relationships* (Colorado Springs, Colorado, Young Life, n.d.) Brochure; *Focus on Youth,* magazine published quarterly.

CHRISTIAN MESSAGE

Since many churches today find it difficult to attract American teen-agers, Young Life attempts to go where they are to bring them the Christian message. The group has no actual membership, since its goal is to integrate young people into an ongoing church program. Recreation plays a large role in attracting the youngsters; camping is an important aspect of the program. Eight camps, operated by the organization in the United States and Canada, cater to thousands of young people each summer. Weekly meetings of the approximately 500 clubs are usually held in homes and include singing and games, as well as speeches and discussions aimed at conversion of the teen-ager. The organization's financial support comes largely from a group of interested wealthy industrialists.

INFLUENCE

Although Young Life has been strongest in the western states and has its national headquarters in Colorado Springs, Colorado, it operates through-out the country and in several foreign countries. Its influence has been growing rapidly, as is evidenced by a growth in budget from less than $600,000 in 1959 to $2,800,000 in 1969.[25]

The staff attempts to make Christianity attractive to the high-schooler, through tastefully done publicity materials, a youthful paid staff, and generous amounts of recreation in the program.

Youth for Christ

Youth for Christ is a nondeminational, evangelical movement begun in Chicago during World War II by Torrey Johnson, a pastor. Johnson was concerned about the large number of wartime G.I.'s on the streets of Chicago and decided to conduct a large meeting for them. Soon Johnson met with others holding similar rallies in other cities, and in 1945 Youth for Christ was officially formed. Billy Graham was hired as YFC's first full-time worker.[26]

In the late Forties, YFC held its first worldwide conference in Switzer-land.

In the early days, rally leaders attracted crowds in any way they could—loud suits, boisterous ways, clowning, and bizarre activities. During the 1950s, the organization's emphasis began to shift from the large rally to more personal evangelism. Several new projects were initiated—literature programs, overseas ministry, film production, Bible clubs, Bible quizzing, and leadership training seminars.

25 From unpublished chart received from John Carter, Director of Development of Young Life, with correspondence dated 12/9/69.

26 *The Continuing Miracle* (Wheaton, Illinois: Youth For Christ International, n.d.) Brochure; *Campus Life,* magazine published 8 times a year.

In the 1960s, the emphasis was "teens reaching teens." Professional staff worked closely with youth to attempt to help them convert classmates. A special program called Lifeline was developed to try to help youth in trouble with the law. Approximately 5,000 such youth attend Lifeline camps each summer.

A magazine, *Campus Life,* attempts to penetrate the teen culture. Articles on sex, pollution, coffee-houses, and other current concerns attempt to hold the teen's interest.

Campus Life clubs are now located in approximately 2,000 high schools; promotion and advising is furnished by over 600 full-time organizers.[27] Although programs are often social and recreational, the group's primary goal remains the same: converting youth to Christianity.

United Boys' Brigades

The first Boys' Brigade was founded in Glasgow, Scotland, in the year 1883 by Sir William A. Smith. The Boys' Brigade was founded in America in 1893, a fact that makes this group one of the oldest organizations in the United States exclusively for boys.[28]

OBJECT AND PROGRAM OF THE BOYS' BRIGADE

The Boys' Brigade is a religious organization in a semi-military form, composed of boys 12 years of age and older. Boys nine to 12 years of age are known as Boys' Reserves, but are entitled to all Brigade Awards. The object of the Boys' Brigade is: "The Advancement of Christ's Kingdom among boys and the promotion of habits of obedience, reverence, discipline, self-respect and all that tends to a true Christian manliness, and to further such principles as will make the youth of the Nation loyal, patriotic and law-abiding." This object is sought by means of a semi-military organization, Bible and mission study classes for religious instructions, drill, physical training, first-aid, signaling, sports, camps, hikes, and other activities of interest for boys. Bugle and drum corps, parades, patriotic formations, and social work are included. A company Bible drill or Bible study class must be a definite part of every company's program.

Every company is connected with a church, mission, or school. Each company is under the command of a captain, who must be 21 years or older, and lieutenants, who must be at least 18. The organization states that it is of vital importance that each officer be a man of Christian character.

Meetings are rather highly structured and include roll call, devotions,

---

[27] Information included in letter from Paul J. Van Oss, Executive Director, Youth For Christ International, dated 12/1/69.

[28] *How to Organize a Company of the United Boys' Brigades of America* (Baltimore, Md.: United Boys' Brigades of America, n.d.) mimeographed brochure.

drill, and merit badge classes. Many companies drill with rifles, although this is optional.

The organization has no paid staff, even in the national office. Membership totals are not kept, but apparently the national membership is under 5,000. In Baltimore, where the national office is at present, there are about 300 members—a decline of about 50 percent in five years.[29]

Internationally, Boys' Brigade is still rather strong. In 1960, it claimed 200,000 members, largely in the British Commonwealth.[30]

Christian Service Brigade

This organization, while much younger than the Boys' Brigade, has enjoyed much greater growth. Founded in 1937 in Glen Ellyn, Illinois, it today has over 2,700 units in evangelical Protestant churches throughout the country.[31]

The Brigade was greatly influenced by the Boys' Brigade and the Boy Scouts. The uniforms and much of the program resemble scouting. The primary difference is in the Brigade's strong religious emphasis. Each rank includes tests related to knowledge of the Bible as well as knowledge of the out-of-doors.

A typical meeting would resemble a typical Boy Scout meeting, except for prayers. The CSB battalion is the equivalent of a Boy Scout troop, while squads function nearly identically to Scout patrols.

The 30-man office staff of the National Headquarters in Wheaton, Illinois, supplies the organization with excellent printed materials, including colorful handbooks for each age level and two monthly magazines—one for leaders and one for boys. The boy's magazine, *Venture,* had a circulation of 60,000 in 1968.[32]

There are three kinds of members in the organization:

1. boys eight to 11 years of age, who are formed into units called "stockades";
2. boys 12 to 18 years of age, known as "brigadiers," who unite to form "battalions"; and
3. those 19 years old and over—leaders and committeemen, who are known as "brigademen."

[29] Letter from Francis L. Butt, National Executive, United Boys' Brigades of America, dated 2/9/70.
[30] *Ibid.*
[31] *Project 70* (Wheaton, Illinois: Christian Service Brigade, 1969) Brochure.
Building Trails (Wheaton, Illinois: Christian Service Brigade, 1968).
Sentinel Trails (Wheaton, Illinois: Christian Service Brigade, 1968).
Frontier Trails (Wheaton, Illinois: Christian Service Brigade, 1969).
Venture, a magazine for boys and young men, published monthly.
[32] Letter from Richard L. Kelley, Program Research and Development Director of Christian Service Brigade, dated December 17, 1969.

Stockade leaders are known as "post rangers" and "chief rangers." Battalions are lead by "captains," "lieutenants," and "non-coms"—sergeants, corporals, and lance corporals.

The purpose of the program is to bring boys into the church, help retain those already there, build leadership, and promote growth in Christian ideals. The religious part of the program is fundamentalist in approach.

The stockade achievement program includes the ranks of Sentinel, Builder, Courier, Lookout, and Ranger. Brigadiers work on achieving the ranks of Observer, Explorer, Trailblazer, and Guide. Sports, physical fitness, wilderness skills, crafts, and Bible study are emphasized at all levels. When a boy completes the requirements for the Guide rank, he begins work on what is referred to as Frontier Trails. These achievements in areas such as mariner, sportsman, woodsman, and technician parallel the Boy Scout Merit Badge program. The highest honor is known as the Herald of Christ award. A boy who enters the stockade at eight and advances through Herald of Christ will have read nearly the entire Bible and memorized over 100 Scripture verses as well as participated in the various group activities.

Pioneer Girls

Pioneer Girls is an outgrowth of the Christian Service Brigade. The *Girls' Guild* was organized in October, 1939, as a division of CSB. In September, 1941, the name was changed to *Pioneer Girls* and it became a separate organization. Today the organization closely parallels the Brigade, and both maintain national headquarters in Wheaton, Illinois, and Burlington, Ontario.[33]

The purposes of the organization are:

1. to win girls to a personal knowledge of Christ as Savior;
2. to build them spiritually through experiences which encourage good habits of Christian living and lead toward Christian maturity;
3. to develop in girls well-rounded lives and gracious Christ-centered personalities;
4. to train them in effective Christian leadership and service.[34]

ACTIVITIES

Operating within local churches, Pioneer Girls includes weekly meetings, special outdoor activities, and a system of ranks and badges. All of these

[33] *The Pioneer Girls Guide* (Wheaton, Illinois: Pioneer Girls, 1963); *Colonist Trail Book* (Wheaton, Illinois: Pioneer Girls, 1963); *Explorer Chart Book* (Wheaton, Illinois: Pioneer Girls, 1964).
[34] *Pioneer Girls Guide,* p. 5.

work together to help the girl apply Christian principles to her entire life. Three types of groups are conducted, according to age—*Pilgrims* for third to sixth graders, *Colonists* for girls in the seventh to ninth grades, and *Explorers* for girls in senior high school.

Clubs hold weekly meetings which include activity leadership training, service projects, and Bible exploration. The achievement program for each age group contains three or four ranks, each having three emphases— spiritual development, personal development, and leadership development. Badges introduce girls to a variety of interest areas, such as personal grooming, food, arts, sports, marriage, Bible exploration, needlecraft, and music.

Pioneer Girls operates 22 camps in various parts of the United States and Canada, all called Camp Cherith. The organization also has a national leadership training center in Michigan and is active in mission projects overseas. More than 20 evangelical denominations utilize the program in their local churches. At present, there are approximately 100,000 members in 2,500 participating churches in the United States and Canada.[35]

J.M.V. Pathfinders

The General Conference of the Seventh-Day Adventist Church officially authorized the Junior Missionary Volunteers Pathfinder Club in 1950.[36]

CHRISTIAN OBJECTIVES

Pathfinders was organized to meet the physical, social, mental, and spiritual needs of the junior youth. It has four prime objectives:

1. to demonstrate the attractiveness of Christian ideals in an activity program;
2. to guide boys and girls into active missionary service;
3. to develop character and good citizenship;
4. to promote the MV classes and honors.[37]

COEDUCATIONAL CLUBS AND CLASSES

Boys and girls who are in the fifth grade or at least ten years old are eligible to join. While the club is primarily for youth of the Seventh-Day Adventist Church, non-Adventists may become members.

Pathfinders are an active group. They work for the harmonious develop-

---

35 Information supplied by national office of Pioneer Girls.
36 C. Lester Bond, *M.V. Handbook* (Washington, D.C.: Review and Herald Publishing Association, 1970).
37 *Ibid.,* p. 15.

ment of the heart, head, and hand. Their fields of activity are many and varied, including agriculture, art, crafts, camping, drill marching, health and safety, hobbies, homemaking, nature lore, vocational exploration, camps, fairs, hikes, nature trips, social events, excursions to places of historical interest, and visits to museums and zoos.

The club leaders include a director, deputy director, and one counselor for each eight members. The Master Guide program is the training outline for the leaders. Classes are taught in areas such as leadership training, Christian story-telling, first aid, denominational history, swimming, and knot-tying. Ten nature honors and five craft honors must be won by a member who wishes to be classified as Master Guide.

The clubs are coeducational and self-supporting, and are run by trained voluntary leaders. Uniforms are worn by all. Meetings are usually held once a week in a meeting hall or the home of the director.

Clubs are expected to hold an outing each month. A system of ranks and awards very similar to those of scouting is in effect. Honors can be won in any of the 150 different fields. Requirements resemble those of the Boy Scouts and Girl Scouts. The two most significant differences between this program and scouting are in its coeducational aspect and the inclusion of religious tests in all requirements.

Camping and service projects are integral parts of the program. Much emphasis is put on the interracial inclusiveness of the organization, and its success in this effort is commendable.

The Pathfinder program is worldwide and has a membership of over 70,000 youths.[38]

Catholic Youth Organizations

The Catholic Youth Organization, or CYO as it is usually called, is one of the largest youth programs in the country. However, it is similar to most Protestant youth groups in that each parish and diocese has a great deal of autonomy and there is no strong national program as such.[39]

Many CYO's are not affiliated with the parent body—the Youth Department of the United States Catholic Conference—which has no compulsory authority. Even among those which are, there is a wide variety of types of program according to local interests and tradition.

[38] Personal interview with Norman Chudleigh, San Diego County Pathfinder Coordinator.

[39] *How to Start a Parish Youth Group* (Washington, D.C.: Division of Youth Activities, United States Catholic Conference, n.d.), brochure.
    Gladych, E. "C.Y.O.: a Progress Report," *Catholic Digest* 27:63–6, Je '63.
    Columbian Squires (New Haven, Connecticut: Knights of Columbus, n.d.), pamphlet. *Junior Catholic Daughters of America,* mimeographed material from Mrs. Margaret Yama, California State Chairman of Juniors and Juniorettes.

The CYO has been strongest in the large, industrial cities of the nation. Emphasis in the large cities has been on sports and other recreation. The New York City CYO, for example, provides six community centers, four summer camps, 17 delinquency recreation projects, swim classes for the handicapped, 48 day camps, leadership training clubs, and a young peoples' symphony and music program.[40] This organization, as well as many others in the East, puts much emphasis on prevention and cure of juvenile delinquency.

At present, the trend seems to be away from recreational programs as such, and the emphasis of the national body and most local groups is now being placed on autonomous parish youth groups. These groups function with adult advisors much the same as youth programs of the Protestant churches and most of the discussion in the section entitled "Protestant Denominational Youth Programs" is applicable to the CYO.

Most parishes try to work closely with the Boy Scouts, Girl Scouts, and Camp Fire Girls and sponsor these groups in their children's programs.

Some communities also promote a youth program known as the Junior Program of the Catholic Daughters of America. This program, established in 1926, is for girls between the ages of 11 and 18. A similar program exists for girls from seven through ten, known as the Juniorettes.

In many ways the programs of the Juniors and Juniorettes resembles the Girl Scout program—uniforms, badges and awards, troops, and so on. However, they are thoroughly Roman Catholic and place a considerable emphasis on religious activities. Charitable service is also emphasized, with each Junior being required to give 30 hours of service annually.

Honors pins can be won in areas such as religion, art, literature, music, civics, nature study, homemaking, health and service. Troops are kept small —eight to ten members—and usually meet in a home.

Another Catholic youth program is the Columbian Squires. This group had its beginning in 1922, when the Knights of Columbus, a Catholic fraternal and service club, adopted boys' work as a part of its functions. The objectives of the program are similar to those of most other youth groups—responsibility, leadership development, and so forth.

The adult leadership is provided by the local Knights of Columbus council. Catholic boys between the ages of 13 and 18 are eligible for membership. Considerable emphasis is put on ritual in secret ceremonies of investiture and installation. Officers elected are: chief squire, deputy chief squire, notary, bursar, marshal, sentry, pole captain, arm captain, and three auditors.

Standing committees plan programs such as sports' nights, career days, hobby shows, dances, parties and service projects.

[40] *1965 Annual Report* (New York, N.Y.: Catholic Youth Organization of New York, 1966), p. 10.

American Youth Foundation

The American Youth Foundation was founded in 1924 to carry out a program of Christian leadership training and character development for young people. It is nondenominational and, like all the other voluntary agencies, nonprofit.[41]

Four basic areas of interest and concern in life—mental, physical, social, and religious—are identified in the philosophy of the AYF. The organization attempts to help youth develop to the fullest in each of these areas in order to become creative and responsible individuals. Two camps are operated to implement this philosophy. One is located in Michigan and the other in New Hampshire. Emphasis is placed on the training of Christian leaders for all walks of life.

Figure 9-3

Rap sessions are always popular with members of religious-oriented youth groups.
Courtesy B'nai B'rith Youth Organization.

[41] *General Information* (St. Louis, Missouri: American Youth Foundation, 1971), mimeographed; *The American Youth Foundation* (St. Louis, Missouri: American Youth Foundation, n.d.), mimeographed.

ORGANIZATIONS SERVING
THE DISADVANTAGED

Chapter 10

Awareness of social responsibility toward the disadvantaged—the cultural-ly and financially deprived, minority racial groups, the physically and mentally handicapped, and others whom society has set apart—has bur-geoned. The principal youth agencies have given emphasis to programs for these youth, often with financial help from federal agencies, while still continuing their work with youth in general. Certain agencies, however, consider work with the disadvantaged young people to be their most im-portant service; and their programs and efforts are directed primarily or, in some cases, exclusively toward them in an attempt to bring them into the mainstream of society. This chapter focuses upon these organizations.

Boys' Clubs of America

The Boys' Clubs, like many other large national youth agencies, began with the establishment of several local programs which were completely indepen-dent of each other. The first Boys' Club was established in Hartford, Con-necticut, in 1860. In 1906, the existing clubs banded together to form the Federated Boys' Clubs. They elected as their president Jacob Riis, a social worker of international renown who played a leading role in the establish-ment of public recreation in this country.[1]

Today, Boys' Clubs of America is one of the fastest growing of all youth

---

1 Boys' Clubs of America, *Manual of Boys' Club Operations*, 2nd ed. (New York, N.Y.: Dodd Mead & Company, 1956); *One Hundred Boys' Clubs Tested Programs for Disadvantaged Youth* (New York, N.Y.: Boys' Clubs of America, 1969); E. J. Stapleton, Director, Public Information, Boys' Clubs of America, *Boys' Clubs of America*, unpublished article prepared for authors, 1970; "What Is Different About a Boys' Club," *The Journal*, Boys' Clubs of America, II, No. 4, Fall, 1967, pp. 3–4.

agencies. The number of Boys' Clubs has more than doubled during the last decade, and there are now almost 900 clubs with about a million members (Figure 10–1).[2] A large percentage of these clubs are in urban areas.

SERVING THE DISADVANTAGED

The Boys' Clubs pride themselves on offering needy boys, regardless of race, creed, or color, "a place to go and a way to grow." They are intended largely to serve disadvantaged boys and are therefore usually located in the less favored sections of cities and towns. Through the years, despite the complexity of the problems confronting youth, the Boys' Clubs' philosophy and mission have not materially changed. Essentially, they offer boys from seven through 17 a wide variety of programs and projects conducted by professional youth workers in clubs designed and operated solely for boys. Under the guidance of skilled and friendly leaders, the boys relax into everyday relationships in a place that offers them "a home away from

Figure 10–1
Nearly 900 Boys' Clubs give about a million boys like these of every shape, size, color, and condition a place to go and a way to grow.
Courtesy Boys' Clubs of America.

2 Stapleton, *Boys' Clubs of America*, p. 3.

home." The leaders' informal guidance and example often give the boys the lift they need at moments that matter.

A building where boys may gather is basic to the Boys' Club program. While Boys' Clubs largely reflect the ambitions and resources of those responsible for their operation, full-sized gymnasiums and swimming pools are not unusual. Almost every club has a wood shop, library, music room, and game room. The boys' needs and interests are filled through physical programs, arts and crafts, music, drama, painting, woodworking, photography, ceramics, and other programs.

Small clubs may be formed within a Boys' Club. For example, many Boy Scout troops are sponsored by the Boys' Clubs. Keystone Clubs, which are service-oriented clubs for senior high school boys, are sponsored by local Boys' Clubs and affiliated with the National Association of Keystone Clubs.

Each club is governed by a board of directors that hires the Boys' Club executive and other staff members and is responsible for financing the program.

FINANCING

Financing is a major concern. Because the Boys' Club program is building-centered and uses professional leadership extensively, it is expensive in terms of the numbers of boys served (Figure 10–2). Moreover, dues are kept very low—generally only one dollar a year—so that even the poorest boy may join. Most of the money must come from outside sources.

Usually Boys' Clubs participate in united fund drives and depend largely on these funds for their operation. United funds give stability to many budgets, and yet sometimes they limit the expansion of programs and facilities. The means of raising adequate funds are numerous. One club raises its entire budget in one evening as each board member traditionally writes out a check for one thousand dollars. Less fortunate clubs supplement united fund drives with everything from pancake breakfasts and car washes to one-hundred-dollar-a-plate dinners.

JUVENILE DECENCY

Most youth agencies and public recreation departments avoid making claims that their programs reduce juvenile delinquency because of the difficulty of proving such claims and the possibility that emphasis on delinquency might repel some would-be members. The Boys' Clubs, however, feel that crime and delinquency rates can be lowered by the opening of a club in a community. At least one study, one conducted by New York University in Louisville, Kentucky, substantiates this claim.[3] At national, state, and local levels, Boys' Clubs proclaim their positive program of

[3] *Ibid.,* p. 3.

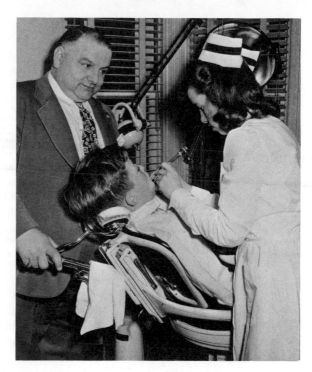

Figure 10-2
Many Boys' Clubs operate free dental clinics offering needy boys extensive and expensive dental care under expert volunteer supervision. Thousands of Boys' Club of America members benefit each year from the program. *Courtesy Boys' Clubs of America.*

combatting juvenile delinquency by building Juvenile Decency. Boys' Clubs attempt to locate where juvenile delinquency is high, recognizing that a very high proportion of the nation's thefts and burglaries are committed by boys in the age range they are trying to reach.

NATIONAL SERVICES

Boys' Clubs have a professional staff in national headquarters in New York. Regional offices with professional staffs are maintained in Boston, New York, Washington, Atlanta, Chicago, Minneapolis, Dallas, Los Angeles, San Francisco, and Seattle. The professional staff establishes standards of personnel and operation, originates and develops programs, and plans and conducts personnel training institutes and conferences.

The national professional staff also recruit and train personnel; conduct national programs and projects; plan buildings, camp equipment, and furnishings; publish periodicals, bulletins, and pamphlets; advise and assist individual Boys' Clubs with their plans and problems; and publicize the Boys' Club movement throughout the United States.

In addition to offering a place which the boys can think of as their own and in which they can engage in wholesome activities, Boys' Clubs are more and more becoming involved in service programs such as People-to-

People, Brotherhood Week, United Nations Day, Get-Out-the-Vote campaigns, and similar projects. Individual clubs and the national organization are repeatedly singled out for awards in recognition of their community service.

PROFESSIONAL LEADERSHIP

The preparation of professional leadership is conducted in cooperation with colleges and universities, and a special graduate program related to New York University provides practical experience. In spite of such educational efforts, there continues to be a shortage of professional leadership of the quality desired. Salaries have improved in recent years, and with fringe benefits now incorporated, they are now comparable to those of other employment; but the work requires irregular hours, and professional workers must have a commitment to serve and must regard the satisfactions of their work as part of the compensation.

Herbert Hoover, one of the guiding forces during his 28 years as board chairman, once said, "Boys' Clubs are the greatest character-building institutions in our country today."[4] Richard M. Nixon, Hoover's successor as board chairman for almost five years prior to his election to the Presidency, said, "Of all the things I have done, nothing has been more heartwarming, nothing has meant more to me than to be the Chairman of the Boys' Clubs of America."[5]

Girls Clubs of America, Inc.

Girls Clubs of America, Inc. is one of the newest and fastest-growing of the youth-serving agencies. Although a Girls Club was started in Waterbury, Connecticut, in 1864, it was not until 1945 that 19 independent clubs joined together to form a new national organization. Today there are over 150 clubs serving approximately 100,000 girls. Girls Clubs are building-centered, serving girls from the first grade through high school.[6]

Though the organization caters especially to girls from low-income areas, all girls are eligible for membership.

PURPOSE OF THE NATIONAL ORGANIZATION

The stated purpose of the national organization is:

1. to foster the character development of all girls of all races and religions from all social and economic backgrounds, through a program of educational, vocational, health, social, and recreational activities;

---

4 *Ibid.*, p. 4.
5 *Ibid.*, p. 4.
6 *Why Girls Clubs?* (New York, N.Y.: Girls Clubs of America, Inc.), brochure; *Handbook For Organization and Administration of Girls Clubs* (New York, N.Y.: Girls Clubs of America, 1969).

2. to help them become responsible mothers, homemakers, and citizens of the community;

3. to coordinate the programs of member clubs;

4. to encourage and assist in the promotion of new clubs; and

5. to help establish and maintain high standards for all Girls Clubs in programming, leadership, and sponsorship.[7]

ACTIVITIES IN THE CLUB BUILDING

Helping girls to grow up to be good citizens, wives, and mothers is the core of the Girls Clubs' program. This is accomplished through classes in cooking, sewing, arts and crafts, sports, and personal grooming. Most well-established clubs feature swimming pools, craft rooms, libraries, game rooms, athletic facilities, and kitchens. The importance of counseling and guidance is stressed.

As in most other youth agencies, policy is set by a volunteer board of directors. The board is responsible for hiring the staff, raising money for the budget, setting policy, and interpreting the club to the community.

As adult professional and volunteer club leaders become increasingly aware of opportunities for civic and community service, teen-age members are encouraged to develop leadership abilities. They work with groups of younger girls at the club and frequently organize activities at school and in the community.

Club members who are in high school and at least 15 years old compete annually for the national Girls Club Citizenship Award. The national winner, selected by a panel of judges for her outstanding record of community service and her ability to describe in a short essay what active citizenship means in her own life, is awarded a trip to Washington, D.C., where she meets government officials and receives a firsthand view of Congress, the Supreme Court, and the White House.

The biggest obstacle to the advancement of Girls Clubs has been lack of finances. Working in low-income communities and not yet widely known, the Girls Clubs have found it difficult to raise funds for adequate buildings and staff. There is, perhaps, more popular interest in helping boys than girls; as a society, we tend, unreasonably, to be more concerned about the problems of boys than those of girls.

The organization tries hard to reach more older girls, since its greatest successes to date have been with girls of elementary school age. Greater emphasis is also being given to serving the entire community in which the club is located. Community service is an integral part of Girls Club activities. Girls Club members all over the country have taken part in planting, landscaping, and conservation and beautification programs. In inner-city

[7] *Giant Steps for Youth* (New York, N.Y.: Girls Clubs of America, 1968) p. 18.

areas where many clubs or branches are located, Girls Clubs are becoming important centers for community activities. During school hours, golden-age clubs, health clinics, nurseries for pre-school children, and adult education courses are being scheduled in many buildings.

At least one club, in Springfield, Massachusetts, has expanded to serve boys and families as well as girls. It has changed its name to the Springfield Family Center Girls Club, Inc. As their National Executive Director explained, "Clubs will always be primarily concerned with girls, but Girls Clubs now see their service to the inner city in terms of maximum use of staff, buildings, and facilities. We expect this new pattern of response to community needs to accelerate in the future."[8]

Settlement Houses

The settlement movement originated in England in a spirit of religious service and philanthropy.

A group of students at Saint John's College, Cambridge, wanted to do something for the poor, and so they asked the advice of Samuel A. Barnett. He suggested that they might rent a house in an industrial district where they could stay for short or long periods of time to "sup sorrow with the poor." This was the idea that led to the founding of the first settlement.[9]

A NEIGHBORHOOD MOVEMENT

The settlement thus began as a center established by these advantaged persons, who desired to help the people in deprived neighborhoods. Groups of religiously motivated people sought to settle among the poor in the crowded cities, and to bring to them, through friendly relations, the advantages of the "better life of which they had been deprived."

The founders of the social settlement movement sought to know the neighborhood in which their neighbors lived and the conditions under which they lived as well. This prompted them to take action and to help their neighbors to act in order to improve their living conditions.

At the National Conference of Charities and Corrections in 1902, there was, for the first time, a section devoted to neighborhood work. After the convention there was a rapid increase in the number of settlements in the United States. There were 103 in the year 1900. In the succeeding five years the number of settlements almost doubled, and between the years of 1905 and 1911 the number doubled again so that by 1911 there were 413 settlements in the United States.

[8] "Girls Clubs Move to Meet New Community Needs," *Community* (Newsletter of the United Community Funds and Councils of America), March-April, 1969, pp. 15–16.
[9] Woods, Robert A., *Handbook of Settlements* (New York, N.Y.: Charities Publishing Company, 1956).

The settlement assumed a special responsibility for all the families living within the radius of a few blocks of the settlement house. It was concerned primarily with the developing of institutional resources that were suited to the needs of a working-class community. This included relief of distress, removal of unsanitary conditions, the care of neglected children, and recreation.

Settlements were not considered activity centers but centers of neighborhood initiative, experimentation, and coordination. They have always been interested in the smaller units of society, including the family, small groups, and the neighborhood.

INFLUENCE ON EDUCATION, RECREATION, AND HEALTH

In the early 1900s, the settlements provided leadership in the establishing of playgrounds for children and recreational facilities for adults. The settlement houses were a powerful influence in supplementing the wider activities of the public schools. They demonstrated how educational facilities could be extended to include the adults of a community. They were influential in raising standards of sanitation and hygiene, and they fostered interest in public health.

CONTRIBUTIONS TO GROUP WORK

In the history of the settlement movement, the trend is toward the distrust of mass activities and toward stress upon work with small groups and the individual.[10] The emphasis is on clubs, group discussions, and the election of the neighborhood leaders. This emphasis gave birth to the techniques that led to the development of the group-work method in social welfare.

Although settlement houses are generally not classified as youth-serving agencies, they have had a tremendous influence on the youth in low-income areas; and much of their program has been and continues to be in the area of club and recreational activities for children and youth. Many settlement houses have become deeply involved in the "war on poverty" and have initiated projects which have been financed by the federal government.

The National Federation of Settlements and Neighborhood Centers is the national organization serving such agencies.

Police Athletic League

The Police Athletic League is a recreational adjunct of police departments. Organized in the 1930s as part of the juvenile aid bureaus, police recreational programs gradually became disassociated from such specialized

---

[10] Kraus, Richard, *Recreation Today* (New York, N.Y.: Appleton-Century-Crofts, 1966), p. 408.

agencies. Today, PAL's are private, nonprofit organizations supported by the adult associate members, private donations, and proceeds from benefits.[11]

SERVICE IN HIGH-DELINQUENCY AREAS

The PAL program aims at providing recreational facilities in areas with a high rate of juvenile delinquency and seeks to give children in such areas a more favorable image of the police.

The Police Athletic League program has been strongest in New York City and other large cities of the East. In New York, professional staff serves approximately 100,000 children and youth through 35 youth centers and several playgrounds.

There is considerable disagreement over whether police officers should be involved in recreational projects. More and more, the functions of the PAL are being assumed by city recreation departments. While officers are encouraged to be interested in recreational programs of all kinds, it is recognized that the typical policeman has neither the time nor the ability to run sports leagues and other youth programs. Use of on-duty officers is very difficult to justify in the light of other needs. Use of policemen in their off-duty hours often works well for awhile, but interest tends to wane over a long period of time.

The trend is to encourage policemen to become involved as individuals in the programs of other community agencies, rather than trying to run a recreational program such as PAL.

Big Brothers of America

The Big Brother movement came into existence on December 3, 1904, through the efforts of Ernest K. Coulter, a clerk of the Children's Court in New York City. His work brought him into daily contact with the problems of youngsters who had become involved with the law. Believing that these boys could be helped through friendship, he enlisted 40 men from the Men's Club of the Central Presbyterian Church in New York City, who each agreed to take a personal interest in one boy, offering him sympathy, understanding, and friendship on a highly personal one-man-to-one-boy basis.[12]

After a few years of this experiment, it was found that few of these first

---

[11] *Ibid.,* p. 405.

[12] *The Art of Friendship—Official Guidebook for Big Brothers* (Philadelphia, Pa.: Big Brothers of America, 1969); Goesta Wollin and Ephrain H. Royfe, "Volunteers in Big Brother Work," *The Citizen Volunteer,* Nathan E. Cohen, ed. (New York, N.Y.: Harper & Row, Publishers, 1960), Ch. 11, pp. 110–123; *Introducing the Big Brother Movement and Big Brothers of America* (Philadelphia, Pa.: Big Brothers of America, n.d.), brochure.

youngsters came into conflict with the law again. Though at first the Big Brother program was carried on entirely by laymen, it was soon discovered that the program could be more effective if a professionally trained staff worked in partnership with the volunteers.

The organization grew slowly, but it received fresh impetus in 1946, when 13 Big Brother associations in the United States and Canada united to form the international Big Brothers of America, with headquarters in Philadelphia. Big Brothers are found today in over one hundred cities, and the movement is growing rapidly. It was chartered by Congress in 1958.

ONE MAN—ONE BOY RELATIONSHIP

A basic belief of the Big Brothers is that boys can best be helped through the personal influence of a mature and stable man. In the words of Wollin and Royfe, "The most important element in Big Brother work is the one-man-one-boy concept of a therapeutic friendship between a volunteer and a boy who is in difficulty because he has no adequate male figure to help him (Figure 10–3). The influence of the character and personality of one

Figure 10–3
For a boy without a father, having a "Big Brother" fulfills an important need. *Courtesy Big Brothers of America.*

man (the volunteer big brother) is utilized for the development of one boy (the little brother) under the direction of a professional staff."[13]

The organization attempts to match the interests of the boy and the man. The Big Brother does not try to be a father; rather, he is a friend to the boy. He plays with him and shares his interests. The two might go together on trips to fish, camp, or boat. The Big Brother might help the Little Brother with schoolwork or take him to a ball game. If possible, they meet weekly. The Big Brother's first task is to dispel the natural suspicion of a boy who has not hitherto been treated kindly by adults. Through the warmth of his friendship and his patience when rebuffed, the Big Brother builds confidence and encourages wholesome growth toward responsible maturity.

Monthly or oftener, the Big Brother confers with the professional staff regarding his relationship to his Little Brother. Group discussions with other Big Brothers enable him to learn through shared experiences how to understand and help his little friend.

GOALS

The objectives of Big Brother work are:

1. To help reduce juvenile delinquency by providing individual guidance in sound character development to boys who lack wholesome adult male companionship, and who have shown delinquent or pre-delinquent tendencies, or other emotional disturbances;

2. To help boys with problems who lack the influence of a mature responsible man to reach their highest physical, mental, emotional, and spiritual development; and

3. To provide for men the opportunity to participate in a happier new generation, through volunteer work that helps them in their character growth.[14]

A trained professional staff studies and selects boys that would be most benefitted from the program and carefully matches each boy to each man, considering not only the interests of both but cultural, religious, and racial factors.

The staff counsels parents and guardians regarding family relationships. If needed, referrals to other agencies are made for help in social and mental adjustment, vocational guidance, and health problems.

THE LITTLE BROTHER

Little Brothers are boys, frequently fatherless, between eight and 17 years of age who need the guidance of a well-balanced, mature male. The

---

13 Wollin and Royfe, "Volunteers in Big Brother Work," p. 110.
14 *Introducing the Big Brother Movement,* p. 3.

boy may be in difficulty with the law, failing in school, poorly adjusted to his family or his peers, or emotionally disturbed. The ages included are those at which a man's influence is most needed and most effective. During these sensitive growing years a Big Brother can redirect a boy's life into constructive channels.

Since Big Brother agencies do not have resources enough to help all boys who lack wholesome adult male influence, their service is restricted to cases in which the absence of the male influence is seen as contributing to a problem. However, not all boys who use the program are delinquent.

THE BIG BROTHER

Wollin and Royfe write, "In affirmative terms, the big brothers are mature, stable, personable men of good character who are willing to take time to help unfortunate youngsters along the road to good citizenship without assuming any legal or financial responsibilities. Big brothers provide the affection, security, sympathy, understanding, and guidance so necessary and important to a young boy. By offering a troubled youngster the assurance that someone cares, that the future is not necessarily dark or hopeless, a big brother becomes the fundamental source for new hope and faith in a young boy."[15]

Most Big Brothers are between 25 and 50 years of age, though it has been found that older men are also successsful Big Brothers.

The Big Brother does not try to be a pastor, physician, psychiatrist, or social case worker. When problems beyond his competence arise, the professional staff is there to help or to refer a boy to another agency if necessary.

The primary expense of the organization is for professional staff to recruit, screen, and train Big Brothers, since the Big Brothers themselves receive no remuneration.

Big Brothers of America is convinced that its program helps boys develop into responsible citizens. It estimates that the cost of its services to each boy annually ranges between $150 and $500 as compared with a cost of $4,000 to $6,000 for maintaining a boy in a state correctional or mental institution.[16]

Youth Organizations United

Emerging from the confused pattern of youth movements today is a unique group working "as a constructive alternative to revolution in building up as well as dignifying the so-called ghettos that they call home." The groups

15 Wollin and Royfe, "Volunteers in Big Brother Work," pp. 113–114.
16 *Introducing the Big Brother Movement*, p. 5.

comprising Y. O. U. were originally ordinary street gangs in constant tangles with the law.[17]

The organization began with the work of Carlos "Chino" Garcia, a gang leader on New York's Lower East Side, who believed that outside agencies wanted to help ghetto youth but that real improvement had to begin with the youth themselves. He brought together other gang leaders under the name of the Real Great Society. In the fall of 1967 a few gang leaders from various parts of the country met in New York to form the Y. O. U. Financed by numerous charitable groups and the U. S. Department of Labor's Coalition for Youth Action, the Y. O. U. members became recruiters throughout the country, getting to know the gangs.

The groups have set up shops, training programs for school dropouts, and recreation centers. They try to train younger members to become leaders of the future, assigning them as "shadows" to leaders. They depend heavily on volunteer help, as financial help is inadequate for the program to which they aspire.

Many nationalities are represented among the members—Puerto Rican, Chinese-American, Mexican-American, white, black, and Indian.

[17] Ellen Ferber, "It's Y.O.U." *American Education,* V, No. 7 (Washington, D.C.: U.S. Department of Health, Education and Welfare, August-September, 1969), pp. 17–21.

VOCATIONALLY-ORIENTED
ORGANIZATIONS

Chapter 11

Although most of today's major youth organizations had their beginnings in the early 1900s, the formation of new groups has been continuous since then. Most of those organized since World War II have been concerned with careers or vocations. Examples of such new groups are Future Scientists of America, Future Business Leaders of America, Future Teachers of America, and Future Engineers. The rapid growth of these organizations can be traced to a combination of increased interest by teen-agers in careers, plus the desire of many professional groups to recruit for their professions.

Other agencies have also capitalized on the teens' career interest. Many YMCA's employ vocational counselors. The entire program of Explorer Scouting was revised to try to be more in tune with teen-agers' interests, foremost of which appeared to be careers. Most Explorer posts today are specialized in an area such as dentistry, banking, police work, or business (Figure 11–1).

This chapter describes a few of the largest vocationally-oriented organizations existing today.

4-H

4-H is the largest youth organization for rural and small-town youth found in America today. It has an estimated membership of four million members.[1] The movement developed in this country in the early 1900s.[2]

[1] *The 1971 World Almanac* (New York, N.Y.: Newspaper Enterprises Association, Inc., 1970), p. 195.

[2] G. L. Carter, Jr., and Robert C. Clark, *Selected Readings and References in* 4-H *Club Work* (Madison, Wis.: National Agricultural Extension Centers for Advanced Study, University of Wisconsin, 1961); *Working Together for 4-H* (Washington,

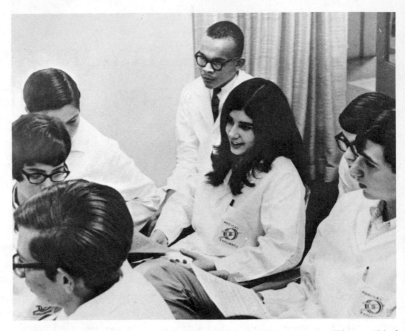

Figure 11–1

Explorers pursuing the study of medicine—one of the many vocational fields to which Exploring relates. *Courtesy Boy Scouts of America.*

Several factors led to the development of 4-H. First, there was a feeling that rural schools were inadequate for the needs of farm boys and girls. Second, colleges of agriculture were urged to pass on new techniques. Third, there was concern for the needs of adolescents, a factor, incidentally, which also resulted in the formation of the various Y's, Scouts, Boys' Clubs, and so on. Fifth, there was a worry about the drift of farm youth to the cities. And finally, the drive to lift rural cultural standards received impetus from the *Report of the Country Life Commission,* published in 1909.[3]

The 4-H idea did not happen all at once. It took shape slowly, step by step. Crop contests for boys were conducted as early as 1828. Horace Greeley, famed newspaper editor, sponsored one in 1865. In the spring of 1882, Delaware College announced a statewide corn contest for boys, each boy to plant a quarter-acre according to instructions set out by the college. In the early 1900s, in the southern portion of the United States, there were

D.C.: U. S. Federal Extension Service, 1962); *This Is 4-H* (Washington, D.C.: Department of Agriculture and State Land Grant Universities Cooperating, revised 1969).

[3] *Report of the Country Life Commission, Special Message from the President of the United States Transmitting the Report* (Washington, D.C.: Government Printing Office, 1909).

sporadic outcroppings of various corn, canning, and poultry clubs which provided learning-by-doing experiences for rural boys and girls between the ages of ten and 21. To the common, everyday work of these youngsters was added the deeper, more rewarding purpose of outstanding achievement. In 1914, the Smith-Lever Act was passed, which established the National 4-H Club, uniting the rural youth of America. Even before its official beginning, there were 73,000 boys and 23,000 girls enrolled in clubs of various kinds, including poultry, cotton, and potato clubs.[4] At this time there was little or no club organization as we know it today.

It was not until 1918 that requirements for 4-H Club membership were drawn up. These included: 1) a club must have a leader; 2) a club must have five or more members working on the same project; 3) a club must have its own officers; 4) the club must meet six regular times per year; 5) at least 60 percent of the members must complete their projects. Members were also required to exhibit annually, to do judging of projects, and to hold an annual achievement day. Since its beginnings in the early 1900s, more than 20 million members have participated in 4-H in this country.[5]

A summary of the various accomplishments of 4-H Club work is impressive. The organization has:

1. trained young men and women for leadership.
2. improved farms in rural communities through the introduction of better agricultural and homemaking practices.
3. helped build a finer rural home life.
4. improved scholarship.
5. helped revive state and county fairs.
6. increased attendance of rural youth at colleges and universities.
7. encouraged cooperative community effort.
8. provided boys and girls the incentive of ownership.
9. implanted the concept of citizenship.
10. helped to keep the right boys and girls on the farm.

The 4-H program is conducted by volunteer men and women under the careful supervision of the Cooperative Extension Service of the State Agricultural Colleges, the Federal Extension Service of the U.S. Department of Agriculture, and local county Extension agents. Hence, 4-H is unique in that it is supported by federal and state money, as well as by local contributors. Any boy or girl 9 through 19 years of age may join.

4-H members today have more than 100 different projects from which to choose. A 4-H-er may raise an experimental crop, grow a vegetable or flower

---

[4] F. M. Reck, *The 4-H Story* (Ames, Iowa: Iowa State University Press, 1951).
[5] Information received from national office of 4-H.

garden, raise a dairy heifer to maturity, or raise a flock of turkeys, and, in the end, realize a handsome profit.

Although profit often provides the initial incentive on the club member's part, it has nothing to do with the organization's objectives. The emphasis is placed on constructive citizenship, leadership, and ability to cooperate for the improvement of services in the home, on the farm, and in the local community. The pledge, which is given before all meetings and on special events, clearly states the purposes and ideal of the 4-H Clubs: "I pledge my Head to clearer thinking, my Heart to greater loyalty, my Hands to larger service, and my Health to better living, for my club, my community, and my country."

The purpose of 4-H Club work originally was to help boys and girls become good, useful, and productive citizens, farmers, and homemakers. Today's program envisions a population more urban in the future and therefore includes city career possibilities. Specifically, the objectives of 4-H are to enable boys and girls to:

Appreciate the value and dignity of work.
Acquire knowledge and skills.
Develop attitudes and ability to cooperate with others.
Recognize the value of rural life.
Develop healthy personalities.
Learn to accept and discharge responsibility.
Be of service to others.

Each year there are state and national meetings of 4-H members, in addition to the local meetings. In most states, from 250 to 2,500 outstanding club members are brought to the state agricultural colleges for a week or more of meetings each year. There is also a National 4-H Club Congress held each year in Chicago, and a National 4-H Conference in Washington, D.C. Originally, clubs were small in size, ten to 15 members, and specialized in one project area. Today an average club has 22 members and may have several project groups within it. Members may be all boys, all girls, or both. Meetings are usually held in members' homes, schools, or community centers.

Although 4-H Club work is usually considered a rural program, many cities and small towns have tried a 4-H program. Approximately 75 percent of 4-H Club members are from farm homes. One of the biggest problems facing 4-H is the shift in population from rural to urban areas. While this may be a hindrance today in terms of maintaining growth, 4-H will undoubtedly continue its fine work among the youth who still remain in rural United States while at the same time enlarging its program for urban youth. 4-H Club work today encourages boys and girls to develop fully their potential by helping them to appreciate the value and dignity of work, acquire knowledge and skills, explore careers, develop attitudes and ability to cooperate with others, learn to accept and discharge responsibility, develop leadership, and be of service to others.

The 4-H Club idea has spread to about 74 countries throughout the world, involving several million youth. Through the International Farm Youth Exchange, many of these foreign youth come to the United States to live for a few months with American families, while American youth, in turn, live in foreign countries.[6]

The Future Farmers of America

The Future Farmers of America is the national organization, of, by, and for students of vocational agriculture in public secondary schools which operate under the provisions of the National Vocational Education Acts. It is an educational, nonprofit, nonpolitical farm youth organization of voluntary membership, designed to develop agricultural leadership, character, thrift, scholarship, cooperation, citizenship, and patriotism. FFA is an integral part of the instructional program, a teaching tool. Students must be enrolled in vocational agriculture to become eligible for membership. They may retain their membership for three years following their graduation from high school, or until they are 21 years of age, whichever length of time is greater.[7]

The FFA is sponsored by the Agricultural Service of the Vocational and Technical Education Division, Office of Education, U.S. Department of Health, Education, and Welfare, in cooperation with the various state boards for vocational education and local high-school departments of vocational education and local high-school departments of vocational agriculture. The Head of the Agricultural Education Service serves as the National FFA Advisor, and a member of his staff serves as the National FFA Executive Secretary. The state advisor for each state association of the FFA is the State Supervisor of Vocational Agriculture, and the advisor of each local chapter is the high school teacher of vocational agriculture. The FFA staff is located at the National FFA Center near Mount Vernon, Alexandria, Virginia.

The national FFA organization was launched at Kansas City, Missouri, in November, 1928, following many years of development of vocational agriculture student organizations in the states and local communities. Originally incorporated under the laws of the State of Virginia, the FFA was granted a charter of incorporation by Act of Congress in 1950 (Public Law 740, 81st Congress).

6 Univ. of Calif. Agricultural Extension Service, *California 4-H Leaders Manual* (Davis, California: Extension Service, 1964), p. 1.
7 *Agricultural Education Magazine,* XLI, No. 9, March, 1969. The entire issue is devoted to Future Farmers of America.

In 1970, the FFA had approximately 430,000 active members in 8,176 local high school chapters located in farming areas throughout the 50 states and Puerto Rico.[8] Similar organizations have been established in Japan, the Philippines, Panama, Mexico, Thailand, Colombia, and other countries.

Through participating experiences in the Future Farmers of America, members learn how to take part in meetings, to follow parliamentary procedure, to speak in public, and to cooperate with their fellow students in programs for individual and community betterment. Local chapters sponsor recreational activities, organize educational tours, conduct safety and home improvement campaigns, and hold parent-son banquets. They have been known to organize a local chamber of commerce where none existed, and to organize and manage a community fair. They frequently take on jobs such as the landscaping and beautification of school and church grounds in the community.

There are four degrees of active membership: Green Hand, Chapter Farmer, State Farmer, and American Farmer. The individual advancement in the first two degrees of membership is determined by the local chapters, while the title "State Farmer" is conferred by the state association and "American Farmer" by the national organization. The requirements for each of the levels of attainment are determined with respect to farming, earnings, investment, leadership, and scholarship. The boys elect their own officers annually.

Throughout the year, the boys of the FFA raise animals and grow crops for the county and state fairs (Figure 11–2). At the local fairs they compete in showmanship, quality of product, and many other areas of competition. During the year, they also visit and work with the advisor and local farmers in helping to improve farming techniques, repairing farm buildings and equipment, and improving livestock and crop production. Unlike many of the other youth organizations, finances and leadership seem to be no great problem, since the programs are run through the schools with school vocational agriculture teachers as advisors.

One of the big incentives to membership is the organization's awards program (Figure 11–3). To further this activity, an FFA foundation was established in 1944. Each year, about $300,000 is raised to provide medals, cash awards, and scholarships to FFA members. Other awards money is made available at the state and local level.

The primary aim of the Future Farmers of America is the development of agricultural leadership, cooperation, and citizenship. The specific purposes for which this organization was formed are as follows:

1. to develop competent, aggressive, rural, and agricultural leadership.
2. to create and nurture a love of country life.

8 Information received from A. Daniel Reuwee, Director of Information for national office of F.F.A., dated 11/19/1970. Mimeographed sheet.

Figure 11–2
Through contests and other activities sponsored by the FFA, students gain practical experience in evaluating and selecting quality livestock and animal products. *Courtesy Future Farmers of America.*

3. to strengthen the confidence of farm boys and young men in themselves and their work.

4. to create more interest in the intelligent choice of farming occupations.

5. to encourage members in the development of individual farming programs and establishment in farming.

6. to encourage members to improve the farm home and its surroundings.

7. to participate in worthy undertakings for the improvement of agriculture.

8. to develop character, train for useful citizenship, and foster patriotism.

9. to participate in cooperative effort.

10. to encourage and practice thrift.

11. to encourage improvement in scholarship.

12. to provide and encourage the development of organized rural recreational activities.[9]

Realizing the trend toward bigger farms and fewer and fewer farm families, vocational agriculture is attempting to diversify its program to cover training in a large number of agriculture-related careers. Machinery

[9] *Official Manual for Future Farmers of America* (Alexandria, Virginia: Future Farmers of America, 1969), p. 11.

Figure 11–3
Earl M. Weaver, 21, of Middletown, Pennsylvania, was named Star Agribusinessman of America at the 1970 National FFA Convention in Kansas City, Missouri. Star Agribusinessman of America is the FFA's highest award for a student preparing for a career in agribusiness. *Courtesy Future Farmers of America.*

sales and service, food marketing and processing, feed and fertilizer production, and landscape gardening are a few of the areas now included in addition to farming, as such.

In line with this change in vocational agriculture, there is a proposal to change the name of the organization to "Federation of Future Agriculturists." Sponsors of the proposal if successful may help to counteract a slight trend toward decreasing membership.

National Grange Youth Programs

The National Grange is a membership organization for farm families which strives to foster progress and enrichment in farm life. Its present membership is approximately 1,000,000 persons aged 14 and over. Youth membership figures are not kept, but youth service is considered an important aspect of the program.[10]

The local organization in each farm community is known as a *Subordinate Grange*. Many Subordinate Granges sponsor *Juvenile Granges* open to children five to 14. Juvenile Granges have their own ritual and degree

[10] Information received in a letter from William S. Steele, Director of Youth activities of the National Grange, dated 1/29/1970.

work, conduct an educational hour at meetings, carry on social activities, and undertake community projects under the guidance of adults selected by the Subordinate Grange.

Other local Granges sponsor Scout troops or 4-H Clubs. Many special activities are planned for the younger members, including camp-outs, dances, bowling tournaments, and leadership schools. Youth travel scholarships are provided as recognition of outstanding accomplishment by youth members. These are awarded by state committees and are open to members from 14 to 29 years of age.

The Grange Interstate Youth Exchange and its International Hospitality Plan are two other National Youth Department projects. The organization prides itself in the fact that youth over 14 are considered full-privilege members eligible to hold office and participate in every way. Many local Granges have received new transfusions of energy and enthusiasm from their young members.

Junior Achievement

The short, successful history of 4-H Clubs in the year 1919 intrigued Horace Moses, president of the Strathmore Paper Company in Springfield, Massachusetts. Why not apply the same principles of "learning by doing" to the business world? If an organization could be formed in urban areas, youngsters could learn more about possible futures for them in industry and business.[11]

Along with Theodore N. Vail, former president of American Telephone and Telegraph Company, and the late Senator Murray A. Crane of Massachusetts, Moses initiated the first Junior Achievement program, incorporated as a nonprofit, educational program under the state laws of Massachusetts in 1926.

In 1929 the program was brought to a large metropolitan area, New York. The eight through 12 age limit was extended to include six through 21-year-old boys and girls. From the start the main objective of Junior Achievement has been to allow youngsters to discover the benefits of the free enterprise system.

Expansion into a national organization was through the efforts of Charles Hook, president of Armco Steel. This program was launched December 5, 1941 at the Waldorf-Astoria Hotel, and was attended by 750 top businessmen. This was the Friday before Pearl Harbor; thus expansion was slight for the next five years.

[11] *Junior Achievement Company Manual,* Advisor Edition, 5th printing (New York, N.Y.: Junior Achievement, Inc., 1970); *Junior Achievement—What's It All About?* (New York, N.Y.: Junior Achievement, Inc., n.d.), brochure.

Junior Achievement saw its most rapid growth following World War II. By the early 1960s, it was operating in 250 cities. Today, more than 150,000 high school students are enrolled.[12]

The basic unit of Junior Achievement is the company. A company is usually made up of about 15 members and is advised by three adults. These adult advisors are volunteers from business or industry in the community. The young people of the company make up their board of directors, labor force, sales staff, and any other positions which are needed.

The company begins operating in the fall. Members meet and elect officers, such as president, vice-president, and treasurer. They also decide what product their firm will make and sell. At the same time they determine how much capital they will need to begin production. The average company needs about $100 to get under way.

To get the capital they need, the members sell stock. Stock sells for 50¢ a share. No one person is allowed to own more than five shares and each member of the company must own at least one share. Members usually sell the stock to their family and friends and door-to-door in their neighborhoods.

When the group acquires its needed capital, it opens a bank account and begins to buy raw materials. At this time the company applies for its Junior Achievement charter, pays a minimal rent, and buys the tools it will need. The rent is usually a fee of $3 per month. Shop machinery can be leased from the Junior Achievement organization by putting down a deposit that is proportionate to the value of the machinery.

The company can now begin production and selling (Figure 11–4). Junior Achievement companies usually make household products which can be sold door-to-door. Many times they make Christmas decorations, such as centerpieces or decorated candles. These products may also be sold in bulk to stores in the community. The members decide on how much wages they will pay themselves and the amount of commission on sales. From the very beginning until the end, complete record books are kept. Every company uses a standard record system developed for Junior Achievement by the American Institute of Certified Public Accountants. The system includes an operating budget; balance sheet; profit and loss statement; stockholder, inventory and payroll records; and stockholder and liquidation reports.

In the spring, just before school gets out, the company goes out of business. All inventory is sold and all debts are paid. If there is a profit, the stockholders are repaid their investment plus the liquidation dividends. Between 75 and 80 percent of Junior Achievement companies do end up with a profit. The average sales for a company is about $700. If a company loses money, special efforts are made to teach the teen-agers the reason for their loss.

12 *Dateline/Junior Achievement*, newsletter published by the national office, n.d.

Figure 11–4
A Junior Achievement company production line. *Courtesy Junior Achievement.*

Although members of Junior Achievement do not usually make a lot of money, they develop a realistic understanding of the organization and operation of a business enterprise. They learn—through their own experience—the problems involved in the manufacture and sale of a product. They build self-confidence and develop leadership ability. They acquire a realization of the importance of risk capital to the economic growth of our nation. They gain understanding, based on personal experience, of the responsibilities and rewards of initiative and enterprise. Finally, they receive the opportunity to measure their vocational desires in real-life business activity.

Junior Achievement is supported financially by over 70,000 subscribers—mainly corporations and business people. Thousands of business men and women serve as advisors to Junior Achievement companies and on local boards of directors. The organization's national headquarters is in New York City.

Future Homemakers of America

Future Homemakers of America was incorporated in 1945, making it one of the youngest of the national programs for youth. Probably because of its close tie-in with high-school home economics, it grew to half a million members within ten years. Most schools including home economics in their curriculum participate in FHA. Membership is open to any girl or boy in high school or junior high school who is taking or has taken home economics.[13]

The organization is sponsored on the national level by the American Home Economics Association and the Home Economics Education Branch of the U.S. Office of Education.

Normally the local clubs function as a school extracurricular activity. The school home economics teacher serves as advisor with the members running their own club.

The national goal is "toward new horizons." The FHA purposes are:

> to promote a growing appreciation of the joys and satisfactions of homemaking.
>
> to emphasize the importance of worthy home membership.
>
> to encourage democracy in home and community life.
>
> to work for good home and family life for all.
>
> to promote international good will.
>
> to foster the development of creative leadership in home and community life.
>
> to encourage wholesome individual and group recreation.
>
> to further interest in home economics, home economics careers, and related occupations.[14]

Future homemakers serve their school through many activities, such as helping with the school lunch program, serving in nursery schools, assisting needy pupils, and sponsoring assemblies and discussions on boy-girl relations.

In the field of community service, chapters undertake projects on their own, or in cooperation with other community agencies. They have sponsored clean-up campaigns, Brotherhood Week, UN Day; planted flowers in parks; and served as assistants to organizations such as the Red Cross, PTA's, and united fund drives (Figure 11-5).

National projects adopted every four years provide a framework within which local chapters operate. The goals for 1969-1973 were: (1) Our Future as Homemakers; (2) Stable Home—Stable Life; (3) Make Time Work for You; (4) Decisions That Count; (5) To Dare is to Care; (6) Our World—A Growing Heritage; and (7) Preparedness—The Key to Opportunity.[15]

---

[13] Carolynn J. Girtman, "The Program, the Teacher, and FHA," *American Vocational Journal*, XLIII, No. 3, March, 1968, pp. 26–27; *The Future is Our Bag* (Washington, D.C.: Future Homemakers of America, U.S. Office of Education, n.d.), 1967–69 Biennial Report.

[14] *Official Guide for Future Homemakers of America* (Washington, D.C.: Future Homemakers of America, n.d.), p. 9.

[15] *1969–1973 National Program of Work* (Washington, D.C.: F.H.A., 1969), pp. 1–27.

Figure 11–5

An FHA chapter in Georgia conducted a community antilitter and beautification campaign. This photo was taken just before they went on camera for a television program to publicize the campaign. *Courtesy Future Homemakers of America.*

The organization is governed by a national executive council composed of 12 youth officers. Each is elected for one year. Fourteen adult representatives serve on a national advisory board. State and local organizations also have their youth officers and adult advisors.

Dues are low—only 25 cents per year. The official magazine of FHA is the *Teen Times,* published four times per year. Each issue contains a theme related to FHA's overall goal. Typical themes are "You as a Family Member;" "Youth and Identity;" "Opportunities Unlimited." The national office also publishes many other materials such as *An Advisor's Guide, The Chapter Handbook,* and *National Program of Work.*

The organization has historically been strongest in rural areas but is making an effort to charter more clubs in urban areas.

Future Scientists of America

Future Scientists of America clubs were organized in 1959 to give interested students an opportunity to meet together and benefit from the common sharing of scientific interests and abilities with their fellow club members. FSA clubs are a scientific community in miniature. Though nationally organized and identified, each club is free to develop a program most suited to its own needs.[16]

Individual membership statistics are not kept; since enrollment is only through the school clubs, however, and some 2,000 clubs affiliate each year, about 100,000 students may be involved.

FSA is sponsored by the National Science Teachers Association—a professional society. It is one of a number of programs that organization offers to help the teacher do a more effective job and to encourage young people who have the potential to enter a science career.

All school science clubs, grades five through twelve, are eligible for affiliation. New clubs may be chartered for an initial fee of $6.00; renewal membership is $3.00 per year per club. The sponsor is mailed suggestions for planning meetings, projects, and activities. Students receive a copy of the national newsletter, *Centrifuge*, each month.

Government Work Programs

During the Great Depression, millions of youth who had finished school were unable to find employment. The Roosevelt administration established the Civilian Conservation Corps, or CCC, to gainfully employ thousands of young persons in worthwhile conservation projects. World War II, of course, ended the program when all manpower was needed for the war effort.

In the late Fifties, large numbers of school dropouts were again finding difficulty gaining employment, and many leaders became interested in reviving the CCC, or in starting a similar program.[17] In 1964, when 16 percent of the out-of-school 16-to-20-year-olds were unemployed, President Johnson inaugurated the Job Corps as a part of his "War on Poverty."[18]

National recruitment for the Job Corps began in January, 1965, with motion picture, radio, television, newspaper, and magazine coverage. During the new agency's first month, 88,000 postcards poured into Washington, and by February they were arriving at the rate of 10,000 per day. Unfortunately, the program could accommodate only 40,000 the first year.

Although the Job Corps is not a youth agency as such, it is included here because it is national in scope and has aims similar to those of many youth agencies.

16 Brother Joseph D'Agostino, Victor M. Showalter, *et al.,* "Youth Activities and NSTA," *The Science Teacher,* XXXV, No. 9, December, 1968, pp. 41–44; *Student Development Programs of the National Science Teachers Association* (Washington, D.C.: N.E.A. Publication Sales Section, n.d.), brochure.
17 "Youth Corps Bill Gets Fresh Start," *Business Week,* March 30, 1963, p. 79.
18 "Congress and the Johnson Poverty Program," *Congressional Digest,* XLV, (March, 1966), p. 67–96; Leddick, W.C., "Job Corps on the Job," *Parks and Recreation,* Vol. I, No. 10, (October, 1966), p. 839.

Job Corpsmen are recruited mainly from city slums. The program places a stronger emphasis on job-training than did the CCC. Many of the camps are located in urban areas or on former army posts. It is felt that the recruits will benefit from the nutritious diet and healthy living conditions as well as from the skill-training and the feeling of becoming productive members of society.

On the assumption that conventional school methods failed, a new set of teaching tools is being devised in an effort to bring the recruits' reading and writing skills up to at least seventh-grade standards.

Many of the training centers were contracted out to industry. Among the companies involved were Ford Motor Company, Philco, Litton Industries, and Federal Electronic Corporation. Some of the service skills being taught include auto repair, building maintenance, welding, cooking, business machine repair, and small appliance repair.

The program has proven costly, and hence controversial. Critics were quick to point out that it cost more per year to keep a girl in a Job Corps camp than it would cost to send her to Vassar. Much other adverse publicity resulted from riots and reports of shakedowns in one or two of the first camps opened.

In the spring of 1969, the Administration ordered the Corps to cut spending by $100 million per year. To this effect, 59 of the 160 training centers were closed, and 30 new centers tied to existing training facilities were created.[19]

President Nixon called the Job Corps a "failure" in his election campaign, and it was shortly after his election that it was shifted from the Office of Economic Opportunity to Labor Department jurisdiction.

The purpose of the 1969 shifts were to reduce the cost per trainee from $8,000 to $5,000 or $6,000 per year, and to provide a more relevant work-training experience. Criticism had also been leveled at the Corps' high dropout rate and the poor job placement record.

A program known as the Youth Conservation Corps was inaugurated in 1971. This Federal program provides summer employment for teens in the national forests and other federal lands. Youths work on projects such as erosion control, brush thinning, and minor construction. The program is administered by the U.S. Departments of Agriculture and the Interior.

It is likely that the future will see more and more involvement in work programs for older youth as job opportunities for the young continue to decline in the age of automation. The Neighborhood Youth Corps, Peace Corps, Vista, and the Teachers' Corps are other governmental attempts at solving this job dilemma.

---

[19] "Job Corps Gets a Working Over," *Business Week,* April 19, 1969, p. 96.

Candy-Stripers

The Candy-Stripers are another example of a vocationally-oriented youth group. The organization is directly related to the field of medical service, and is open to girls of high-school age. The girls have varied duties, including working in hospital coffee shops or gift shops, reading to and writing letters for patients, working at the receiving desks, delivering flowers and packages to the rooms, and comforting and listening to the patients. Their duties are very similar to those of the adult Gray Ladies or Pink Ladies, found in hospitals throughout the country.[20]

Each hospital sets its own requirements, such as that Candy-Stripers must be high-school sophomores and must volunteer at least 100 hours each per year. The girls provide a very valuable service for the hospital and for the patients, and in turn have the opportunity to discover whether nursing is a career which might appeal to them.

The Candy-Stripers are normally trained and supervised by the hospital coordinator of volunteer service. It is not unusual for a hospital to have more than 100 Candy-Stripers, many of whom may put in 500 or more hours per year of volunteer service.

[20] Interview with Mrs. Constance Salerno, Associate Professor, School of Nursing, San Diego State College, Feb. 4, 1971.

OTHER ORGANIZATIONS
FOR YOUTH

With a few exceptions, this book focuses on voluntary, non-governmental agencies, national in scope, non-profit, dependent primarily on voluntary financial support, and offering year-round programs for large numbers of children and youth. Similarities among certain agencies have justified discussing them under the headings of "outdoor-oriented," "religious-oriented," "serving the disadvantaged," and "vocationally-oriented," in Chapters 8 through 11. This chapter reviews some of the large national voluntary organizations that fall outside these categories—the youth programs of the American National Red Cross and American Legion, Masonic youth organizations, national honor societies, junior sports programs, and youth work of service clubs and conservation organizations. High school fraternities and sororities are also considered.

There are myriads of other organizations—local and national—for young people. There are programs for children with special problems—the crippled, the blind, and the mentally retarded. There are organizations that serve children indirectly by pressing for needed legislation and for community action to secure advantages for youth. There are cultural and educational organizations—music clubs, language clubs, art clubs, drama clubs, and numerous hobby groups. Among older youth are political groups, the student activists, and groups advocating radical change. Beyond the scope of this book are the thousands of tax-supported park and recreation programs that are in many ways similar to those of the voluntary agencies.

One wonders how anyone could be overlooked by these numerous organizations. Yet some children are missed, despite the tremendous efforts of the organizations. Most children, however, encounter one and probably more of these groups in the course of growing up. A child may belong to several of them simultaneously. As he matures, he may shift membership from one to another in accordance with his changing interests. As the home-centered interests of the small youngster widen into the community and outdoor interests of the pre-teen and these, in turn, give way to the teen-ager's exploration of adult careers and life styles, organizations at every hand give support and guidance. Their influence can hardly be over-estimated.

The organizations supplement the work of the school and provide a channel whereby parents can have a part in the education of their children. They are a worthy outlet for the need of a great part of our adult popula-tion to give altruistic service, direction, and money.

Youth Programs of the American National Red Cross

During World War I, leading educators approached the American National Red Cross in quest of a means through which school work could be related to the national emergency. As a result, the Junior Red Cross was born.[1]

Today, Red Cross Youth programs are primarily concerned with three broad areas of interest: (1) health and safety, (2) services to others, and (3) intercultural and international friendship. Through first-aid, water safety, and mother's aide courses and related activities, boys and girls learn health and safety rules. They study and campaign for safety, courtesy, good nutrition, and beautification. Red Cross Youth programs also encourage children to lessen the loneliness of others by sharing creative materials and fun with the hospitalized, the handicapped, and the aged; to make friends with boys and girls in other areas of the United States and overseas by the sharing of tokens of friendship and ideas through various types of com-munications; and to develop leadership skills by participation in these programs.

Red Cross Youth programs in junior and senior high schools are guided by Red Cross Youth councils and clubs or through student government committees. Young people contribute hours of volunteer service—both in and out of school—as tutors for younger children, as participants in school and community service projects, and as aides in hospitals, nursing homes, and blood centers. In-school activities include packing school chests for shipment to disaster areas in the United States and overseas, recruiting faculty blood donors, and promoting health and safety programs for the student body.

To enroll, an elementary, junior high, or senior high school has only to

---

1 *Presenting...Red Cross Youth* (Washington, D.C.: American National Red Cross, 1969); *American Junior Red Cross News,* magazine for elementary schools published monthly, October through May; *American Red Cross Journal,* magazine for secondary school members published monthly, October through May.

make the request; the local Red Cross chapter will then provide program and promotional materials. Students are considered members of the American National Red Cross when they participate in programs and/or make voluntary contributions to the chapter's Red Cross Youth Service Fund.

The organization publishes two student magazines, the *American Junior Red Cross News,* for elementary schools, and *The American Red Cross Youth Journal,* for junior and senior high schools. Both magazines are published monthly, October through May. Distribution to school classrooms is based on subscriptions entered by chapters annually.

The *News* contains curriculum-related articles of interest to elementary school students and stories of life in the United States and other countries. Other monthly features include a primary graders' selection, a historical calendar, a fun page, student-written materials, and articles and photographs describing activities of Red Cross Youth at home and abroad.

The *Journal* presents discussions of subjects of interest to young people. Each issue of the magazine features an in-depth study of a particular topic. Included also are articles related to school, growing up, career opportunities, and social concerns of youth, together with program suggestions for teenage volunteers.

A monthly Braille edition of the *News* and *Journal* and an annual talking book edition of the *News* are published for free distribution to blind or visually handicapped children and youth.

Red Cross Youth also provides a number of program materials—films, filmstrips, safety posters, and promotional aids. Local Red Cross chapters can provide information about these materials.

Teachers play an important role in Red Cross Youth programs. On the elementary school level, teacher-sponsors coordinate Red Cross Youth activities within the school. On the secondary school level, faculty advisors work with student leaders in Red Cross clubs or councils.

Student contributions in support of Red Cross Youth programs are deposited in the chapter's Red Cross Youth Service Fund. Money in this fund is used (1) to pay the annual subscription fees for the Red Cross Youth magazines, (2) to finance local youth service projects and programs, and (3) to make voluntary contributions to the American Red Cross Youth Fund, a special national fund maintained since 1919 by these voluntary contributions. The American Red Cross Youth Fund makes possible many nationally sponsored programs and services for young people at home and abroad.

No membership totals are compiled, although at one time the organization claimed that more than 19 million children and youth were involved.[2]

[2] M. M. Chambers, *Youth Serving Organizations* (Washington, D.C.: American Council on Education, 1948), p. 10.

Youth Programs of the American Legion

The American Legion promotes Americanism among youth through various channels, including support of Boys' Clubs and sponsorship by Legion Posts of over 4,000 Boy Scout units. In addition the Legion conducts *Boys' State,* in which high school juniors receive training in the functioning of local, county, and state government. Similar training is offered on the national level by *Boys' Nation,* held annually in Washington, D. C.[3] The American Legion Auxiliary conducts a corresponding program in *Girls' State* and *Girls' Nation.*

American Legion Baseball is a youth activity in which championship teams from throughout the nation compete for the national championship. The program is promoted by local posts and legionnaires.

The Legion cooperates in American Education Week, conducts a national high-school oratorical contest for thousands of participants, and maintains a program of awards to encourage good citizenship and leadership.

The *Sons of the American Legion,* open in membership to sons of legionnaires and of deceased veterans, promotes the "Ten Ideals" of patriotism, health, knowledge, training, honor, faith, helpfulness, courtesy, reverence, and comradeship. A national award of recognition is given those who complete the Ten Ideals program, which requires such accomplishments as participation in specified Legion events, leadership, good conduct, and service. The official uniform includes a white shirt and "Legion blue" trousers. A five-point program of patriotism, citizenship, discipline, leadership, and legionism leads to the Five-Star Award for older members. Each SAL squadron is permitted flexibility in planning its programs to meet the needs of its own age groups.

Masonic Youth Organizations

During the nineteenth century many fraternal organizations developed. Two of these which saw rapid growth were the Masons and Eastern Stars. One of the members, W. Mark Sexson, a minister, became very active in the two organizations. In fact, he had such a deep sense of their importance, he went on to hold the highest office possible in both organizations. His concern deepened when he realized that in order to attract members, an interest should be stimulated among the youth. Other members of the fraternal organizations felt as Reverend Sexson did; so in 1922 he was asked to write

---

3 *Action Programs of Americanism, Sons of the American Legion, The Legion Extends Its Hand to Boys, The American Legion and Boys' Clubs of America, The Legion and Scouting* (Indianapolis, Indiana: The American Legion, n.d.), brochures.

a ceremony for girls (since DeMolay had already been established for boys).
Thus, the International Order of the Rainbow for Girls was created.[4]

RAINBOW GIRLS

The founder of Rainbow Girls knew that girls love ritualism and felt that
they want to be identified with a secret organization that could be part of
their lives. Like its parent organizations (the Masonic Lodge and the Order
of the Eastern Stars), therefore, the Order of the Rainbow is very ritualistic
and is secret.

The rainbow is used as the symbol of the organization because it represents "the first visible sign that God gave to His creatures;" according to
Genesis 9:16: "And the Bow shall be in the cloud; and I will look upon it
that I may remember the everlasting covenant between God and every living
creature of all flesh that is upon the earth."

Girls between the ages of 12 and 20 are eligible for membership. A potential member must be either a daughter of an Eastern Star or Mason, or a
friend of another Rainbow Girl. In the latter case, the girl petitions the
local assembly she wishes to join and after an interview with an adult and
two members, the total assembly votes (by secret ballot) to accept her as a
member. She pays a nominal dues fee and is initiated during an elaborate
ceremony at which time secret signs, passwords, and lessons are revealed
to her. The International Order of the Rainbow for Girls is a Christian
organization, but other denominations are not barred. It is essentially Protestant (since Catholics are not allowed, by their Church, to join secret
organizations).

Like most fraternal orders, the Order of the Rainbow has a hierarchy,
ranging from the Supreme Assembly (whose headquarters are located in
McAlester, Oklahoma) through the Grand Assemblies (in each state or
jurisdiction) and the local assemblies (classified according to districts).

Within each local assembly are 20 officers (seven of these elected offices;
13 appointed offices) and an adult advisor. There is also an adult board of
advisors and a Service Club composed of interested parents of the girls.

The local assemblies are entirely self-supporting. The girls must earn
approximately $300 each term. They choose and plan the fund-raising
activities themselves. These range from selling baked goods or candy to
holding dinners, luncheons, and fashion shows. The assemblies also have
service or charity projects, fun projects, and courtesy affairs (work with
other fraternal organizations).

The qualities of leadership that a young lady gains from being an active
member are emphasized. The ritual, speeches, and floorwork help a girl

---

[4] *The World Book Encyclopedia* (Chicago, Illinois: Field Enterprises Educational
Corporation, 1967), Vol. 16, p. 127; Interviews with members and advisors.

to acquire ability in public speaking. Since many meetings are formal, and etiquette is stressed, she also develops poise.

There is an intricate reward system by which the girls can earn points and eventually medals for their efforts. They earn points by helping on committees, performing various duties or extra service work. They can receive demerits as well for failing to do something or behaving in an unladylike manner.

DEMOLAY

Building better citizens of teen-age boys is the goal of the Order of DeMolay, an international youth organization founded on March 18, 1919, in Kansas City, Missouri, by Frank S. Land and nine teen-age boys.[5]

The organization was named for Jacques DeMolay, the last Grand Master of the Knights Templar, who was burned at the stake by King Phillip of France on March 18, 1314, as a martyr to loyalty and toleration. Today, members of DeMolay strive to carry on the fine ideals for which DeMolay gave his life—loyalty and service to God and fellow man.

Frank Land served as the Secretary-General for DeMolay until his death on November 8, 1959. By 1920, the Kansas City Chapter had grown to 3,000 members, and chapters were soon instituted from coast to coast and in several foreign countries. Today there are over 2,500 active DeMolay chapters and nearly three million boys have taken their obligations at the DeMolay altar.[6]

DeMolay membership is open to any boy of good character who is between the ages of 14 and 21. Although DeMolay chapters are sponsored only by Masonic bodies or individual Masons, it is *not* necessary that a boy be a son or a relative of a Mason to belong to DeMolay.

The Order of DeMolay is a nonprofit corporation with International Headquarters located in Kansas City, Missouri. Under the guidance of the Grand Secretary, a small office staff acts as the clerical and administrative group to maintain central office records and promote the growth and development of the organization.

The youth movement is governed by an International Supreme Council composed of over 200 outstanding Masons located around the world. They meet in annual session to review and approve the actions of the staff.

DeMolay's slogan is "Young Men of Action!" Its ritual is what sets the organization apart from other youth groups.

The ritual was written in 1919 by Frank Marshall, a prominent Mason and newspaper man in Kansas City. It has been termed ageless, and is

5 "Special DeMolay Issue" *The New Age Magazine,* June, 1969, Vol. LXXVII, No. 6, DeMolay News Release "The Founding of DeMolay;" *Cordon,* a monthly magazine published by and for the International DeMolay.
6 DeMolay News Release "What the Order of DeMolay is," p. 1, mimeographed.

divided into the Initiatory and DeMolay Degrees. The Initiatory Degree is one of solemnity and consecration, during which the initiate dedicates himself to uphold the virtues of filial love, reverence, courtesy, comradeship, fidelity, cleanness and patriotism. The DeMolay Degree is a dramatic and historic portrayal of the trials, tortures, and martyrdom of Jacques DeMolay, and teaches a lesson in fidelity and comradeship.

As the officers of a chapter, young men are taught responsibility and given the opportunity to express themselves before a group of their fellows. Although DeMolay ritual and meetings are serious and reverent, the organization does not advocate any particular creed, but teaches only a profound faith in the one living and true God.

DeMolay has a three-way program designed to benefit the individual DeMolay, the chapter, and the community. Various awards are given to individuals for achievement, and Merit Bars are awarded for distinction in civic service, athletics, music, dramatics, religion, and other fields. Special keys are given for obtaining new members. The Degree of Chevalier is the highest honor an active DeMolay can receive. It is earned by outstanding service in a chapter and to fellow DeMolays. The top honor in DeMolay is the Legion of Honor. This is conferred on Senior DeMolays, over 30, for outstanding service to their community and their fellow men.

International and jurisdictional membership, ritual, efficiency and athletic competitions are held for the chapters. Each chapter is encouraged to have a balanced program of social activities. Each social event, like all other DeMolay activities, is supervised by an adult advisor of the chapter.

Chapters and individual DeMolays are also required to observe certain obligatory days annually. These include Devotional Day, Patriots' Day, DeMolay Day of Comfort, Educational Day, Parents' Day, and Frank S. Land Memorial Day.

The participation of DeMolay chapters in community projects has been extensive and is sometimes carried out on an International basis. Teen-age traffic safety programs have been especially successful. These involve campaigns aimed at making safe drivers of all teen-agers. Such efforts have received high praise from the National Safety Council and local law enforcement agencies. Other projects that have been carried on include charitable fund drives, blood donations, civil defense, anti-narcotics and anti-Communist campaigns, and distribution of safe-driver pledges.

Each chapter is supervised in all of its functions by an adult advisory council. One man is designated as the official "Chapter Dad" to handle the supervision of chapter meetings and to council the members. Another helping hand for most chapters is the Mothers' Clubs. These now number over 2,000. The Mothers' Clubs primarily help the boys to raise money for their activities, and they usually handle the purchase and repair of robes and regalia.

DeMolay publishes an international magazine called the *Cordon*, which serves as a medium for distributing information from international headquarters and furnishing information on chapter activities.

DeMolay does not attempt to take the place of the home or church, but rather to supplement them. The organization's purpose is to offer young men of today: (1) a wholesome occupation for their spare time; (2) worthwhile associates; (3) the best of environment; and (4) an interesting and complete program of all-around youth development.

JOB'S DAUGHTERS

A third large Masonic organization for youth is Job's Daughters. This order was started in 1921 in Omaha, Nebraska, by Mrs. Ethel Mick. Members of the Eastern Star and the Masons were instrumental in the organization's formation.[7]

Job's Daughters, for girls between the ages of 12 and 20, is very similar in program and philosophy to Rainbow Girls with the important difference that members must be related to a Master Mason. As with the other fraternal orders, great faith is placed in the power of ritual to leave a lasting impression on the members. The ritual is based on the book of Job. The organization's motto is "Virtue is a quality which adorns woman."

The local groups are organized into "bethels." Each bethel is required to have a money-raising project twice a year. One-third of the proceeds is given to an educational fund, one-third to a promotional fund, and the remaining third to the bethel's treasury. Social functions also play an important role in the organization. Frequent parties and dances are an attraction to membership.

At present, there are approximately 150,000 girls in Job's Daughters. There are about 1600 chartered bethels in the United States, Canada, Labrador, Guam, the Philippines, and Australia.[8]

High-School Fraternities and Sororities

Although most organizations for children and youth are generally accepted as beneficial and socially desirable, there is widespread agreement that secret social clubs on the high-school campus should be discouraged, if not banned. These secret organizations date back as far as 1876. California passed a law in 1908 banning secret clubs in high schools when a girl shot herself after being rejected from a sorority. Many other states have similar statutes.[9]

Despite laws and rules against them, secret societies have continued to

---

[7] William J. Whalen, *Handbook of Secret Organizations* (Milwaukee, Wisconsin: The Bruce Publishing Company, 1966).

[8] *Ibid.,* p. 72.

[9] "Schools Open War on Secret Clubs," article in *San Diego Evening Tribune,* December 20, 1967, pp. 1–2.

exist in many cities. In 1967, San Diego was shocked to hear that a boy had been scarred for life in a hazing ritual, which took place in a high-school parking lot.[10] Similar incidents have occurred throughout the nation.

High-school students organize secret societies for many reasons. The societies' restricted membership give students a feeling of acceptance and prestige. Meetings are closed and secret, which adds an element of glamor. Pins and insignia provide a certain amount of status and identity. The social recognition achieved through membership is a big factor, especially among those who tend to be insecure and need ego bolstering.

The arguments waged against such groups are impressive: (1) They are undemocratic in both their method of election and in conduct of the organization. Members are usually selected on the basis of socioeconomic background, looks, or status in the school, rather than on individual merit. (2) The organizations produce cliques, factions, and snobbishness, which are detrimental to school spirit and harmony. (3) There is generally little or no adult supervision. This typically results in excesses of drinking, hazing, and other undesirable forms of conduct. Values and standards of behavior in these clubs are questionable at best.

Very few of these groups, if any, emphasize good study habits or scholastic achievement. A San Diego State coed confessed that out of 45 girls in her high-school social club, only three went on to college. She stated that she herself would not be in college if she had not dropped out of the group in her senior year.[11]

At present, there appears to be a lessening of interest in secret social clubs. This may be due in part to pressure from school authorities and parents, but is probably due more to a current trend among young people against any highly organized activities. College fraternities and sororities are witnessing a rapid erosion of their influence on campuses, and fraternal groups of all kinds appear to be losing popularity. Students are seemingly becoming more critical of social values and are more interested in "doing their own thing" than in conforming to a structured organization of any kind. Not only fraternities and sororities, but nearly all school clubs are experiencing a general loss of interest. It would appear that the successful club of the future must have highly appealing short-range goals, and a loose membership structure.

If secret social clubs are soon a memory, few will mourn the loss.

Service Club Work with Children and Youth

One of the prime reasons for the great expansion of youth programs in this country has been the strong support afforded by the nation's service

10 *Ibid.,* p. 1.
11 Personal conversation with author.

clubs. Most service clubs and civic organizations give boys' and girls' work a high priority. The Optimist Club alone devotes over $4,000,000 per year to projects in this area.[12]

Typical service club projects are programs such as sponsorship of Scout troops, donation of buildings to camps, sponsorship of junior sports teams, sending underprivileged children to camp, providing expenses of participants to such events as Youth and Government or Scout Jamborees, sponsoring *Kids' Day* (Kiwanis), and assisting in international youth exchange programs.

A few of the larger service clubs which place major emphasis on boys' and girls' work include Kiwanis, Rotary, Lions, Optimists, Jaycees, Civitan, Y's men's clubs, and Zonta. Fraternal and civic groups with a similar emphasis include the Moose, Elks, VFW, American Legion, chambers of commerce, and others. While most of these groups support existing youth programs rather than starting their own groups, a few sponsor clubs of their own for youth. The two most noteworthy of these—Key Club (Kiwanis) and Junior Optimists—will be covered here.

KEY CLUB INTERNATIONAL

The Key Club is a service club for boys only, from the tenth to the twelfth grades in high school. The objects of the Key Club are: (1) to develop initiative and leadership; (2) to provide experience in living and working together to serve the school and community, (3) to cooperate with the school principal, (4) to prepare for useful citizenship, and (5) to accept and promote certain ideals.[13]

The organization's ideals are:

1. to give primacy to the human and spiritual, rather than to the material values of life.
2. to encourage the daily living of the Golden Rule in all human relationships.
3. to promote the adoption and the application of higher standards in scholarship, sportsmanship, and social contacts.
4. to develop, by precept and example, a more intelligent, aggressive, and serviceable citizenship.
5. to provide a practical means to form enduring friendships, to render unselfish service, and to build better communities.
6. to cooperate in creating and maintaining that sound public opinion and high idealism which makes possible the increase of righteousness, justice, patriotism, and good will.[14]

12 *Boys Work Statistics of 1964* (mimeographed report of Optimist International), p. 1.
13 *Key Club Manual* (Chicago, Illinois: Key Club International, n.d.). *Keynoter,* magazine published by the national office, monthly except June, July, and August.
14 *The Key Club* (brochure), p. 2.

Operating under school regulations, the Key Club draws its membership from the student body. Each club is sponsored in cooperation with the school officials by a local Kiwanis Club.

The Key Club's service program is unique in that, besides serving the school, it extends into the community and international scene. The Club feels that leadership, good citizenship, education, and fellowship are best acquired through actual participation in service programs. This idea gives support to its motto, "We Build."

The first Key Club was sponsored in May, 1925, in a Sacramento, California, high school by the Kiwanis Club of that city. Its function was to carry an active vocational guidance program directly to the whole student body on a year-round basis. In the beginning, the Key Club's only means of expansion were for those Kiwanians visiting the Sacramento Club to take the idea back to their own communities. Slowly, clubs began to be sponsored throughout the country. By 1939, Florida had enough Key Clubs functioning to call a state convention and form a district. Finally, in 1943, an international organization was started with Malcolm Lewis as the First International Key Club President. In 1946, at New Orleans, a Constitution and set of bylaws were adopted at the third International Convention. The present Key Club organization has been built to include 30 organized districts with over 3,400 clubs and 90,000 members.[15] The membership roughly doubled from 1960 to 1970, making it one of the few groups for high-school age students which is experiencing rapid growth.

Two or more Kiwanians should be present at every Key Club meeting. The sponsoring Kiwanis Club is not expected to carry any of the club's financial expense. There are also Kiwanis District and International Committees devoted to the Key Clubs.

The Kiwanis Clubs also help sponsor the Key Clubs' general office in Chicago, which edits and prints the Key Clubs' official publication, *The Keynoter.*

An International Convention is held each year. Two voting delegates from each Key Club are seated at the convention. The organized districts also hold conventions each year.

The Key Club is primarily a service club. Each year every Key Club makes out an achievement report which is a list of its services for the year. The average report lists about 50 separate activities. Annual awards are given to those clubs whose reports indicate the most outstanding service. The Key Club at Bartow High School, Bartow, Florida, was judged the top club in competition during 1968–1969 on the basis of the following list of activities:

1. Held separate appreciation night banquets for parents

<hr>

[15] *Key Club in Action* (brochure, n.d.), p. 1.

2. Conducted four model programs at the regular meeting of sponsoring Kiwanis Club

3. Attended church as a group 14 times

4. Had several speakers come to the school to speak about their vocations

5. Presented two special school assemblies during the year

6. Had a banquet for school leaders

7. Participated in several interclubs in the local area

8. Held a Teacher Appreciation Banquet

9. Moved, counted, and distributed 7,500 textbooks

10. Assisted teachers to clean up classrooms

11. Helped teachers grade papers

12. Held welcome breakfast for new teachers

13. Installed sprinkler system, resodded large area of school's front lawn and cared for the upkeep of this area

14. Provided garbage cans for campus, held cleanup drives for various areas of school, assisted teachers by washing blackboards

15. Painted lines on parking lot

16. Moved desks for classroom relocation

17. Trimmed hedges and cut grass periodically

18. Sanded and repainted bulletin boards

19. Cleaned and arranged trophy cases

20. Painted lines on new track

21. Cleaned storage room of gymnasium, also press box and ticket booth

22. Sanded and refinished school desks

23. Helped install sidewalks at front of school

24. Coordinated formation of student committee for merger of school

25. Assisted PTA with bake sale, manning booths, setting up and cleaning up after

26. Aided with Swim Meet, providing judges, manning starting stations

27. Sponsored dance for those attending Swim Meet

28. Drove in parade, provided escorts for homecoming sweethearts

29. Sold ads, printed and sold football programs

30. Provided referees and scorers for Student-Faculty Basketball game

31. Reserved space for band members at games

32. Coached, officiated, and announced at girls' football game

33. Assisted with set up for both swim and track meets

34. Set up and took down 800 chairs for graduation exercises

35. Club worked a great deal at neighboring junior high school, sanding and repainting desks, washing blackboards, moving and rearranging books in library, cleaning auditorium and replacing lights, cleaning band room and washing windows, packing and sorting school records, hauling dirt for campus, and cleaning and rearranging book room

36. Cleaned up after class play
37. Provided entertainment for Junior Classical League Banquet
38. Presented program for school service club assembly
39. Designed, took pictures, sold ads, and distributed "Spring Supplement" for school annual
40. Conducted a forum on the integration of school to discuss and clear the air of problems from both schools involved
41. Made posters for homecoming to build spirit for hometeam
42. Carried good sportsmanship sign at football games
43. Presented program at cheerleaders' assembly
44. Every Sunday from October to May, led boys at a migrant workers' mission in educational, sports and spiritual activities (Buddy Program)
45. Sponsored, organized, provided ribbons and trophies for "Bike Rodeo"
46. Helped organize and conduct a Christmas party for children of migrant workers
47. Attended meetings of city commissioners to discuss problems of youth
48. Cleaned grounds of local park
49. Provided clowns for Halloween parade
50. Cleaned grounds for Girl Scouts' hall
51. Organized a junior choir for a local group
52. Collected trading stamps for Boys Ranch
53. Worked with Little League teams
54. Assisted with the organization of and/or collection of funds for the following groups: United Fund, Mothers March of Dimes, Cancer Drive, Teens Against Dystrophy, Bike Race for Mental Health Center, and Heart Fund
55. Donated services to Polk County TB Association
56. Held interclub breakfasts with several other clubs
57. Directed a "Used Articles" campaign for Church Service Center
58. Folded 100,000 pamphlets for Civil Defense organization
59. Assisted with Civic Club Sport's Day
60. Aided Chamber of Commerce with Miss Bartow Contest
61. Provided concession workers, coordinated and directed talent show for Crickette Club Halloween Carnival
62. Assisted with Garden Club Flower Show
63. Helped Goodwill with clothing drive by picking items up, also assisted with the moving of a Goodwill Store run by Junior Service League
64. Aided University of Florida with their scholarship banquet
65. Cleaned and weeded the grounds, served at suppers, moved equipment for 11 different churches with a total of over 150 man-hours of work involved
66. Prepared and printed model programs for churches

67. Collected magazines for servicemen in Vietnam

68. Conducted extensive "Interclub by Mail" project, corresponding with over 150 Key Clubs

69. Sponsored extensive "Get-Out-The-Vote" campaign for new state constitutional election

70. Held an "Attend Church Campaign" throughout community

71. Conducted a "Keep America Beautiful" campaign

72. Cleaned up trash from city streets and parks

73. Cleaned up railroad track roadbed in town

74. Had Key Club Week declared in city, offered service to over 500 groups and business leaders

75. Conducted a "God Is Alive" campaign

76. Coordinated food and recreation for Kiwanis Family Reunion Day Picnic

77. Assisted Kiwanis Club with their Ladies' Night

78. Worked with their Kiwanis Sponsors on the Kiwanis Foster Children's Christmas project

79. Helped Kiwanis Club with special project to raise money for local Crippled Children Society

80. Washed and waxed cars, cut grass, cleaned up yards of Kiwanians

81. Provided Key Club members for Kiwanis Slave Day free of charge

82. Played game of touch football with Kiwanis Club (and lost)

83. Participated in five Kiwanis socials

FUND-RAISING ACTIVITIES

84. Three talent performances and 18 special performances $4,375
85. Two car washes 208
86. Work with Kiwanis on projects 3,510
87. Operating men's clothing store for a day 311
88. Promoting Florida Orange Juice at International Convention, Montreal 800
89. Selling football programs 600
90. Football dance 175
91. Raising and selling young steer 187
92. Band for Halloween float 75
93. Moving law books on three separate occasions 300
94. Miscellaneous (putting up political posters, checking coats, selling cokes, parking cars, etc.) 142

TOTAL FUNDS RAISED $10,683[16]

16 Youth Services Club Committee Materials, *Key Club #15: Condensation of Key Club International Winning Achievement Reports, 1968–69.* (Mimeographed materials issued by the office of Kiwanis International.).

JUNIOR OPTIMISTS

"Friend of the boy" is a slogan which has been adopted by the Optimist Club. In 1924, this slogan was put into action when the Optimists formed the Junior Optimist Club, a community service organization for teen-age boys. Prior to this the Optimists had cooperated with existing community agencies, but had not directly sponsored youth activities.[17]

The Optimists are dedicated to good government, to civic affairs, and to the development and rehabilitation of boys. They are interested in safe-guarding the American way of life, encouraging respect for law, and pro-moting patriotism. These are the principles that serve as the foundation of the Junior Optimist program.

The Optimists strive to aid in the rehabilitation of youths who have gone astray. However, the Junior Optimist program is more directly aimed at showing appreciation to, and helping, youths who do not get into trouble and who are a credit to themselves, their city, and their nation. Optimists feel that too much attention is given to delinquent teen-agers and not enough to the majority of youths who stay out of trouble. The tools used by the Optimists in working with the Junior Optimist Clubs are encouragement, fellowship, and sincere interest in young boys.

The Junior Optimist Clubs usually operate at junior high schools and are advised by Optimist Club members. Awards are presented to members for outstanding contributions to Optimist activities, for scholarship, and for citizenship.

The Junior Optimist program manifests three major goals. These are sportsmanship, leadership, and responsibility. The first goal, sportsmanship, is promoted by means of a year-round program of athletic events (Figure 12–1). Competition is held in football, basketball, softball, volleyball, and other sports. Club activities are designed to inspire the boys toward the second goal: leadership. Boys are encouraged to become officers in their clubs and also to participate in their school student body government.

The club's third goal, responsibility, is one to which Optimist Club members give special attention. Club members are aided in the sponsorship of numerous campus and community service projects. They are urged to participate in any school functions in which responsibility is involved, such as hall monitor and safety patrol.

Throughout the year, the Junior Optimist Club may hold various special events, such as kite contests, talent shows, pot-luck suppers, parties, camp-ing and fishing trips, and speech contests. These activities, like the others, are contributed to by Optimist Club members who are willing to give their time to help boys learn to become useful citizens.

[17] *Junior Optimist Club Manual* (St. Louis, Missouri: Optimist International, n.d.)

Figure 12–1
Each year, the Optimist Club of Downtown, Toledo, Ohio, donates at least $1500 worth of ice time at the Toledo Arena so that the Optimist Junior Hockey League can go about its business of teaching the game and skating arts to youngsters. Pictured here are but 15 of the 450 boys who take advantage of the Optimist program. In addition, the club sponsors an active Boy Scout Explorer post, two baseball teams, and it furnishes eight annual memberships in the Toledo YMCA.

It would appear that Junior Optimist Clubs are not growing in popularity. In 1950, the Optimist magazine stated that the total membership was about 35,000 in 775 clubs. In 1964, the last year that statistics were compiled, there were only 567 clubs with 14,257 members.[18] It is significant, however, that Optimist youth work is branching into many varied avenues. In 1950 there were only two activities widely promoted—the Junior Optimists and Optimist Oratorical Contest. In 1964, Optimist Clubs reported working with over 50 different kinds of youth groups—boys' clubs, YMCA's, athletic clubs, bowling clubs, Junior Achievement, boys' bands, rifle clubs, Scouts, youth centers, model airplane clubs (Figure 12–2). Regular contact was reported with 254,399 boys and occasional contact with 2,571,811 others.[19]

[18] *Boys Work Statistics of 1964*, p. 3.
[19] *Ibid.*, p. 1.

Figure 12-2
For more than 20 years, members of the Optimist Club of Ann Arbor, Michigan, have sponsored an Optimist Rifle Club for area youngsters between the ages of 11 and 15. Affiliated with the Junior Division of the National Rifle Association, the club has an annual membership of 45 to 50 and there's always a long waiting list. *Courtesy Michigan Rifle Club.*

Work of Conservation Organizations with Youth

Youth groups, particularly the outdoor-oriented agencies, have long been active in environmental protection. There can be no doubt that the seeds from which sprang today's swelling concern for the earth's ecology were sown among many young adults when they were Boy Scouts, Girl Scouts, or Camp Fire Girls. Many national conservation organizations have cooperated with the youth organizations in the preparation of materials, training of leaders, and offering consultation services.

Concentrating upon one particular service in conservation and nature education is the Natural Science for Youth Foundation. The Foundation is an outgrowth of the efforts of John Ripley Forbes who, in 1935, began a program of encouragement to communities in establishing natural science centers, children's museums, and school nature centers. After various reorganizations, the present Natural Science for Youth Foundation was set up in 1961 to help in planning, programming, funding, and staffing these "gateways to nature." The Foundation and its predecessors have helped establish over one hundred centers throughout the country.[20]

A part of the widespread services of the National Wildlife Federation is directed toward young people. Significant contributions to children's conservation programs have been made through *Ranger Rick* magazine, games, stamps, charts, slides, and booklets such as *My Land and Your Land Conservation Series.*

The National Audubon Society, founded in 1905, is one of the oldest and largest national conservation organizations in the United States. Among its many activities are educational services for children as well as training programs for teachers and other youth leaders. The Society maintains four nature education demonstration centers at wildlife sanctuaries where school children and youth groups come by busloads for scheduled outdoor sessions. About 80,000 children visit the centers each year. The centers are located in California, Connecticut, and Ohio.[21]

The Audubon Camps are summer workshops for adults, particularly teachers and other youth leaders. The four camps are situated in Maine, Connecticut, Wisconsin, and Wyoming. The Society also prepares *Audubon Study Programs* for children which, since 1910, have been used by 12 million children. The Nature Centers Planning Division encourages the establishment of nature centers throughout the country.

National Honor Societies

The National Honor Society and the National Junior Honor Society are school affiliated programs which allow school faculties to give recognition for outstanding scholastic achievement. To those students who are chosen, the Honor Societies offer association with other outstanding schoolmates. Since most chapters undertake programs of service, they offer their members stimulation to begin upon a lifetime of service consonant with their great abilities. The organizations hope that their presence in a school will provide a respect for academic excellence, and motivate intellectual achievement.[22]

Both groups are sponsored by the National Association of Secondary School Principals, which also makes available 150 thousand-dollar scholarships each year to senior members.

20 *Natural Science for Youth Foundation—Programs and Purposes* (New Canaan, Conn: Natural Science for Youth Foundation, 1970); *Open Wide to Youth All Gateways to Nature* (New York, N.Y.: Natural Science for Youth Foundation, 1966).
21 *What is the National Audubon Society?* (New York, N.Y.: National Audubon Society, 1970), brochure.
22 *A Primer for the National Honor Societies* (Washington, D.C.: National Association of Secondary School Principals, 1968), brochure.

Membership is based primarily upon grade average, but consideration is also given to citizenship, leadership, and character. A minimum of a "B" average is required, and many chapters set higher standards. In 1969, there were about 15,000 members—up about 40 percent in ten years.[23]

The national office publishes a newsletter entitled *Student Life Highlights,* which contains news of state and regional meetings and articles of interest to student leaders.

Greek names or letters are not allowed, and selection of members is by the faculty and is never subject to student vote. Membership in the Junior Honor Society is open to students in grades seven through ten, while National Honor Society accepts tenth graders as provisional members and students in grades eleven and twelve as active members.

Junior Sports Programs

The years since World War II have seen a fantastic increase in organized sports competition for elementary age boys and, to a lesser extent, girls and older boys. Little League baseball alone attracts nearly two million boys each spring—up from a quarter million in 1955.[24] Biddy Basketball, Pop Warner Football, Babe Ruth Baseball, and Pony League Baseball have also enjoyed rapid expansion.

Although they lack national organizations, junior soccer leagues, age-group swimming competition, junior wrestling, junior hockey, and other sports programs are also showing phenomenal growth in many parts of the country. Many of these ventures are sponsored by adult organizations in the community which are interested in furthering a particular sport. In many cases, sponsors are the Amateur Athletic Union, the YMCA, or city recreation departments (Figure 12–3).

When they are properly conducted and under good leadership, junior sports programs offer many benefits. They give boys and girls the opportunity to learn the joy of participating in an active sport, teamwork, fair play, and sportsmanship. Competition can improve a child's self-confidence. Many of the activities contribute greatly to the development of basic skills, coordination, strength, and endurance. In addition, being a member of a team enhances new friendships, helps break down social barriers, and can enrich the father-son relationship. Little League, for example, has been praised by such notables as J. Edgar Hoover, Herbert Hoover, Dwight Eisenhower, and the Chicago police chief as a major contributor to the prevention of juvenile delinquency.

On the other hand, many persons have been critical of the junior sports

23 Correspondence from G.M. Van Pool, national staff, dated December 5, 1969.
24 *This is Little League* (Williamsport, Pennsylvania: Little League Baseball, Inc., n.d.) p. 9.

Figure 12–3
Baseball is a popular activity with youngsters at The Salvation Army's youth centers across the country. *Courtesy The Salvation Army.*

programs. Dozens of articles have been written against Little League Baseball, and many of the arguments are applicable to other activities as well, in varying degrees. Most of the arguments are put forth by professional educators and child psychologists.

The most criticized aspect is that of parental involvement. Most leagues are run almost entirely by fathers of the participants. Although well-meaning and hard-working, a high percentage of the dads are not qualified either as coaches or as youth leaders. Far too often, the "win at any cost" philosophy creeps in. Psychologists feel that too much pressure is put on the youngsters to win. It is not uncommon to see a parent cursing the officials, or angrily yelling instructions to his child from the stands. Too many fathers become ego-involved, trying to push their children to heights of glory they were never able to achieve themselves.

Another frequent criticism is that the programs often become over-organized and too competitive. The primary reason for a child's participation—fun—is often lost in the flurry of post-season play-offs, all-star teams, and national championships. It is charged that an excessive amount of money is spent on complete uniforms, official equipment, grandstands, dugouts and trophies. Many times, the junior program is emphasized to the point that participation in later years is a letdown. Money spent on a few could be used to provide a chance for all boys who are interested, say some critics.

An unfortunate aspect of junior sports programs is the tendency to keep lowering the age of participation. Competitive swimming for six-year-olds is not uncommon. Boys begin to play baseball before they are old enough to hit a moving ball, and consequently must use a batting-tee. This early entry into organized sports poses two major problems. First, it robs many children of their childhood. They never experience the childhood joys of free and imaginative play and childhood games. Second, it tends to make sports programs seem "old hat" and "kid stuff" to children at an early age. Many adolescents who have tired of organized sports or who are far behind the level of achievement of their classmates may undoubtedly find their thrills in socially undesirable activities.

A great deal of criticism has also been leveled at the physical health aspect of these programs. Much of this criticism has proved invalid. Studies have shown that a healthy, growing child is seldom injured by strenuous activities, although there is a difference of opinion as to whether bones and joints are injured by body contact in the rapid-growth years. Many baseball coaches feel that a boy can permanently damage his arm by throwing curve-balls at too early an age.

Since sports programs for children are undoubtedly here to stay, it would appear more fruitful to discuss desirable standards than to quarrel over their existence. Professional educators, recreation administrators, and physical education teachers should become more involved and do what they can to improve programs, rather than sitting back and condemning them. The unqualified parent who is running a detrimental program is probably in charge because qualified, trained leadership did not come forward.

Recreation directors and school administrators who often control the facilities may be able to insist on policies which will promote the well-being of the participants.

The most important factor in the quality of a program is leadership. Coaches and managers who are trained in working with children and who are more concerned with the growth and attitudes of the players than with winning and losing are essential. College students, young teachers, and others who are skilled in a sport and are interested in children are generally more satisfactory leaders than parents. If parents help a team their children should play on another team, if at all possible. Coaches should agree on objectives of the program before the season starts, so that one team is not losing all its games because the coach plays each boy an equal amount, while the other coaches use only the better players.

Programs for older players should be progressive, involving better uniforms, longer trips, and so on.

Competition should be organized so that as large a number of participants as possible can take part. No boy or girl should be "cut" for lack of ability.

League officials must realize that their activity is only one of many activities in which the child may be interested, and from which he can benefit. Incidents of coaches telling a boy he will be dropped from the team if he goes to summer camp or on a family vacation are far too common. Practices and games should not consume so much time that a child cannot continue music lessons, belong to a club, or spend some time with his family and friends. Junior sports leagues should not have as a goal the producing of major league professional ball players or Olympic Games champions. The numbers of children for whom this is a real possibility are too small, and efforts to accomplish such a goal would most likely just wear out the child at a tender age.

More emphasis needs to be placed on the so-called "minor sports" and sports with carry-over values. A very small percentage of people will be able to participate in baseball, basketball, football, or track after graduating from high school or college. Individual and dual sports offer much wider opportunity for a lifetime of participation.

COOPERATION, COORDINATION, AND PLANNING

Chapter 13

In a complex society, beset with a wide variety of social and educational problems, the need for social planning and cooperation among agencies at all levels—local, state, regional, and national—is increasingly apparent. By and large, social planning lags far behind technical and scientific planning. Cooperation among agencies, although recognized as desirable, is often perfunctory. It is probably natural that this situation exists, since the study of human beings and their needs and of the social structures designed to meet those needs is less than an exact science. The agencies working with youth have developed programs and procedures that meet particular needs; and cooperating with other, often competing, groups may seem secondary in importance to expending energy on their own programs.

Although the youth-serving agencies have many similarities in program and structure, each organization's program contains distinctive qualities or serves particular interests or segments of society that make it unique. Because the organizations are, for the most part, nongovernmental and voluntary and have to make their appeal through their distinctiveness, attempts to secure cooperation among them often generate problems.

Competition and Cooperation

Agencies find themselves competing with one another in many areas. They may compete for members and, in some cases, for leadership. Because of their need for community support, the agencies sometimes must compete for board and committee members who have community status and access to funds. They may compete for publicity in the mass media of communication in order to keep their agencies in the public eye. Finally, and extremely im-

189

portant, they usually must compete for funds. Even with the united fund approach, each agency must present its budget in a favorable light to secure what it considers its fair share of financial support.

Competition between organizations serves some important functions. It gives a choice to the participant, keeps agencies on their toes, and stimulates the development of new ideas. Agencies afraid to compete and too eager to keep the status quo could stifle new ideas, bar new organizations that offer needed services, and become insensitive to the changing environment.

WHY AGENCIES SHOULD COOPERATE

Cooperation in many areas has, however, become essential. Individual agencies must recognize this and devote some of their energies to cooperation, even to the extent of surrendering some of the traditional prerogatives of their agencies for the good of the community. The following are some of the reasons why agencies should participate in any attempts to cooperate.

1. Any single agency, public or private, working with youth, is unable to meet total community needs. Increasing leisure time and mounting social problems in our society necessitate the best use of all social, educational, and recreational resources of the community.

2. There is a limited amount of money available for youth services in any community. The money must be used to the best advantage of all children and youth and not for the advancement of the services of one agency. Of course, some youth have particular needs, requiring unique services, and provision should be made to meet these needs.

3. Agency workers need to keep informed about the services provided by other agencies in order to make their own programs more effective. It is easy for an agency to become routinized, locked into its own rigid patterns of procedure. As a result, it may be unable to meet newly developed needs. Only through constant awareness of changing social needs and the stimulus of contact with other agencies also interested in meeting these needs can the agency remain flexible and adaptable enough to serve the community. Many times new agencies must be formed merely because existing agencies have been unable to adapt their outmoded programs to new conditions.

4. Communities must be looked at and served as a whole as well as by parts. The needs of all groups can be met only through cooperative planning and action.

5. Joint planning is much more effective than individual planning by youth-serving organizations. Immediate needs are important; but plans must not ignore the future of ten, 20, or 40 years hence. Planning for youth services must be coordinated with planning for other facets of community life, such as schools, highways, open spaces, and industry.

6. Cooperative development of facilities for joint use is often the most efficient means of providing needed facilities. For example, a camp may

be used by two or more organizations, or a YMCA and a YWCA may find it feasible to operate a building in common.

7. Recruitment and training of volunteers on a joint basis may save time and money for the individual agencies and may also produce superior results.

8. Research into the needs of a community can be carried on more thoroughly and with less duplication of effort through the combined efforts of all concerned agencies.

Planning and Cooperation on a Local Level

The most important form of cooperation among agencies takes place on a local level. Such cooperation has the most direct effect on the people in the community and is most effective in terms of long-range community services. Local cooperation exists on several planes.

INFORMAL COOPERATION

As agencies and agency personnel understand and develop respect for one another, a great deal of planning and cooperation may take place without the formality of highly organized structures. Often two or more agencies can plan joint ventures that serve the interests of both groups. Examples of cooperative efforts include cooperative studies of neighborhood needs, with attempts to allocate responsibilities; joint use of facilities; joint neighborhood meetings and publicity to interpret programs, social events, and other special activities. The programs of the major youth organizations stress help to other organizations as well as receiving help from them.

In some ways informal cooperation between agencies with common interests is the most effective form of cooperation. Unfortunately, the preoccupation of agency staffs with their own programs and their reluctance to make new contacts without some outside stimulus often limit such cooperative action.

STRUCTURED COMMUNITY-WIDE COOPERATION

COMMUNITY COUNCILS

In many communities, community councils have been developed to bring together agencies with interests in all types of community problems to exchange information, study, plan, and recommend action. The community council is generally comprised of representatives from a wide variety of groups such as civic and social clubs, lodges, and philanthropic societies; interested individuals; and representatives of health, welfare, education, and recreation agencies. Both public and private organizations are included. The concerns of the council may be exceedingly broad, embracing problems of economics, education, health, correctional services, welfare, and youth services. Within the broad structure may be found special interest committees and study groups. Group work and recreation often constitute one of the committees within the community council. The committee may include both professional and lay members of the council.

Similar in function but differing in their basis of membership are the community service councils, in which the voting membership is open to any dues-paying individual. Agencies are non-voting affiliates. This pattern of organization is intended to make possible more representation from industry, labor, and business than the traditional community council secures.

One benefit of the community council is that it makes possible the interpretation of youth services to representatives of numerous community organizations with varied interests. The council thus helps secure a broad base of support, both for ongoing programs and for programs to meet special needs that arise from time to time.

The functions of the community councils vary from community to community but usually include the following:

1. *Education.* Through regular meetings of the whole group and through conference and committee meetings, the members become better acquainted with the problems and needs of the community and the available services of the various agencies. The council may become a significant force in developing lay leadership with an understanding of community problems.

2. *Coordination.* Elimination of overlapping programs and the coordination of scheduled programs is a logical outcome of meeting together.

3. *Studies.* As community needs become apparent, the council may itself undertake or may authorize the undertaking of research into various areas of their concern. Such studies may determine what services are available as well as those that are needed. Often conflict arises between the wills of the national office of an agency and the desires of a local coordinating body. It is generally accepted that the national organization shall have as its primary function the development of standards for staff and program, whereas the primary function of the local planning council will be the determination of priorities.

   Councils are often requested to study issues such as "Is a new Boys' Club needed in the east part of town?", "Do the Girl Scouts need another district with resultant staff increases?", and "Does the YMCA need another youth worker?"

4. *Recommendations.* The studies will usually result in the council's recommendations of definite steps to meet a need or correct an undesirable situation. The recommendations may be implemented through the programs of member agencies or may require the establishment of new agencies for their fulfillment. By acting together through a council, the individual agencies attain a strength that none of them possesses individually.

What puts teeth in the recommendations of the local planning councils are their relationships to the communities' financing organizations.

5. *Action.* Though the councils are primarily advisory in nature, they may on occasion initiate action, especially in new areas in which no existing agency is prepared to act.

6. *Special Coordinating Services.* There are also other coordinating services which the community council may perform. Among these are the maintenance of a volunteer bureau and the sponsorship of a leadership training program for youth-serving organizations. These activities are discussed in further detail later in this chapter.

Another service sometimes performed by the council is the dissemination of information to newspapers, radio, and television regarding its own activities and those of its member agencies.

The councils are probably more effective in small or medium-sized communities than in large metropolitan areas. They should not and usually do not offer direct service but act in an advisory capacity only and have no authority to compel an organization to follow their recommendations.

HEALTH AND WELFARE COUNCILS

In large cities a second pattern of structured cooperation—the council in which representatives are directly concerned with health, education, recreation, and welfare—is apt to exist instead of a community council. At one time most councils of this type were called "councils of social agencies." Today the more common designation is "health and welfare councils" or "coordinating councils." Their functions are similar to those of a community council. Though both lay men and professionals may serve in such councils, the membership is chiefly derived from representatives of the community agencies. The organizations represented in a health and welfare council are thus less inclusive than those represented in a community council. There is usually a committee or section in the health and welfare council that is concerned with youth services.

ORGANIZATIONS OF EXECUTIVES

The executive heads of the youth-serving agencies may establish a club or committee for themselves alone so that they may meet periodically to discuss subjects of mutual interest.

COUNCILS AND COMMITTEES WITH SPECIALIZED INTERESTS

A third pattern in planning and cooperation takes form through councils specializing in particular programs. An example might be a council concerned with organized camping. The council might make studies of community camping needs, sponsor a joint leadership training program in which all agencies conducting camping programs would cooperate, act as a clearing house for securing and distributing camperships to needy children, or sponsor a "camp week" to promote a better understanding of camping.

Similarly, an arts and crafts council or committee might provide service to all agencies, recruit competent voluntary assistance, or conduct special workshops in arts and crafts. Other cooperative endeavors might be carried on in natural science, dramatics, and music. If several agencies have certain mutual program interests, this type of joint action may produce better programs than does individual action.

ORGANIZATIONS TO MEET SPECIAL PROBLEMS

Agencies often may join together for an effective approach to a particular problem. For example, the dropout and the delinquent pose very special problems that might best be handled by means of a program developed cooperatively by several organizations. These problems could be approached through special committees in the community council or the health and welfare council, but separate organizations may be set up to meet urgent emerging situations demanding concentrated attention.

COOPERATION IN AREA AND FACILITY DEVELOPMENT

There are times when agencies may work jointly to meet needs for open spaces, day-camp sites, centers, or other facilities. These arrangements may be temporary and may be dissolved when the goals are accomplished.

COOPERATIVE LEADERSHIP TRAINING AND RECRUITMENT

When several agencies have similar needs, they may jointly sponsor leadership training workshops or courses. The training programs may offer education in the psychology of leadership, group processes, and special skills, such as social activities, music, arts and crafts, natural science, and camping. By jointly financing and conducting such courses, the agencies may secure better instruction than they could enlist singly.

Since the volunteer agencies depend for their existence on volunteer leadership, recruiting of volunteers is of major importance. Though much of this recruiting must be done by individual agencies, some communities have found it effective to pool their efforts through some type of joint recruiting structure. Appeals through PTA's, service clubs, newspapers, radio, and television often prove effective.

Volunteer bureaus are sometimes maintained for interviewing volunteers, advising them regarding opportunities for service in the community, and referring them to the particular agencies in which their skills and abilities may be most effectively used. In some instances the bureaus are conducted by community councils or health and welfare councils and in other instances they are supported as separate agencies by united funds. The volunteer bureaus may develop comprehensive information on volunteer resources of a community, including up-to-date lists of volunteers available for short-term and incidental assistance as well as those available for long-term service.

Cooperation between Public and Voluntary Agencies

Community councils and health and welfare councils generally include representatives of both public and voluntary agencies. The public agencies that have the closest affinities to the voluntary youth-serving organizations are usually the park and recreation departments and the schools, although public welfare, health, probation, and law enforcement agencies are also vitally interested.

DISTINCTION BETWEEN FUNCTIONS OF PUBLIC AND VOLUNTARY AGENCIES

There is no general agreement as to the differences in function between public and voluntary agencies; or, it might be said, their differences have not been clearly defined. The voluntary agencies in general have been the pioneers, developing experimental programs and new methods of work and setting standards for a high quality of service. This work, however, is now being performed to an increasing degree by governmental agencies with large budgets for research and new laws and regulations that permit them to expand the scope of their services.

Voluntary organizations continue to enjoy the advantage of flexibility. They are not as bound by legal restrictions and civil service regulations as governmental agencies, and they are free to experiment without too much red tape, testing programs which might be adopted later by public agencies when their worth is proven. Voluntary agencies also may be more selective than public agencies in their membership, since tax-supported agencies must be guided by the principle of "service-to-all." The variety of voluntary organizations makes it possible for a person to join a group that caters to those of his particular economic, social, or cultural background, although the major national voluntary organizations have few restrictions beyond those of age and sex. As a rule, the voluntary organizations have more freedom to concentrate on small-group programs than do city recreation organizations, although there are many exceptions. For example, city programs may serve small as well as large groups, and voluntary agencies may not limit themselves to small groups but may delve into mass activities such as Scout fairs and basketball leagues.

By and large, the programs of public and voluntary organizations should not be competitive but rather complementary. The public schools provide a compulsory basic education, and the public park and recreation departments provide a basic recreation service for all ages, with a greatly varied program of activities and facilities, such as parks, playgrounds, and community centers, which it would be difficult or impossible for any nonpublic organization to provide or maintain. Basic recreation areas and facilities in most communities are publicly owned.

HOW PUBLIC AND VOLUNTARY AGENCIES ASSIST EACH OTHER

There are several kinds of assistance often provided by public agencies to youth agencies. Public agencies, particularly the schools, frequently encourage young people to participate in voluntary agency programs, distribute information, and assist by providing meeting rooms. Land and facilities for meetings, field trips, sports, swimming, and camping are sometimes available in public parks and forests. Government-employed naturalists, arts and crafts leaders, swimming instructors, and other program personnel are often borrowed by voluntary agencies for leadership and for leadership training.

In turn, voluntary agency leadership and facilities may sometimes serve public agencies as, for example, when an agency permits a school system to use its camp for a school camp or its pool for the school swimming program. Service to the community is a major program area in many youth organiza-

Figure 13–1
Community service activities are very much a part of Boys' Club membership. Hundreds of Boys' Clubs of America annually take part in a nonpartisan "register, inform yourself and vote" campaign. Boys' Clubs also cooperate on clean-up campaigns, community chest drives, etc.
Courtesy Boys' Clubs of America.

Figure 13–2
Girl Scouts from Bergen County,
New Jersey, cleaning up a
portion of the Hackensack River.
*Courtesy Girl Scouts of the
United States of America.*

tions (Figure 13–1). It may take the form of planting trees in public parks
and school grounds or assisting in clean-up campaigns and similar projects
(Figure 13–2). The youth organizations may be among the most forceful
and vocal advocates of public recreation programs and facilities.

COMPETITION FOR TIME

One of the ever-growing problems of cooperation lies in competition for
the time of young people. The increasing number of summer school programs accentuates the problem, making it difficult for summer camps and
other summer programs of voluntary agencies to secure participants. The
proposed school year of 11 or 12 months, if adopted, will squeeze the agency
summer programs even further. The expansion of park and recreation
department services also reduces time available for the voluntary agency
programs. Public school educators and recreation leaders need to consult
with youth agencies to reduce possibilities of friction. Where summer schools
are in operation, there should be some agreement whereby children may
attend summer camps. It should be recognized that summer camp programs
may be fully as significant educationally as school programs, and every effort

should be made to make it possible for youth wishing to attend camp to do so. Similarly, the public summer recreation program should be scheduled to offer minimum interference with the program of the voluntary agencies, and vice versa. Although some competition for the time of young people is invigorating, cooperation in scheduling is necessary if the maximum opportunities are to be made available.

The fact that public agencies have often incorporated into their programs many aspects of the programs of voluntary agencies does not mean that voluntary agencies are unneeded. Essential elements of American democracy are voluntary choice and the opportunity for free agencies to conduct programs that meet special desires and needs, to experiment in new programs, and to serve minority as well as majority interests.

During the depression of the 1930s there occurred a very extensive development of governmental services in welfare and recreation. Since that time, governmental services have grown more rapidly than private services. Most social planners agree that both sectors are necessary, even though no clear definition of the responsibilities of each has been made.

Relationships with Religious Organizations

Three types of relationships exist between the voluntary youth-serving organizations and religious groups. First, a large number of organizations are an extension or part of the faith groups. The Catholic Youth Organization and the Young Men's Hebrew Association fall into this category. In such instances the programs generally have specific religious aspects. Membership is derived primarily from the religious group sponsoring the organization, and religious education and observation of religious customs may be an integral part of the purpose of the youth agencies.

A second type of relationship may be illustrated by the Young Men's Christian Association and the Young Women's Christian Association. Although they are Protestant-inspired organizations and have religious implications in their programs, they are open to people of all faiths. In some cases a fairly large percentage of the members may be non-Protestant. Some associations encourage participation of members in the religious observances of their own faith, even though not Protestant.

A third type of relationship is one in which a youth-serving organization does not adhere to any specific faith group, although units within its structure might be sponsored by synagogues, Catholic churches, Protestant churches, or community groups without any religious affiliation. For example, a Boy Scout troop might be sponsored by a church and meet in the church. An organization such as the Boys' Clubs of America is not allied with any religious group but encourages its members to worship with their own religious groups.

It should be noted that the religious organizations of America have generally provided much of the community support for the youth-serving organizations. Much of the leadership comes from religious bodies, and the facilities of churches and synagogues are often made available to the youth-serving organizations. Members of religious groups have often been very influential in providing financial assistance.

Joint Financing

In the early history of the youth-serving organizations, funds were raised for their support by the individual efforts of the organizations. Board members were often selected because of the financial assistance they might give. A great deal of the time and energy of board members and staff had to be given to organizing an annual campaign and securing solicitors. The amount of money raised was related more to the effectiveness of the promotion than to the needs of the community. Moreover, it was difficult to secure solicitors, since many of the organizations sought the help of the same people. The public tended to become deaf to the multitude of appeals. Increasingly, therefore, agencies began to be interested in joint campaigns. Interest in such means of financing began before World War I and was spurred on by the organization of war chests during the war. Though most of the war chests were dissolved after the war, interest in cooperative financing continued and grew through the 1920s and 1930s. A National Association of Community Chests and Councils was formed in 1927. During World War II, the local community chests joined the National War Fund, which supported the war emergency services as well as the permanent agencies.

After World War II, with the emergence of many new national health agencies that conducted separate campaigns, the membership of many of the federated agencies was enlarged to include some of the new agencies; and many of the "community chests" gave way to "united funds." These self-governing local funds formed a national organization, the United Community Funds and Councils of America, which provides services to its members but has no administrative relationship to them. Its services include field consultations, conferences, institutes, correspondence, and publications.[1]

The local united funds are usually incorporated as voluntary nonprofit associations. They may serve several counties or a single community. Because they must decide which agencies to admit and how to budget the funds they raise, the united funds are involved in community planning. If they are to benefit from the work of other planning groups, they must work closely with the community councils. In some instances the same staff serves both

[1] Harry L. Lurie, ed., *Encyclopedia of Social Work* (New York, N.Y.: National Association of Social Workers, 1965), pp. 327–329.

agencies. Professional staffs are maintained except in very small communities.

In joint financing, emphasis is placed on one big campaign each year with one big gift from each donor to meet the needs of all of the voluntary agencies in the areas of health, welfare, and recreation. Though some agencies, particularly those devoted to the eradication of particular diseases, continue to conduct their own campaigns, united fund drives have considerably reduced the number of campaigns in a community and the administrative expense per dollar received. Almost always the united fund has raised more money in its first campaign in a community than the separate agencies had been able to raise the previous year.

The success of the united funds is evidenced in their growing acceptance by the public, which is relieved from the burden of numerous financial appeals. The agencies benefit, not only from improved financing, but also from being able to devote more of their time to the purposes for which they were founded.

One of the greatest values of the united fund is that cooperation in fund-raising has led to cooperation in other areas of community planning. Each agency is forced to look at itself in relation to the other services of a community. Moreover, in presenting its budgets to the united fund, each agency must justify its programs and its expenditures. Wastefulness in procedures and programs is exposed, and there is incentive for self-improvement.

There is a continual need for a hard look at existing organizations so that only those effectively serving the community receive financial support. It is often difficult to cut off funds from organizations that have been admitted to a united fund, but organizations that have outlived their usefulness must be dropped. Further, organizations serving important community needs must not be penalized by being forced, through cooperative agreements, to protect or assist organizations offering inferior programs.

Organizations may fail to join cooperative drives for several reasons. Some organizations can raise more money by acting alone. Others have programs that cater only to a limited segment of the community—for example, a religious sect—and therefore they do not feel justified in appealing to the general public for support. Still others do not wish to give up the freedom they enjoy, for in joining a united fund they must adhere to certain financial policies and perhaps even alter their programs, inasmuch as a united fund authority may withhold money from an organization which departs from its principles. Also some organizations may prefer to stay out of a united fund because they believe that individuals should have the right to give to agencies of their choice rather than to have all agencies share their gifts. The national health organizations that have refused to join the united funds carry on their own campaigns, making effective national appeals and using local sponsors and solicitors.

Guiding Rules for Local Cooperation

When local cooperative organizations are established or expanded, certain general principles should be followed. The national voluntary agencies have had a long history of service, and their particular modes of action must be given consideration. Some guiding rules are:

1. There must be recognition of the right of each agency to plan and operate its own internal affairs.
2. Cooperation should not be compulsory. It is the right of an individual agency in a democracy to operate independently of any other agency.
3. National agencies assume a major responsibility in setting standards for their local groups, but local agencies must work out their own relationships with local planning bodies.
4. Public and private agencies should find a means of working together for the total good of the community, recognizing the unique contribution that each has to make.
5. The total resources of the community should be studied, and the services of its component parts should be evaluated.

Cooperative Endeavors on the State Level

The most effective coordination and planning takes place on the local level. This, however, does not mean that coordination and planning at the state level is unimportant. Many important relationships include public agencies of the state government. As state government expands its services to children and youth, these increasingly affect the voluntary youth-serving agencies. In some cases voluntary agencies may have their own statewide means of cooperation largely independent of state government agencies.

JOINT PLANNING AND COORDINATION WITH PUBLIC AGENCIES

The increasing participation of state agencies in youth problems should be accompanied by closer working relationships with the voluntary agencies, both for the improvement of total services and for the expansion of resources of importance to voluntary agencies. Some of the reasons for such joint cooperative action and planning are:

1. to exchange information in order to promote a better understanding of functions and programs of public and private groups in the state.
2. to contribute the wide experiences of the voluntary youth agencies to the solution of statewide problems of children and youth.
3. to secure passage of legislation that would be in the best interest of children and youth.

4. to participate in state conferences, institutes, and workshops that will contribute to improved services.

5. to organize and conduct leadership training programs.

6. to protect agencies from undesirable usurpation of functions by public agencies. Historically, voluntary agencies have been innovators and have experimented with programs that have been later assumed by public agencies. There are, however, certain functions that remain primarily the prerogatives of the voluntary agencies.

7. to participate in planning for the protection of the health and safety of children and youth.

8. to plan for land and resource conservation that has an important bearing on the programs of voluntary agencies.

Voluntary agencies have helpful contacts with numerous state agencies and structures. A few of these are described here.

STATE RECREATION DEPARTMENTS, BOARDS, OR COMMISSIONS

A number of states have created state government agencies concerned with the development and expansion of community recreation. The functions of such agencies often include the following:

1. *Services to local communities.* Although these are primarily services to local public agencies, they often also include assistance to local planning groups and social welfare councils.

2. *Leadership training.* Many types of local institutes are conducted in which voluntary agency leaders participate.

STATE PLANNING AGENCIES

Although much of the work of state agencies is devoted to economic and physical development of the state, voluntary agencies are affected by their actions.

INTER-AGENCY OR STATE COORDINATING COMMITTEES

Many states have developed coordinating committees to provide an exchange of information among the state government agencies. In some cases the representatives of voluntary agencies are included on these committees.

STATE BOARDS OF HEALTH

State boards of health are concerned with setting standards and protecting the health and safety of the people of the state. As a result, their work is related to that of all agencies conducting programs for children or operating swimming pools, camps, and other facilities.

DEPARTMENTS OF NATURAL RESOURCES

There are various agencies of state government related to forests, parks, fish, and wildlife; yet all of them share certain functions. They administer public outdoor areas for recreation purposes and are responsible for land, water, and wildlife conservation policies and activities. They are concerned with the federal Land and Water Conservation Fund, which provides matching federal funds for outdoor recreation purposes. Participation in the Land and Water Conservation Fund is contingent upon the development of state and local plans for future projects. Organizations using public outdoor areas for camps and outings are of course affected by such developments.

STATE DEPARTMENTS OF EDUCATION

Although primarily concerned with public education, the activities of the state boards of education have a relationship to local youth agencies, insofar as they are concerned with matters such as use of buildings and extended school services.

STATE YOUTH COMMISSIONS OR COUNCILS

In some states youth commissions or councils have been organized particularly to attempt to ascertain and meet unfulfilled needs of youth. In many cases the voluntary youth-serving agencies occupy a prominent role in these organizations. Their "know-how" and leadership are important assets. Although the youth commissions are often primarily concerned with problem youth, they are also interested in providing desirable leisure opportunities for all young people.

OTHER AREAS OF STATEWIDE COOPERATION

Statewide cooperation also takes place in organizations related to social work, camping, and conservation. Such groups provide opportunities for joint planning, either in specialized programs or in general program development and planning. Both voluntary and state governmental agencies with common interests may cooperate in this fashion.

Cooperation and Planning on the National Level

There is much similarity between cooperation on a national level and that on the state level. Here again the relationships lie between agencies themselves and between agencies and government, and these relationships may be either structured or informal. Informal cooperation is common. For example, the Boy Scouts and the Girl Scouts assisted the Camp Fire Girls in its recent revamping of its local council structure, and the Camp Fire Girls and Girl Scouts cooperated in a project for training women for community agency work. The YMCA was helpful in the establishment of the Boy Scouts and the Camp Fire Girls. Individual Boys' Clubs and YMCA's sometimes are chartered to operate local Boy Scout units.

NATIONAL VOLUNTARY ORGANIZATIONS CONCERNED WITH PLANNING

Structured cooperation takes place through special organizations. The National Assembly for Social Policy and Development, Inc., accomplishes on a national level many of the things that a community council does locally. Superceding the 22–year old National Social Welfare Assembly, the National Assembly for Social Policy and Development began functioning in January, 1968, as a voluntary, nonprofit association of individuals and organizations concentrating on national planning and coordination of policies and programs in the area of social work.[2]

The Assembly's corporate authority resides in 300 trustees chosen from throughout the United States. Regional and national meetings are held to formulate policy and program ideas. Publications emerge as the result of task force, committee, and conference work.

The Assembly focuses upon three broad areas:

1. national social planning, policies, and programs in both the governmental and voluntary areas;
2. strategies for action and implementation, including legislation;
3. strengthening of citizen participation.

There are 77 organizations associated with the Assembly, which provides them with a mechanism for working together and assists them in developing ideas and programs. The organizations work through the Assembly in developing guidelines and standards in such areas as personnel, field service, salaries, volunteers, and finance.

Other national organizations such as the United Community Funds and Councils of America, described earlier in this chapter, and the National Association of Social Workers, also perform coordinating functions. The latter organization, established in 1955 as the single professional membership association for social workers in the United States, is devoted to promoting the quality and effectiveness of social work practices.

On the national level, the voluntary youth-serving agencies participate in the activities of organizations representing and coordinating special program interests. Among these organizations are groups concerned with conservation, camping, natural science, recreation, the arts, and music.

---

2 Mrs. Louise N. Munn, ed., *Service Directory of National Organizations* (New York, N.Y.: The National Assembly for Social Policy and Development, Inc., 1969), pp. 3–4.

Examples of such national groups are the National Audubon Society, the American Camping Association, the National Art Education Association, the Children's Theatre, and the National Recreation and Park Association. National organizations concentrating on delinquency, crime, mental and physical health, safety, racial discrimination, and other social problems are often supported by the youth-serving organizations. Representatives of the national organizations may also serve as representatives of numerous educational and child study associations.

IMPORTANCE OF VOLUNTARY AGENCIES TO FEDERAL GOVERNMENT AGENCIES

In spite of the great increase in the activities of the federal government and in the availability of federal funds for services that impinge on voluntary effort, there is increasing need for the voluntary agencies. Federal governmental activity cannot be effective except as it works through individual citizens and voluntary agencies, as well as through states, cities, and community institutions. The long experience and resources of the voluntary agencies are of particular value in reaching the community. The concept of government and the voluntary sector sharing responsibilities and each rendering its distinct service needs continual reiteration and strengthening.

The following are some agencies of the federal government that depend for their effectiveness on a cooperative relationship with voluntary agencies.

Department of Health, Education, and Welfare. In much of its social planning for youth, this department depends upon the cooperation of the youth-serving organizations. Provision for the mentally and physically handicapped, as well as for normal youth, is related to efforts of the youth-serving organizations.

Bureau of Outdoor Recreation. As a relatively new agency of government, established in 1962, the Bureau of Outdoor Recreation needs to develop a much closer working relationship with youth-serving agencies that will help to interpret land and facility management in terms of the best human uses of the land. All conservation and outdoor recreation programs of the federal government similarly need this cooperation.

Poverty-related agencies. The voluntary youth-serving agencies have a particular concern for services to culturally deprived children. Through the funds of the Office of Economic Opportunity, many children have been provided with day or resident camping. Members of youth organizations have given assistance in VISTA and Head Start; and hundreds of local agencies have conducted special projects supported primarily through the Office of Economic Opportunity.

Many members of voluntary agency boards are reluctant to accept federal government aid for at least three reasons: (1) general opposition to this type of government expenditure and a reluctance to become a part of it, (2) fear of government control, (3) fear of the impermanency of the grants, with the danger of possibly building an expanded operation from which, with a change in government policies, the financial base may suddenly be removed.

On the other hand, many agency leaders feel that government grants provide an excellent means of expanding into badly needed programs not financially feasible otherwise. Their attitude is, "If we don't get the funds, some other community will, depriving our city of badly needed funds; or else some other local agency will get the grant and overshadow what we are trying to do."

In spite of the high degree of conservatism on the part of most agency boards, it seems likely that the latter viewpoint will prevail and that more and more federal funds will be channeled through private agencies.

Programs with children from poverty areas require heavy subsidies. Although there has been some resistance to the use of federal government monies, most of the voluntary agencies working with disadvantaged youth have participated to some extent in the federal "war on poverty."

In 1965, the National Council of the YMCA adopted the following policy, which illustrates the attitude of many voluntary agencies. It states the necessity for retaining the integrity of the agency while recognizing the desirability of cooperating in certain government programs.

> Recommendation 1: The National Council of YMCAs reaffirms its policy of cooperation with governmental agencies for the common good, providing such cooperation does not compromise the objectives or status of the YMCA as an independent, voluntary, and lay-Christian organization. The Council believes that the most important contributions of YMCAs to such cooperation will be through sharing their methods and experience in working with young people, and the service ideals of their members.
>
> Recommendation 2: The National Council of YMCAs welcomes and encourages the cooperation of public and private organizations in developing plans for community action to deal with the underlying causes of social problems and urges YMCAs, especially those in downtown and inner-city locations, to share in these efforts, including the use of government funds for disadvantaged youth where appropriate.
>
> In instances where such associations are convinced of their qualifications in goals and competence to participate in programs or projects involving the use of government funds, careful consideration should be given to guides set forth in this committee's report, bearing in mind that imprudent or imcompetent action by one association could be a disservice to the movement as a whole.
>
> Recommendation 3: The National Council of YMCAs commends and encourages continuation of the general practice of financing "normal" YMCA programs and operations through earned income, United Fund and Chest appropriations, contributions, membership dues and program fees.[3]

3 *YMCA Yearbook, 1966* (New York: Association Press, 1967), pp. 40–41.

In 1966, 282 YMCAs reported that they were participating in the neighborhood youth corp. Many others were involved in Community Action Programs, VISTA, the Job Corps, tutoring programs and work-study programs.

OTHER AREAS OF COOPERATION WITH THE FEDERAL GOVERNMENT

There are numerous areas of national importance in which national public and private agencies could pool their efforts. The following are a few of these.

Research and studies. Numerous types of problems such as needs of disadvantaged youth, or the problem of delinquency, need cooperative approaches to achieve maximum results.

Joint national conferences and workshops. Joint conferences such as the White House Conference on Children and Youth and the National Youth Conference on Natural Beauty and Conservation, in which many of the leading national youth agencies cooperated, have pointed the way toward further national gatherings in which government and voluntary agencies meet to define problems, develop policies, and endeavor to mobilize resources to meet the needs. Continual study of the relations and functions of public and voluntary agencies is a part of such conferences.

Summary

All agencies give recognition to the desirability of cooperation and coordination; but their achievements are usually less than satisfactory, both on the national and the local levels. Strenuous and imaginative efforts are needed to improve the communication among agencies and to increase their joint endeavors. This action is essential if agencies are to merit the trust placed in them by the communities that support them.

Far too often youth-serving agencies have tried to conduct their activities in a social vacuum. The typical volunteer club leader has little knowledge of or concern for programs offered by other agencies. Even most local professional leaders have been guilty of nearsightedness in looking only at their particular agency needs instead of overall community needs. Some of the results have been overlapping services, wasteful competition, and failure to reach many young people at all.

Most communities in America of over 10,000 population have some structure to facilitate coordination. Youth agencies have a responsibility to do their best to make such cooperation effective.

WHAT OF THE FUTURE?

Chapter 14

Without question, the great majority of Americans hold the voluntary youth-serving agencies in high esteem. Parents may not always encourage their own children to be members, but they nevertheless regard membership in youth organizations as important for young people in general. The large numbers of men and women who serve as volunteers—as leaders, as committee or board members, or as money-raisers—for the organizations is convincing evidence of public support.

Educators are usually strong advocates of youth agencies. The methods and content of youth programs generally follow approved practices in educational psychology. Current thinking favors the responsible participation of youth in programs that meet felt needs. The inclusion in school programs of many types of activities that have long been used by youth agencies attests to educators' recognition of the agencies' success and importance in meeting these needs.

The apathy of certain portions of the population toward services for youth is a serious handicap to their effectiveness. It has always been difficult to obtain adequate volunteer leadership; and, in spite of the increased leisure possessed by today's adults, there has been no lessening of this difficulty.

Another limitation to the effectiveness of the agencies lies in the image they too often project to the eyes of poor people—those who have the greatest need for the agencies' services. Parents in deprived areas often maintain that youth agencies are organs of middle-class thinking and morality and that the cost of membership excludes their children. The youth agencies need make no apology for their services to the middle-income segment of society. This group represents a major portion of the population of the United States, and the development of leadership and of sustaining values in children of this group is of great consequence. Nonetheless, there lies a tremendous need in the disadvantaged segments of society; and the youth agencies must accept the challenge for expanded services in this area and must alter the image that has developed in some places (Figure 14–1).

The high membership in the many youth organizations indicates their popularity with youth themselves, despite a tendency among some older youth to think of membership as being "square." Being held in high esteem today will, however, not be sufficient for the future. The American social scene is changing at an ever-accelerating pace. The youth agencies themselves realize that if they are to survive they must continually study social trends, their own functions, and the suitability of their programs to new needs and interests. Planning for the future can be successful only if based upon such examination.

Because of their voluntary nature and freedom from many restrictions, the youth organizations may find it easier to remain flexible and to meet new conditions than public organizations. The Boy Scout research study, *Is*

Figure 14–1

The Girl Scouts, like most youth groups, are becoming more involved in community service projects. These girls are donating time to a tutorial reading project.
Courtesy Girl Scouts of the United States of America.

Scouting in Tune with the Times?[1] and their program of expansion, called *BOYPOWER '76*, illustrate the efforts of agencies to keep pace with evolving needs. All of the major youth-serving organizations are, to a greater or lesser extent, engaged in similar projects.

Social Changes that Concern the Youth-Serving Organizations

Peering into a crystal ball has its hazards, but only through attempting to anticipate changes can we make plans for the future. The following are some of the factors that will probably influence youth agencies in the coming years.

POPULATION FACTORS

The population may be expected to expand in spite of a recent slowing down of the birth rate. Unless some new and unforeseen factor enters the picture, we may expect in the United States a population of 300 million by the year 2000. The percentage of people in metropolitan areas will continue to increase, with suburban growth most rapid and the inner-city somewhat static. Most of the population will inhabit the great megalopolis areas. Problems of housing, slums, transportation, and air pollution will continue to plague our crowded urban centers. Experiments with model cities, new cities, and decentralization will ameliorate somewhat the plight of the cities, but for the foreseeable future many of the most serious problems will remain.

Population age groups are shifting. Between 1970 and 1980, the numbers of young adults in their 20s and 30s will increase by 34 per cent, whereas people in all other age groups will increase by only six percent.[2] Youth will be better educated, more knowledgeable, and more sophisticated than before.

WORK AND LEISURE

As automation eliminates more and more drudgery, coming years will find fewer and fewer blue-collar workers. There will be more white-collar workers, and more people will be engaged in the service occupations. The industrial workweek decreased by over 20 hours, dropping from 60 hours to 39.7 hours, between 1913 and 1971.[3] If this rate continues, today's workweek

[1] Daniel Yankelovich, Inc., *Is Scouting in Tune with the Times?* (New Brunswick, N.J.: Boys Scouts of America, 1968).
[2] "What U.S. Will Be Like by 1980," *U.S. News & World Report,* LXX, No. 2, pp. 38–40, January 11, 1971.
[3] Archibald A. Evans, "Work and Leisure, 1919–1969," *International Labour Review,* 99, No. 1, January, 1969, p. 56.
New York Times, Feb. 6, 1971, p. 22, col. 2.

will decrease to about 30 hours by the year 2000. There will be some groups of people, however, who will not benefit from the decreased work week. They are the executives, the highly skilled, and the people in the professions, upon whom technology and sciences will place greater demand.

Longer vacations and long weekends, with holidays on Monday or Friday, will make possible more activities away from home. Improved transportation will provide more travel opportunities but will place great pressures on outdoor resources.

Throughout American history it has been generally assumed that the great satisfactions of life should come through meaningful work. From the time of the Puritans, Americans have generally frowned upon idleness. Today a new attitude is in the air. Certainly meaningful work will remain life's greatest reward for many people. For others, however, leisure rather than work will provide fulfillment. The preparation of youth so that they may use their leisure wisely is an increasingly important function of youth agencies. A hedonistic search for pleasure is self-defeating; but leisure used in learning, attaining new skills and interests, sharing enthusiasms, and giving service to others may provide an enrichment of living never attainable for many in a work-oriented society.

AFFLUENCE AND POVERTY

Economists tell us that we are moving toward greatly increased family purchasing-power. A typical family income by the year 1979 may reach $15,500, as compared with $9,000 in 1969.[4] Better homes, education, foods, and medical care should result. An increased percentage of family income will doubtless be spent on travel, television, better cars, and other luxury items. The percentage of poor in the population should continue to decrease; and there should be greater concern for the unemployable, the ill, the aged, and the handicapped.

The great discontent of the poor lies not so much in their lack of money as in the disparity between their status and that of others. The children of the disadvantaged will need to be allowed opportunities of education and youth services now enjoyed by the more affluent. The next 20 years may well be a testing period as to whether it is possible to give underprivileged youth those experiences that will bring them into the mainstream of American life.

The Boys' Clubs have concentrated on services to the disadvantaged, and their impact has been significant. Most of the other agencies have also directed attention to disadvantaged youth. In view of still-existing inequalities, however, the agencies will need to focus greater attention on these

4 "The Spectacular '70s'," *U.S. News & World Report*, LXVI, No. 25, June 23, 1969, p. 42.

young people, make them feel accepted, and offer them programs that will captivate their interest and meet their needs.

RACIAL JUSTICE

The struggle for racial justice is one of the signs of our times. The black, the chicano, and the American Indian are grasping for equal opportunity in a society that has too long discriminated against and, in some cases, abused them. In varying degrees, the youth agencies have entered the arena of this battle. The agencies labor under the handicap that, with a few exceptions, theirs has been a long history of service to primarily white, middle-class groups. There have been many cases of discrimination within local sections of agencies, even though not sanctioned by the national organizations.

The fact that agencies have taken a stand for racial justice does not mean that they have achieved it, even within their own organizations. The problem of implementation is complex, and years may be required to equalize opportunity.

Efforts made in the summer of 1968 to provide camping for disadvantaged children led to fruitful results for the youth-serving agencies. Many of these children were from minority groups. The Battelle Institute study indicated that over 1.1 million children from disadvantaged homes attended resident and day camps. In most agency camps these were integrated programs.[5]

It is to the credit of the major youth agencies that they all declare better service to the disadvantaged to be a major goal at this time. Examples of publications designed to further these aims are *One Hundred Boys' Clubs Tested Programs for Disadvantaged Youth* and the YMCA's *Programs for Urban Action*.[6] Both books contain examples of what local groups have done in an effort to inspire new and creative ways for meeting better the urgent problems of the inner city.

The traditional, building-centered approach of the typical YMCA has not fit the needs of lower-class youth. Many of these youth have lacked the necessary funds for memberships, and often their behavior has resulted in their eviction. Realizing a responsibility to these youth who do not possess the funds or behavior patterns to fit into the traditional YMCA program, several Y's have developed street-worker programs. The largest and best known Detached Worker Program is run by the Chicago YMCA. It grew from an initial two-man effort to 32 workers by 1966.[7] The theory

5 Reynold E. Carlson, *National Camping Survey for Disadvantaged Youth* (Bloomington, Indiana: Indiana University, 1968), mimeographed.

6 *Programs for Urban Action* (New York: National Board of Young Men's Christian Association, 1969); *One Hundred Boys' Clubs Tested Programs for Disadvantaged Youth* (New York: Boys' Clubs of America, 1969).

7 James M. Hardy and Richard L. Batchelder, eds., *1966 YMCA Year Book and Official Roster* (New York, N.Y.: Association Press, 1966), p. 21.

behind the street-worker programs is that the organization must go to the youth—serving them where they are, rather than hoping the youth will come to the agency.

Several other Y's have followed Chicago's example, and undoubtedly many more would if they felt they could afford it. The necessity of balancing a budget often gives priority to income-producing programs, even though they may not meet as great a need as other activities.

EDUCATION

Public education increasingly pervades the lives of children and young adults. Children enter school at an earlier age and continue until a later age than heretofore. The school has shouldered more and more of the functions formerly borne by the home or social agency. One reason given for assumption of these responsibilities is that through the school all children, not just a few, will benefit. Another is that the knowledge explosion of the present day requires more learning time, although schools are wrestling with the problem of what should be taught.

The tremendous financial investment in school buildings and grounds has led many people to the conviction that, for greatest efficiency in use of the tax dollar, afternoon, evening, week-end, and summer programs should be conducted in the schools. Innovative programs have begun, and a 12-month school year has been seriously considered. The summer vacation, once justified as a time when children could help with crops, no longer serves this purpose in most of the country.

Expansion of the school year and increased usurpation of children's time pose serious problems for youth agencies, which have difficulty fitting their programs into already crowded schedules. The question may well be raised as to the right of schools so to preempt the time of children that these agencies, as well as the homes and religious institutions, find their influence waning. America has traditionally offered freedom of choice, with opportunities for families to pursue their own special religious and other interests. Adequate time must be kept available for *all* of our major social institutions to carry on their work with children and youth.

Summer camping programs are seriously threatened by the proposed 12-month school year and an emphasis on summer school attendance. About eight million children now attend summer camps, chiefly under the auspices of the voluntary agencies, religious organizations, and private groups. Summer playground programs would also suffer from any compulsory 12-month school year. The argument that schools can provide programs for all children, not for only those who participate in the offerings of the various agencies, has validity. It does not, however, recognize the right for children to choose, from a variety of opportunities, those that meet their particular needs or those that their families wish them to enjoy. It is difficult to assess the significance of youth agencies as an educational force in American life. How much do they contribute to what we may consider our American value system? How much do they assist in the personal growth and development of the qualities of leadership? What contribution do they make to helping young people learn to live together and to find solutions to problems on a democratic basis? These and other questions might well be asked in any effort to evaluate the youth programs that are such an evident part of American life.

The American system of free public education is relied upon as the major thrust of our democratic society. Yet by its very nature it has limitations in what it can do. The voluntary youth agencies are complementary to public education in that they can give primary attention to those personal qualities that are essential to the more complete education of youth. They also provide a place for direct parental leadership and a place for varied religious and social concepts to find their place as a part of education.

The very principles of democracy are concerned with respect for diversity. There are dangers of an overwhelming government bureaucracy stifling the creativeness and diversity of youth through the uniform control of all education.

THE NEW CONSERVATION

Today's broadening concept of environmental conservation encompasses not only the traditional aspects of land, water, forests, and wildlife, but also the acute problems of overpopulation, air pollution, urban sprawl, litter, and sheer ugliness. Here is an area in which the youth agencies, because of their methods and ideology, are particularly fitted to make important contributions. Through the youth agencies, young people can find social causes in which to invest their abilities; and few causes can be so readily incorporated into the youth agency program as conservation. There are several reasons for this fact. In many agencies, the outdoors, with camping, hiking, learning outdoor skills, and studying animals and plants, is essential to the program. Also, because youth agencies may often have time to schedule field trips and lengthy outdoor experiences, they have more freedom than the schools to expose young people intimately to situations revealing ecological relationships and the need for conservation. Moreover, they have time to carry out conservation projects—time which the schools often do not have to spare. Finally, because of their dependence upon natural lands in their own programs, the youth agencies have a particularly great responsibility toward the retention of their beauty and usefulness.

The urbanization of American culture has divorced a major part of society from direct relationship with the natural environment; yet there seems to remain a deep-seated need to seek out, in leisure, just such a relationship. As we become more and more urbanized, we try more and more to escape from the city during weekends and vacations. Helping young people to establish a relationship with the environment through which they will not only use and enjoy it, but also understand it and accept responsibility for the preservation of its quality, may well be one of the most significant services the youth agencies can render.

The agencies have already taken strides in conservation. Their interest was evidenced at the National Youth Conference on Natural Beauty and Conservation, held in Washington, D.C. in 1966, as a result of which youth adopted beautification and conservation projects throughout the country.

FEDERALLY-FINANCED PROGRAMS

Through the emergency relief programs of the 1930s and the poverty programs of recent years, federal funds were made available to youth-serving organizations for experimental programs and programs such as summer camps and clubs for deprived children. As a general rule the agencies have accepted funds that provided for some special need rather than for their ongoing programs. The youth agency is in somewhat of a dilemma in accepting federal funds. The agency is usually eager to assist in alleviating problems, particularly if the program of assistance is temporary and will not impede the agency's permanent program. However, the acceptance of federal funds means a certain control of program that is contrary to the long-established principle of independence and voluntary support. The freedom of the youth agency from government control is one of its most cherished attributes.

CONFUSION IN THE STANDARDS OF YOUTH

More sophisticated than their counterparts of earlier generations, many young people today are rejecting established institutions, the materialistic philosophy of their elders, organized religion, and the authority of home, school, and government. Though the world of their parents is unacceptable to them, they are confused in their search for a brighter one. Within most of them, however, lies a strong strain of idealism, a desire for justice, and a longing for causes in which to believe. Their apparent indifference to organized religion stems not from a lack of spiritual concern but from a criticism of structure and dogma. The youth agencies can step into the generation breach to help these young people find their moral and spiritual footing and retain that which is significant in the field of religion.

WAR, PEACE, AND LOVE OF COUNTRY

The youth of the land have been torn by wars which many of them have felt were unjustified. Their disillusionment has been at the bottom of many of their criticisms of the government. The old virtue of love of country has been submerged in the tide of their discontent. As nongovernmental institutions, the youth agencies have an opportunity beyond that of the schools to explore our American goals and to keep alive the American dream of a better world (Figure 14–2). Not content with "my country, right or wrong," the agencies can do their share toward making our country right and affirming the high purposes for which we should stand.

Figure 14–2
Since 1928 the FFA has held its annual National Convention in Kansas City, Missouri. In 1970, more than 14,000 FFA members and guests were on hand for the 43rd National Convention. The theme of the convention was "Involved in America's Future." *Courtesy Future Farmers of America.*

Competing Interests for the Leisure of Youth

In the complex urban society of today, competition for the leisure of youth has risen to dizzying heights in the cities and even higher in the suburbs. Parents who feel obliged to give every so-called advantage to their children and must keep up with the neighbors are caught in a whirlpool of demands. The children themselves are often frustrated by the myriads of decisions they must make between competing interests. Children, it has been said, no longer have time to be children.

The following are a few of the kinds of programs offered to young people.

Summer School. We discussed the summer school earlier in this chapter. Even though attendance of young people is voluntary in most cases, the requirement for early registration that commits their time for six or eight weeks in the summer often eliminates the possibility of participating in summer camp and many other summer activities.

Programs of Religious Organizations. Summer has traditionally been the time for Bible schools, camps sponsored by religious organizations, and special church events. Many parents and religious educators feel that the daily summer program has an impact that the once-a-week-on-Sunday instruction of the rest of the year cannot match.

Cultural Programs. Lessons in music, dancing, and dramatics outside of school are an essential part of education in the thinking of many parents. Although some of these programs take place after school and in the evenings, they are intensified in the summer.

Sports Programs. Little League Baseball, Junior Golf, Pop Warner Football, Age-group swimming, and numerous other sport leagues claim a share of the time of growing boys. Special lessons in tennis, bowling, and swimming attract both boys and girls. Home swimming pools and other recreation facilities at home give further opportunities, particularly to the middle and upper segments of society.

Outdoor Recreation. Swimming, boating, scuba diving, surfing, hiking, camping, bicycling, skiing, skating, water skiing, and fishing find their devotees among the young, either on their own or with their families. Family camping has grown to major proportions, and many families take off to the mountains or beaches with their children. Some parents regard family camping as a substitute for organized youth camps for their children. Desirable as family camping may be, it is a different type of experience from the organized youth camp, in which children live with and work with their peers; the one experience is no substitute for the other.

Travel. Travel, one of the major industries of the United States, is no longer restricted to the wealthy or to adults. Parents take their children with them whether they are going to nearby parks, across the continent, or overseas. Older young people are traveling in great numbers in both organized groups and as individuals.

Public Park and Recreation Programs. Community centers, playgrounds, and public parks have expanded their offerings enormously. Facilities and programs are available near the homes of most children. Particularly in the crowded sections of large cities, public parks attain an important place in the leisure activities of young people; and they offer not only facilities but also classes and club programs under leadership.

VOLUNTARY YOUTH AGENCIES IN RELATION
TO OTHER PROGRAMS

The youth agencies have amazingly continued to expand despite the variety of demands on youth. This growth is one of the surest indications of the high respect in which these organizations are held. It is also an indication that they offer something of special value. Their methods—the peer groups, the volunteer leaders, the democratic planning, the specialized attention— and their programs, designed around the interests of youth, assure them success. There is evidence, however, that some aspects of their programs, such as summer camps, have suffered from the competition of other activities.

Both public and voluntary agencies have important services to give to young people. If the tax-supported agencies, including the schools, begin to edge out the voluntary agencies, it is time for the latter to raise their voices and affirm their place in the affairs of youth. In most communities, if the channels of communication are kept open, the public agencies will recognize the need for the youth agencies and will cooperate with them in working out their schedules. The programs should be complementary rather than competitive; and there should be room for flexibility so that the best interests of youth may be served.

Challenges to the Youth Organizations

The problems of our uncertain age gravely challenge the strength of the youth agencies. How they meet these challenges will determine the future influence of these organizations on individuals and on the character of American society.

The Challenge of Innovation. The technological advances of American society have not been matched by social adjustments, all of which lag far behind. Agencies find it difficult to relinquish the structures, methods, and programs that have proven successful in the past but are no longer applicable. To keep an active and growing membership, however, they must be pliable and innovative in facing new conditions.

The Challenge of the Disadvantaged. To equalize opportunity and reduce poverty to its lowest possible level will be problems of all business, educational, and social agencies. Because of their influence on youth, the youth-serving agencies bear a great responsibility for the building of attitudes and for offering opportunities within their programs.

The Challenge of Older Youth. Here is a particularly difficult challenge. Few of the agencies are able to hold older youth. If we do not want an alienated generation, unsympathetic with their elders, efforts will be needed to understand these young people. Providing opportunities for participation in and service to the adult world should help youth to bridge their years between childhood and adulthood and make it easier for them to assume adult responsibilities. Much consideration needs to be given to the image projected by clubs for older youth. If the group does not establish an image of "young adult" rather than "advanced kid's stuff," it will never stand a chance.

The Challenge of Changing Values. With old moral values toppling in some sections of American society, it is time to reexamine those standards by which generations have lived. The youth agencies can act as stabilizing forces, fostering that which is essentially good while rejecting that which is harmful in the long run to the individual and to society.

The Challenge of World Friendship. The world shrinks as air and space travel annihilate time and distance. Steps beyond the earth poignantly remind us that we are fellow travelers on a lonely planet, bound together. Old barriers between peoples must fall. The building of international friendships and respect for people of different cultures is a task to which the youth agencies must unfailingly turn (Figure 14–3).

Figure 14–3
As long distance travel becomes more feasible, international youth exchange programs offer promise of better understanding between nations. Pictured here is a group of students from Israel, hosted by B'nai B'rith Youth Organization. *Courtesy B'nai B'rith Youth Organization.*

The Challenge of Democracy. Through their group practices, their services to communities, and their teachings, the youth agencies have been strong forces in the preservation of American democratic ideals. In a world that is today by no means safe for democracy, their help is needed in steering the nation on a stable keel. Potentially no finer structure exists for the learning of democratic procedures than in a youth organization.

The Challenge of Research. To keep pace with the changing social scene, the agencies require continuing research into the behavior and needs of youth. Studies of program techniques and constant re-evaluation of existing programs should be included.

The Challenge of Serving the Family. Most youth organizations that are successful involve parents in the program in some way. Parents must, at least, give encouragement for their children's participation and take pride in their accomplishments. Hopefully they will contribute time and energy toward the supporting work necessary in transportation, communications, and financing.

Unfortunately, all parents do not grasp the importance of their own participation. Many fail to see that even if youth groups could carry on without parental support, they would sacrifice their most important asset if they did. Youth groups must *extend* family relationships, not replace them. The majority of parents are probably ignorant of their responsibility in making the youth agency program effective. Certainly one of the main challenges facing the agencies is interpretation of the need for parental support. This has been a major stumbling block in agency attempts to work more effectively in lower-class neighborhoods.

Peck and Havighurst concluded from their findings that character tends to be firm by the age of ten.[8] If they are correct, a re-evaluation of some of the youth agency claims in the area of character development is needed, since many of the youth organizations' programs do not enroll members below 11 or 12. Perhaps more emphasis should be given to pre-school and lower elementary school programs, and certainly more thought needs to be given to ways in which the agencies can help parents to do a better job while their children are young.

The Challenge of Leadership. It is a cause for deep concern that all youth-serving agencies have difficulty in recruiting and holding professional personnel. Since leadership is the most important factor in the success of an agency, an expanded program of recruitment and training is needed. The status of the professional and the image of the profession held by prospective workers must be improved. Among volunteers, too, the desirability and worth of service must be emphasized.

---

[8] Robert F. Peck and Robert J. Havighurst *et al., The Psychology of Character Development* (New York: John Wiley & Sons, Inc., 1960), p. 157.

The Challenge of Support. More adequate financing is needed, particularly for leadership salaries and programs.

The Challenge of Interpretation. One of the great challenges for the future lies in the area of public interpretation to attain a better understanding of the functions, values, and programs of the voluntary youth-serving organizations. From this understanding there should emerge not only public support, but also better working relations with allied professional groups, particularly in education and recreation. This aspect of interpretation leads to our final challenge.

The Challenge of Cooperation. Better cooperative relations must be sought among the youth agencies themselves as well as with public agencies in order to render the greatest service to the total community.

Youth Organizations in a Changing World

With our world in rapid transition and frequent crises, many older values are subject to disdain and discard. The youth organizations have often been

Figure 14-4

Women of the YWCA—teens, young adults, and the 35 years plus—came to the 25th National Convention of the YWCA of the U.S.A. in numbers—2,500—and with original banners revealing their special needs and concerns. Delegates to the convention, which was held in April 1970 in Houston, Texas, represented community and student associations. *Courtesy National Board, YWCA.*

criticized as bastions of conservatism. It is true that their membership has often been drawn from the middle-income segments of society, but evidence indicates that their vital concern now is to serve in the solution of problems; they are part of the fight against poverty, racial discrimination, and environmental abuse. They recognize increasingly that understandings, attitudes, and active participation in improving our world all go together (Figure 14–4).

Yet the agencies have not forgotten that the basis of social improvement lies in the individual. Certain features of their programs have a profound effect on the personality of participants: the participation by members of their own free will in programs that give more or less immediate satisfaction; the small-group involvement; the leaders who are friends rather than dictators and who care about each member as a person. It is our hope that the development of the individual will continue to be the major thrust of organizations for youth.

APPENDIX

Selected List of Organizations Serving Children and Youth

American Association for Health, Physical Education, and Recreation, 1201 16th Street, N.W., Washington, D.C. 20036.

American Camping Association, Bradford Woods, Martinsville, Indiana 46151.

American National Red Cross, 17th and D Streets, N.W., Washington, D.C. 20006.

American Youth Foundation, 3460 Hampton Avenue, St. Louis, Missouri 63139.

American Youth Hostels, Inc., 20 West 17th Street, New York, N.Y. 10011.

Big Brothers of America, 341 Suburban Station Building, Philadelphia, Pa. 19103.

The B'nai B'rith Youth Organization, 1640 Rhode Island Avenue, N.W., Washington, D.C. 20036.

Boy Scouts of America, New Brunswick, New Jersey 08903.

Boys' Clubs of America, 771 First Avenue, New York, N.Y. 10017.

Camp Fire Girls, Inc., 65 Worth Street, New York, N.Y. 10013.

Christian Service Brigade, Box 150, Wheaton, Illinois 60187.

Division of Youth Activities, United States Catholic Conference, 1312 Massachusetts Avenue, N.W., Washington, D.C. 20005.

4-H Clubs, Extension Service, Department of Agriculture, Washington, D.C. 20250.

Future Farmers of America, Box 15160, Alexandria, Virginia 22309.

Future Homemakers of America, c/o U.S. Office of Education, Washington, D.C. 20202.

Girls Clubs of America, Inc., 133 East 62nd Street, New York, N.Y. 10021.

Girl Scouts of the United States of America, 830 Third Avenue, New York, N.Y. 10022.

Job Corps, 1200 19th Street, N.W., Washington, D.C. 20506.

International Order of Job's Daughters, 719 South Boulevard, Oak Park, Ill. 60300.

Junior Achievement, 909 Third Avenue, New York, N.Y. 10022.

Junior Catholic Daughters of America, 1312 Massachusetts Ave., N.W., Washington, D.C. 20005.

Key Club International, 101 East Erie Street, Chicago, Illinois 60611.

Little League Baseball, P. O. Box 1127, Williamsport, Pennsylvania, 17701.

National Assembly for Social Policy and Development, Inc., 345 East 46th Street New York, N.Y. 10017.

National Association of Social Workers, 2 Park Avenue, New York, N.Y. 10016.

National Audubon Society, 1130 Fifth Avenue, New York, N.Y. 10028.

National Conference on Social Welfare, 22 West Gay Street, Columbus, Ohio 43215.

National Council of Young Israel, 3 West 16th Street, New York, N.Y. 10011.

National Federation of Settlements and Neighborhood Centers, 232 Madison Avenue, New York, N.Y. 10016.

National Honor Society, 1201 16th Street, N.W., Washington, D.C. 20036.

National Jewish Welfare Board, 15 East 26th Street, New York, N.Y. 10010.

National Recreation and Park Association, 1700 Pennsylvania Avenue, N.W., Washington, D.C. 20006.

National Wildlife Federation, 1412 16th Street, N.W., Washington, D.C. 20036.

Natural Science for Youth Foundation, 763 Silvermine Road, New Canaan Conn. 06840.

Optimist International, 4494 Lindell Boulevard, St. Louis, Missouri 63108.

Order of DeMolay (International Supreme Council), 201 East Armour Boulevard, Kansas City, Missouri 64141.

Pioneer Girls, Box 92, Wheaton, Illinois, 60188.

Rainbow Girls, Box 768, McAlester, Oklahoma 74501.

The Salvation Army, 120–130 West 14th Street, New York, N.Y. 10011.

Sons of the American Legion, P. O. Box 1055, Indianapolis, Indiana 46206.

United Boys' Brigades of America, 1211 West 40th St., Baltimore, Md. 21211.

United Community Funds and Councils of America, 345 East 46th Street, New York, N.Y. 10017.

United Synagogue Youth, 218 East 70th Street, New York, N.Y. 10021.

Young Life, 720 West Monument, Colorado Springs, Colorado 80901.

Young Men's Christian Association of the United States of America, 291 Broadway, New York, N.Y. 10007.

Young Women's Christian Association of the United States of America, 600 Lexington Avenue, New York, N.Y. 10022.

Youth Department, National Grange, 1616 H Street, N.W., Washington, D.C. 20006.

Youth for Christ, Box 419, Wheaton, Illinois, 60187.

BIBLIOGRAPHY

Publications of the Organizations

Especially valuable in a study of youth organizations are the handbooks, leaders' guides, annual reports or yearbooks, histories, magazines, pamphlets, promotion materials, and other material available from the youth organizations themselves. These may be obtained from the addresses that appear in the Appendix, pages 223–225.

The Changing World

Burke, John G., *The New Technology and Human Values*. Belmont, Cal.: Wadsworth, 1966.

Chase, Stuart, *The Most Probable World*. New York: Harper & Row, 1968.

Nature and Motivation of Children and Youth

Doty, Richard S., *The Character Dimension of Camping*. New York: Association Press, 1960.

Erikson, Erik H., *Childhood and Society* (2nd ed.). New York: Norton, 1963.

Maslow, Abraham H., *Motivation and Personality* (2nd ed.). New York: Harper & Row, 1970.

Maslow, Abraham H., *Toward a Psychology of Being*. Princeton, N.J.: Van Nostrand Reinhold, 1968.

Peck, Robert F., Robert J. Havighurst *et al.*, *The Psychology of Character Development*. New York: Wiley, 1960.

Survey Research Center, Institute for Social Research, University of Michigan, *Adolescent Girls*. New York: Girl Scouts of America, n.d.

Yankelovich, Daniel, Inc., *Is Scouting in Tune with the Times?* New Brunswick, N.J.: Boy Scouts of America, 1968.

Principles, Techniques, and Administration of Group Work

Blumenthal, Louis H., *Administration of Group Work.* New York: Association Press, 1948.

Glanz, Edward C., *Groups in Guidance.* Boston: Allyn & Bacon, 1962.

Konopka, Gisela, *Social Group Work: A Helping Process,* 2nd. ed. Englewood Cliffs, N.J.: Prentice-Hall, 1972.

Murray, Janet P., *Guidelines for Group Leaders.* New York: Whiteside, Inc., 1954.

Northen, Helen, *Social Work with Groups.* New York: Columbia University Press, 1969.

Trecker, Harleigh B., *New Understandings of Administration.* New York: Association Press, 1961.

Trecker, Harleigh B., *Social Group Work, Principles and Practices.* New York: Association Press, 1955.

Leadership

Corbin, H. Dan, *Recreation Leadership.* Englewood Cliffs, N.J.: Prentice-Hall, 1970.

Frank, Lawrence K., *How to be a Modern Leader.* New York: Association Press, 1954.

Roberts, Dorothy M., *Leading Teen-age Groups.* New York: Association Press, 1963.

Ross, Murray G. and Hendry, Charles E., *New Understandings of Leadership.* New York: Association Press, 1966.

Shivers, Jay S., *Leadership in Recreational Service.* New York: Macmillan, 1963.

Whyte, William H., Jr., *The Organization Man.* New York: Simon & Schuster, 1956.

Miscellaneous

Carlson, Reynold E., Theodore R. Deppe, and Janet R. MacLean, *Recreation in American Life.* Belmont, Cal.: Wadsworth, 1963.

Chambers, Merritt M., *Youth-serving Organizations.* Washington, D.C.: The American Council on Education, 1948.

Duran, Dorothy B. and Clement A. Duran, *New Encyclopedia of Successful Program Ideas.* New York: Association Press, 1968.

Lurie, Harry L., ed., *Encyclopedia of Social Work.* New York: National Association of Social Workers, 1965.

Mumn, Mrs. Louise N., ed., *Service Directory of National Organizations* (10th ed.). New York: The National Assembly for Social Policy and Development, Inc., 1969.

Neumeyer, Martin H., and Esther S. Neumeyer, *Leisure and Recreation* (3rd ed.). New York: Ronald Press 1958.

INDEX